Swin

How Cricket and Baseball Connect

The great I *Play.*

CRICKET.

THIS Leſſon obſerve,
   When you play at *Cricket*,
Catch *All* fairly out,
Or bowl down the *Wicket*.

MORAL.

This Maxim regard,
   Now you're in your Prime;
Look ere 'tis too late;
   By the Fore-lock take *Time*,

C 3   STOOL-

The little k *Play.*

BASE-BALL.

THE *Ball* once ſtruck off,
   Away flies the *Boy*
To the next deſtin'd Poſt,
   And then Home with Joy.

MORAL.

Thus *Britons* for Lucre
   Fly over the Main;
But, with Pleaſure tranſported,
   Return back again.

TRAP-

Swinging Away

How Cricket and Baseball Connect

Beth Hise

Introduction by Matthew Engel
Foreword by Andrew Flintoff

SCALA

This edition © Scala
Publishers Ltd 2010

Text © Marylebone
Cricket Club 2010

Illustrations © Marylebone
Cricket Club 2010 unless
otherwise credited on
page 192

First published in 2010 by:
Scala Publishers Ltd
Northburgh House
10 Northburgh Street
London EC1V 0AT, UK
www.scalapublishers.com

in association with:
Marylebone Cricket Club
Lord's Ground
London NW8 8QN, UK
www.lords.org

and:
National Baseball Hall of Fame
and Museum
25 Main Street
Cooperstown, NY 13326, USA
www.baseballhall.org

ISBN: 978-1-85759-644-1

Coordinated at MCC by
Adam Chadwick
Text by Beth Hise
Edited by Oliver Craske
Designed by Jade Design
Printed in Spain

10 9 8 7 6 5 4 3 2 1

Page 1: Pages from *A Little
Pretty Pocket-Book*, first
published in London in 1744
(see page 30). Shown is the
earliest printed reference to
'base-ball'.

Page 2: Babe Ruth with
Australian cricketer Alan Fairfax
in the cricket nets at Thames
House, London, 9 February
1935 (see page 140).

Below: Lord's cricket ground
in London, with the famous
pavilion at centre, pictured on
17 July 2006 during the last
day of the 1st Test match
between England and Pakistan.

Contents

Preface

Almost three years ago now, towards the end of the hugely successful Ashes Exhibition tour to Australia, I had the first of several conversations regarding a cricket and baseball exhibit. Beth Hise, who became the show's curator, was one of the first to be hugely enthusiastic, as was Tom Morgan to whom the idea had occurred during his regular visits to Lord's from Oneonta, New York.

However it was not until visits to the National Baseball Hall of Fame and Museum and the C. C. Morris Cricket Library that a truly collaborative exhibition seemed possible. Our enthusiasm was reciprocated in Cooperstown not only by Jeff Idelson – the current President – but also by senior curators Ted Spencer and Tom Shieber, and in Haverford by Paul Hensley, Alfred Reeves and all the friends of the Library.

Such goodwill has underpinned the evolution of this unprecedented project and MCC is genuinely indebted to all those on both sides of the Atlantic who have contributed. There is a lengthy and detailed list of acknowledgements at the back of this catalogue but thanks are due of course to all the lenders, photographers, scholars, individuals and organisations who have contributed in such a wide variety of ways.

However, it would be remiss of me not to acknowledge in particular the outstanding work of Beth Hise, the curator, and the terrific contributions of Tom Shieber, Owen Snee, the exhibit designer, Oliver Craske, the catalogue editor, and Erik Strohl, Senior Director of Exhibitions at the Hall of Fame. Without their passion and unfailing commitment we would not have come close to realising what will I hope prove to be a hugely popular show and a catalogue to treasure.

Finally I would like to thank our sponsors for their valuable support.

Adam Chadwick
Curator of Collections
Lord's Ground

This exhibition has been sponsored by:

E. Denis Walsh   **Thomas J. Elliott**

HURFORD SALVI CARR
PROPERTY ADVISORS AND DEVELOPMENT CONSULTANTS

ROBINSONMcCOLL
ARCHITECTS+DESIGNERS

springlaw.

Foreword

Andrew Flintoff

I am delighted to loan my England Test kit to Lord's as part of their joint cricket and baseball exhibition. As a venue, Lord's has always had a special place in my heart and to have my kit chosen as part of this exhibition is a big honour. With the exception of Old Trafford, where I have played my cricket since the age of nine, I would have to say that Lord's is my favourite ground. It's a special place to play, and the facilities, from the playing surface right down to the lunches, are absolutely first rate.

I've been lucky that I've had a few good times at Lord's, starting with the 142 I scored for England against South Africa in 2003, which was my first home Test century. Most people remember that as the match when I broke my bat in two, but although I enjoyed the innings at the time it was tarnished by the fact we lost the Test. The Lord's matches that mean most to me are the two Ashes Tests I played, in 2005 and 2009, as well as leading England out as captain in a Test there against Sri Lanka in 2006. Because it was my last ever Test appearance there, the 2009 victory over Australia would have to be my most treasured memory of all. I had already announced that I was going to retire from Test cricket before the start of the Test, so I knew it was going to be the last time I played at Lord's in the Ashes. Just because of the significance of the match for me, I suppose I was looking around the place a bit more than normal, trying to make sure the experience stayed with me. Maybe it was a sense of the occasion, but knowing I wouldn't be there again seemed to add to my determination to make my mark and I was delighted to get a five-wicket haul to help win the game. Getting on the honours board for that meant so much more to me than my century a few years earlier, simply because we'd won.

Those are my fondest memories of Lord's, and I hope when people visit this exhibition on cricket and baseball they will be equally inspired. It's only when you have a good look around the place that you realise how special a place it is and how privileged we are to be able to play there. I'm not sure what baseball fans will make of it, but it should give them an idea of why cricket is such a popular game. I'm sure the popularity of Twenty20 cricket around the world will help cricket grow in popularity in America because of its similarity to baseball, and hopefully this exhibition will be the first step.

Introduction

Matthew Engel

When, several hundred million years ago, this planet comprised one continent, all the life-forms must have indulged in the same activities. Sex and eating, one presumes.

As the world grew more complicated, it became more diverse. And eventually sport emerged as an expression of that diversity. The games we watch and play are among the defining characteristics of a modern nation. If you made a list of the differences between Britain and the United States, the fact that one plays cricket and the other baseball would be very close to the top.

But it has never been that simple. Jane Austen, writing circa 1799, mentions baseball as well as cricket in *Northanger Abbey*, and there never was a less Yankee writer. It is less contentious to write about religion or politics than the origins of these two games, but it seems safe to say they are both strongly rooted in English folk tradition.

In England, cricket very quickly smothered baseball, and as Britain acquired another empire to replace those uppity American colonies, cricket took root everywhere else that it conquered.

But it was not until the second half of the 19th century that the sporting destiny of the United States was settled. In 1859 John Wisden led an All-England tour that boosted interest in American cricket and might have meant that we would be thinking this summer about the prospects for the Tests in Chicago and Atlanta. Two years later, the Civil War erupted and the game never recovered.

Some historians concluded that the war was the deciding factor. Tom Melville, author of the very thorough history of US cricket, *The Tented Field*, disagreed: 'Cricket failed in America because it never established an American character,' he concluded. Ah, if only they had thought of Twenty20. Instead, baseball became a craze, and then an institution.

Yet in neither country was the wipeout total. Some private American schools continued to favour cricket, because it taught old-fashioned virtues and offered international prestige. High-standard cricket persisted in Philadelphia into the 20th century, but only among the famously hoity-toity Philadelphian upper-class, who were also fond of fox hunting.

But no city in the US has a more raucous set of sports fans, and the idea that many of the Philly locals would ever have hushed, or remembered not to walk behind the bowler's arm, is unimaginable. And for many decades American cricket retreated largely into such British expat bastions as Sir Aubrey Smith's Hollywood Cricket Club.

In Britain, baseball-style games certainly never disappeared. Rounders was always popular in primary schools, and rightly so. Fifty years ago, when even seven-year-olds were expected to play cricket as an eleven-a-side game with a hard ball, rounders offered both more involvement and less fear. And it became an organised sport in Ireland in the 1880s under the aegis of the Gaelic Athletic Association, which promoted non-British sport as a means of instilling anti-imperialist solidarity.

In Wales, rounders mutated into a form of baseball: eleven-a-side, underarm bowling (not pitching), and with a run awarded for each base reached, not just for a full circuit. And that game still quietly thrives around Cardiff. In 1924 the New York Giants and Chicago White Sox met at Stamford Bridge in front of the King and Queen. The *Times* correspondent, however, was full of lordly disdain: 'The long catches into the outfield are too simple for a private school boy to miss, if he has the advantage of a huge glove...The running between the bases was slow.' In contrast, the *New York Times* treated the advent of Don Bradman respectfully and hailed him as the 'Babe Ruth of cricket'. But he could have walked down Fifth Avenue unnoticed.

The mutual incomprehension continued for generations. The cricketing

Albert Pujols of the St. Louis Cardinals batting against the Atlanta Braves, 5 May 2002, at St. Louis.

establishment regarded baseball as some sort of barbarous mutant; Americans regarded cricket as some crazed English joke, a view epitomised by Groucho Marx's famous comment as he sat watching a match at Lord's: 'This is great. When does it start?'

But things slowly changed. In the 1980s, when English soccer was dreary on the field and violent off it, many sports fans began to look for alternatives. American football became a huge hit on Channel 4, and baseball became an obvious next step. There were cheap fares across the Atlantic, so many young Brits began to see for themselves. And locals would join expats in softball games in Regent's Park.

Meanwhile, in the US, cricket surged for totally different reasons. There were waves of immigration from, first, the Caribbean and then the subcontinent. The migrants brought their game with them and used it as a badge of their identity. American cricket became a hard school with an ethos far removed from Sir Aubrey Smith. But soon huge numbers of Asians were playing in all the major cities. And cricket administrators licked their lips at the prospect of this fabulous untapped market (at least until they started dealing with the feuding barons who ran the American game).

The truth, though, was that the overwhelming mass of Americans were as distant from cricket as ever. And the attitude of newspapers has reversed since the 1920s: The *Times* habitually provides good coverage of the World Series; its New York namesake ('All the news that's fit to print') declined to print a solitary word – not one – on even the 2005 Ashes.

Perhaps cricket is like Marmite; unless you are exposed to it by the age of three, you are unlikely ever to acquire a taste for it. And it is hard to imagine even Twenty20 having any impact now. What would it offer Americans that is not already available in baseball? A discerning baseball fan might, however, notice a similarity between Twenty20 and the Home Run Derby, the novelty event (a sort of six-hitting contest) that takes place before the annual All-Star game.

Yet at root baseball and cricket are not that different. I see them as blood brothers, separated at birth but genetically linked. I peered uncomprehendingly at baseball for ages until I suddenly realised there was a wicket – the strike zone. It's just invisible, that's all. Once I saw that, I saw everything. The techniques may be different but the duel is the same: pitcher v batter, bowler v batsman, the one trying to outdo the other using pace and/or duplicity.

The duel is between individuals, but that is hidden inside what is ostensibly a team sport. It is bad form, especially in cricket, to be seen to elevate a century above the needs of the team. Yet what are the most resonant records?

They are individual. Bradman's 99.94 Test average trips off the tongue as does Ted Williams' .406 season. No need to look up Lara's 501 or 400 or Ruth's 60 home runs. What's the highest Test total? Some dreary match on the sub-continent, wasn't it? Must be in Wisden somewhere.

And the appeal to the spectator is the same too. They both have long soporific periods of nothing-much, broken by sudden, unpredictable climaxes. They both offer bottomless strategic profundity. They both have revered traditions, with a rich literature as well as endless statistics. Perhaps above all, they are both sports of summer – in which a magnificent game can become entwined in our minds with the memory of a perfect day.

Cricket offers the advantage of the ball bouncing, making the terrain a crucial extra element, whereas in baseball it hardly matters. Cricket is played over 360 degrees whereas baseball is confined within the 90-degree angle of the diamond. And cricket offers the concept of the draw – as beautiful as a cry of 'Sanctuary!' at a church door, and so scorned and misunderstood by Americans.

Baseball, though, knows what it is. A game is a game: nine innings a side, more if they are level, taking an average three to four hours. Its rhythms are immutable. Cricket is in torment over its format, caught in an undeclared war between those who love it as a game and those who value it as a business. Baseball was lucky enough to get rich quicker. In the 1980s the Hampshire captain Nick Pocock met a big-league American who asked him how much he earned. '£4,000,' he said. 'How many games do you play a year?' Pocock totted up all the different county competitions of the era and reckoned he played about 45. 'Gee, 45 times 4,000, that's not bad.' 'No, no, you don't understand. It's £4,000 a year.' Cricket salaries have gone up, but the average on the New York Yankees roster is now heading for $8m a year.

Many cricketers have thought the grass was greener. Ian Botham fancied his chances, not unreasonably, but he was way too old by then. Ian Pont of Notts and Essex was picked as starting pitcher for the Philadelphia Phillies in a pre-season contest but ultimately became a county bowler with a distinctive baseball snap to his action. Ed Smith's experiences with the big leaguers helped make him a writer, but not a millionaire. There is no reverse flow, though many Australians, including the Chappell brothers, played baseball as kids.

There is every reason why these two games should understand each other better. Cricket people ought to be less snotty about baseball; baseball people should make the tougher journey to grasping cricket. Both sides would gain a lot: by understanding the delights and the problems of the other world, administrators, players and spectators would learn a lot about their own world too. I hope this pioneering exhibition and book help start this process.

1 Sporting cousins

In 1879, an American named J. E. Sprague bowled 'peculiarly puzzling grounders' to the opening batsmen of Lord Harris's visiting English cricket team. Sprague, a member of the Staten Island Cricket and Baseball Club, was playing for a combined New York and Philadelphia team against the far superior English players at Hoboken, New Jersey's celebrated sporting fields.[1] His unusual style took some getting used to, and the English players struggled for some time before they managed to lay bat on ball. This wasn't the first time either that Sprague managed to baffle quality cricketers. The Australian cricket team visiting the year before considered his 'old-fashioned underhand grounders' amusing – until they found they couldn't hit them.[2]

What did this American cricketer have over these international players? The answer seems to lie in the fact that this 'cricketer' was none other than Joe Sprague, the renowned baseball pitcher previously of the pioneering Excelsiors and Atlantics clubs of Brooklyn, who in the 1860s had perfected a turning underhand pitch some considered to be a curveball.[3] Almost 20 years later, the great Philadelphian cricketer J. B. King similarly brought curveball-pitching techniques to cricket with stunning results.

It should come as no surprise that American ball players enjoyed more than one sport in the mid to late 1800s, or that baseball combined so easily with cricket. Apart from the obvious parallels between the two games – summer sports played with bat and ball on a field with two teams and umpires – cricket and baseball also share certain important fundamentals. Their rhythms are dictated by events on the field; neither is a helter-skelter rush punctuated by the clock. Players and fans alike have time to consider, calculate and strategise. Individual performances are celebrated, especially in the one-on-one duel between ball and bat, but players are never soloists; they play in concert with their teammates and every achievement is quickly placed statistically within the greater whole of the game. Context is everything: every ball or play is recorded, no matter how mundane, giving both sports a rich statistical foundation.

What are the reasons for this natural affinity between cricket and baseball? It must be more than coincidence that both sports use words like run, umpire, inning(s) – or, indeed, 'swinging away'. It is now clear that apart from shared ancient ball-playing traditions, the two have no direct evolutionary relationship. Conventional histories, however, have taken only passing interest in the dual baseball and cricket careers of players like Joe Sprague in 19th-century America. Not because the games don't share similarities. It is rather that so much has changed around the games since then. Baseball and cricket have become massive professional and commercial enterprises with highly paid elite players, corporate sponsors, television coverage and passionate fans.

1
The great English cricketer Ian Botham during a Scottish Amicable Cup baseball match, 1987.

Grass-roots enjoyment remains strong and both sports now stand for far more than enjoyable exercise among friends. Just as baseball became America's 'National Pastime', cricket too became more than the game played around the world by Englishmen. Many countries embraced it, adopted it as their own and now play it passionately for their own sense of national pride. To the uninitiated, baseball and cricket are complicated and difficult to understand, so it is unsurprising that as they prospered separately they grew further apart. Most cricket countries do not play much baseball, and vice versa (with a few important exceptions where both are played, such as Australia or South Africa). Thus, as potential players grow up around the world they are rarely faced with choosing between these two sporting cousins. 'I would, I'm sure, have been a baseball player', wrote English cricketer Ed Smith in 2002, 'if I had been born in America.'[4]

All the same, for a short time in 19th-century America these two sports were far more interrelated than many today realise. Because cricket hasn't featured significantly on the American sporting landscape for such a long time it is difficult to imagine anyone playing both sports today, or even to appreciate just how prevalent and popular cricket was in America in the mid-19th century. But the relationship goes deep, as will be illustrated through the careers of several significant 19th-century baseball figures, people like Harry Wright, simultaneously a member of the Knickerbocker Base Ball Club and the St George Cricket Club, and Henry Chadwick, the English-born sports writer credited as the 'Father of Base Ball'. Both of these men, and others, brought elements of cricket directly into the developing game of baseball.

The work of scholars Melvin Adelman, Tom Melville and George Kirsch laid the groundwork for this analysis, and more recently other baseball historians have begun to appreciate this early influence, albeit often hampered by a poor understanding of cricket.[5] On the other hand, cricket histories all but ignore baseball. The chapters of this book often return to the story of cricket in America to better illustrate some of the ways that this 'English' sport contributed to the development of America's game. To those playing and watching both sports at the time, this would seem unremarkable.[6] It is only with the passage of time, and the subsequent popularity of many baseball myths, that we've lost sight of the natural, albeit short-lived overlap of these two sports.

The story doesn't end there, for cricket's influence continued in more subtle ways as baseball professionalised and undertook several international tours in the late 19th and early 20th centuries. American baseball thereafter found an often tenuous place for itself in cricket-playing nations, and the story of baseball in Britain will be examined here. Cricket also maintained a healthy presence on the American sporting scene until the 1920s, albeit isolated to specific urban centres, most notably Philadelphia. Ultimately cricket failed as a mass sport in America, but there are signs of a low-level revival today.

The picture that emerges over time is of a sometimes close and sometimes distant relationship between cricket and baseball at different times and in different places. In many ways it is a story that spans the globe over the past 150-plus years, but this account will limit the focus, with a few exceptions, to the relationship across the Atlantic between the nations claiming these sports as their own – America and England.

This story is not entirely confined to history. The tables have now turned, and to see how the relationship between the sports continues we need look no further than a game of Twenty20 cricket anywhere in the world today. Cricket is in the midst of an astonishing metamorphosis. While several decades of cricketers have benefited from the baseball-like precision fielding actively brought into the game by coaches and players, it is in this newest version, a short and fast form of the game, where the influences of American baseball are most evident: a three-hour match with explosive action, bravado, bright lights, coloured clothes, packed stands and a winner at the end of the day.

*   *   *

On the surface, cricket appears a more conservative sport than its flashy, fast-paced American counterpart. It seems too big and its administration too complicated to be a likely innovator. A quick snapshot shows cricket's federation of nations, administered by the Dubai-based International Cricket Council (ICC), to encompass ten Test match-playing nations, or Full Member countries of the ICC, at the top, followed by 35 Associate Member nations and 59 Affiliate Members. Today cricket alone seems to unite the disparate group of nations that make up the ten Full Members: Australia, Bangladesh, England, India, New Zealand, Pakistan, South Africa, Sri Lanka, the West Indies and Zimbabwe (although Zimbabwe have been suspended from Test cricket since 2005). There is no single defining season's-end championship. Instead, under the ICC's Future Tours Programme, at present all countries must play each other in home and away Test and one-day series over a six-year cycle, and there are official rankings for countries and players based on results. Cricket's worldwide spread takes today's top players to the northern and southern hemispheres, skipping the cold off-season, living a perpetual summer and playing almost year-round.

On closer examination, however, cricket seems to have experienced something of a revolution over the past 40 years. Its mix of centuries-old

2
Andrew Flintoff during his final Test innings, England v Australia, at The Oval, London, 22 August 2009
Andrew 'Freddie' Flintoff retired from Test cricket in 2009 as one of England's most celebrated all-rounders. Flintoff made his Test debut at the age of 20 in 1998, but it was his enthralling 402 runs and 24 wickets in the England–Australia Ashes Test series in 2005 that made him into an international cricketing superstar. He has played all forms of the game for England, has been contracted to the Chennai Super Kings in the Indian Premier League and has represented his home county of Lancashire since 1995. At six feet four inches, Flintoff intimidates batsmen with deliveries in excess of 90mph, excelling in reverse-swing, while as a right-handed batsman he is known for his powerful big hitting. The Australian wicket-keeper pictured here is Brad Haddin, and the fielder is Michael Clarke.

traditions and competing national interests hasn't changed and its foundations run deep – after all playing regulations have been governed by the same private English club, Marylebone Cricket Club (MCC), since 1788. Nevertheless, the sport hurtles along at breakneck speed, embracing sweeping new transformations. Elements of the game today would have been all but unrecognisable even in the recent past.

New versions of the game have been invented, tested and embraced all in the span of a few years, while the worldwide spread of the game grows. Several different Associate Member countries have qualified for major international tournaments in recent years. The United States, for example, qualified for the ICC Champions Trophy in 2004, and in May 2010 Afghanistan first competed at the top level after their unexpected entry into the World Twenty20 finals.[7]

Cricket is now an eclectic mix of three main formats, all played on the international stage. Test cricket, the ultimate 'test' of players' skills, is the oldest version of the game, the first Test match having been played in 1877. It is also the longest format, each match taking up to five days to complete, and even then it may end in a draw. Each side has the opportunity to bat through their entire line-up twice. Players wear 'whites' – long trousers (pants), shirt and pullover – as has been the tradition for over 180 years (see, for example, nos 2–4).

Shorter forms of the game have always been played, but the 1970s marked a real turning point for cricket. The first One Day International (ODI) was played in 1971, a format in which each side batted once for a limited number of overs (today, 50 six-ball overs) and the draw was removed from the possible results. The first World Cup was played in this format in 1975, and has been held every four years since. The game reached a challenging crossroad in 1977 when a short-lived rebel Australian league called World Series Cricket (WSC) signed up many of the world's leading cricketers and played entertaining and vigorously contested matches over two seasons. Its greatest innovation was to play matches over an afternoon and into the night under lights, using a white ball and with the players in coloured clothing, all to the tune of cricket's most successful marketing campaign. Even controversy over player salaries (big paychecks were new to cricket) could not dent the popularity of this format with crowds and television audiences, who luxuriated in plenty of exciting video replays, and enjoyed eight camera angles rather than the usual two. Money flowed into the game. WSC was absorbed into traditional cricket administration in 1979, but it had opened the door to innovation in the game as well as increasing professionalism and commercialisation, a spirit and legacy that, despite considerable unease among purists, remain strong to this day.[8]

An even shorter form of the game, called Twenty20 or T20, each side limited to 20 overs as the name implies, was more recently developed for English county cricket with the aim of making the game faster, more entertaining and accessible to younger spectators and television audiences. First unveiled in 2003, this newest form of the game has become a worldwide phenomenon. Now a part of every international series, Twenty20 is also a highlight of domestic seasons all around the cricketing world. Many feel it has the potential to break into the American market, one of cricket's most enticing challenges. And this is not just because the length and speed of the game seem to fit better into the American sporting psyche. It is also because in Twenty20, as Australian baseball coach Jon Deeble recently noted, 'you are out slogging the ball and running hard and fielding and throwing, just like in baseball'.[9] In 2008, the Indian Premier League (IPL) played its first season of Twenty20 cricket and unleashed a phenomenon entirely new to cricket: privately owned franchise teams, auctions

The great fast bowler Imran Khan in action for Pakistan against England in the 3rd Test at Headingley, Leeds, July 1987. He took 10 wickets in a match-winning performance.

4

England's Andrew Strauss takes a brilliant catch to dismiss Adam Gilchrist off the bowling of Andrew Flintoff, during the 4th England v Australia Test at Trent Bridge, Nottingham, 27 August 2005

for players, international stars paid huge sums to join domestic teams, a short season lasting five or six weeks, stadium music, dancing cheerleaders, movie star patronage and massive television and popular support. The advent of the IPL has significantly increased the incomes of the cricketers involved. Some are paid – for just a few weeks' competition – up to three times what they earn annually from all other aspects of the game. Of the ten top-earning cricketers in 2009, taking into account their match fees, sponsorship deals and other cricket income, five were Indian, and all but one had entered into an IPL contract.[10]

In its first season, the IPL established itself as one of the most popular events in India, attracting new fans, including women, and millions of television viewers. Some in the international cricketing world have mixed views on this newest spectacle and it is hard to know if the shine will wear off in subsequent series, yet there is no denying the unprecedented global interest in an otherwise domestic Indian competition. The biggest impact of Twenty20 cricket is now being seen in the number of matches played in this format as part of the ICC programme and in the creation in 2007 of an ICC Twenty20 World Cup (nos 5–8).

Women's cricket is also increasingly robust. Long active in the game, women have played at Test level since 1934 and their game is also administered by the ICC. Women now play the same three formats at international level, although without the frequency of men's cricket and with more emphasis on the shorter versions of the game. Greater investment has allowed some national teams, especially England, to contract players as part-time professionals and this in turn has lifted playing levels and players' profiles (in 2009 English batsman Claire Taylor was the first woman ever recognised as a Wisden Cricketer of the Year). The Australian Cricketers Association (ACA), the industry body looking after player welfare, granted full membership to women players in 2009, and, with voting rights and potential executive representation, there is certain to be additional institutional support in future.[11] Women in less wealthy cricket countries struggle against far greater disadvantage but still manage to participate, and often perform well, in international competition.

5–6
Twenty20 ICC World Cup jerseys worn by Shahid Afridi of Pakistan and Kumar Sangakkara of Sri Lanka, 2009
Shahid Afridi is renowned for his explosive hitting (he holds the current record for the fastest hundred in One Day Internationals, off 37 balls), as well as his skilful slow bowling, but was composed in compiling match-winning half-centuries for Pakistan in both semi-final and final of the 2009 World Twenty20. Kumar Sangakkara, a highly talented batsman and wicket-keeper, was elevated to the Sri Lankan captaincy in 2009 and led his team to the final, where they lost to Pakistan.

7
Kumar Sangakarra batting against Pakistan during the World Twenty20 at Lord's cricket ground, 12 June 2009

8
Shahid Afridi batting during the World Twenty20 at Lord's, 9 June 2009

England Women's captain Charlotte Edwards during the Women's World Twenty20 final against New Zealand at Lord's, 21 June 2009
Charlotte Edwards captains the English national women's cricket team and has led them in recent years to a series of thrilling victories, including the 2007–08 Ashes series in Australia. In 2009 they won both the Women's World Cup and the Women's World Twenty20 championship, as well as retaining the Ashes. She spearheads a dynamic side blending youth and experience.

The women's and men's games were successfully brought together for the first time in a major championship in the 2009 ICC Twenty20 World Cup in England: the last three matches of each tournament (semi-finals and final) were played on the same grounds and on the same days as each other, as double-headers (no. 9). This was repeated in the 2010 Twenty20 World Cup in the West Indies. Still, press coverage is patchy, and player experiences differ vastly between the men and women in terms of professional contracts, sponsorship opportunities and institutional influence. Women's cricket, while on the rise, will strengthen in future only with continued investment, and it remains vulnerable to funding insecurity.

*   *   *

The baseball-playing nations of the world, of which there are many, get the chance to compete against each other far less frequently. Major league baseball is the pinnacle of professional baseball, and, with its 30 privately owned franchise teams organised into two leagues, it is primarily a domestic American game. Compared to cricket's three very different formats, baseball is much more uniform, differences restricted to the designated hitter rule (adopted in the American but not National League), and the use of aluminium bats in amateur baseball while the minor and major leagues require wood bats. Today, the baseball regular season usually opens on the first Sunday in April and runs through to the first Sunday in October. There follows a month of postseason competition to decide the champions of the American and National Leagues, who then compete with each other in the best-of-seven-game World Series. Some teams make regular appearances in the postseason: the American League New York Yankees (no. 10) have won the World Series a record 27 times; the National League St. Louis Cardinals are a distant second with ten titles. In contrast, as of the end of the 2009 season, eight teams have never won the title and nine have only won it once or twice. The Boston Red Sox, the

Yankees' long-time rivals, had to wait a record 86 years between their fifth and sixth titles.

Outside of the United States, amateur baseball has staged an international competition since 1938 – the first being won, improbably, by Great Britain (see page 109). The relatively recent World Baseball Classic (WBC) is the main stage for international teams today. A professional competition, the WBC was launched in 2006 with teams from 16 countries and held again in 2009. Unlike international cricket competitions, run through a world body, the WBC is under the umbrella of Major League Baseball, through its international arm, and the finals are played on American soil. The competition takes place prior to the MLB regular season and has notable restriction on how much pitchers can participate in games, to protect the valuable arms of various major league pitchers before the season. This American control caused some resentment in its inaugural competition, especially in Japan, but the tournament successfully showcased the strength of international baseball. In 2006, Mexico eliminated the USA team and other powerhouses like the Dominican Republic and Venezuela missed out on the final.[12] Japan has shown its strength by winning both WBC tournaments to date, the first over Cuba, and the second over South Korea in 2009 (no. 11).

One place where there seems little comparison between cricket and baseball is in the women's game. In contrast to the comparative opportunities offered to their counterparts in cricket, girls and women who elect to play baseball in the United States choose a 'rocky path less travelled'.[13] Players who

10
Derek Jeter of the New York Yankees fielding in a game against the Atlanta Braves, June 2001
Derek Jeter is the charismatic shortstop and captain of the New York Yankees. In an outstanding 2009 season, he led his team to their first World Series Championship since 2000, and became the first Yankee to be named *Sports Illustrated* Sportsman of the Year. During the season he also passed Lou Gehrig's record for the most career base hits as a member of the Yankees, was selected for his tenth All-Star Game, and earned many honours including his fourth American League Silver Slugger Award for best hitting shortstop and his fourth Gold Glove Award as the American League's best defensive shortstop. He is widely respected in the game, on and off the field, and has been described as one of the best hitting shortstops in baseball history.

Japanese pitcher Yu Darvish pitching against South Korea at Dodger Stadium, Los Angeles, 23 March 2009
Yu Darvish pitches for the Hokkaido Nippon Ham Fighters in the twelve-team Nippon Professional Baseball League. Despite his youth, he has been dubbed the face of Japanese baseball, although he is far from typical at 6 feet 5 inches tall, with an Iranian father and Japanese mother. Many consider him not only the best pitcher in Japan, but one of the best outside of major league baseball. Here he is pitching during the final of the 2009 World Baseball Classic against arch rivals South Korea in front of a record 54,846 raucous fans, to give Japan its second WBC championship. In five WBC games, Darvish led all pitchers in WBC with 20 strikeouts in just 13 innings pitched.

prefer baseball over softball have limited options, with no robust and stable women's baseball currently on the American sporting landscape and often no female baseball team at the high school or college level. Girls, only allowed to participate in little league baseball after a court ruling against their exclusion in 1974, often have to battle to stay in the game, although there are slowly increasing numbers of talented players competing successfully on boys' teams at high school level and beyond. There are also a number of amateur women's leagues and advocacy organisations supporting women and girls in baseball with some success.[14] Robin Wallace is a good example of a talented player pushing against the odds to achieve the highest possible success in her sport. She was the first female athlete to play on a boys' baseball team in her hometown and went on to play college baseball before playing in the Women's New England Baseball League (WNEBL). She played on the gold-medal USA team in the inaugural Women's Baseball World Cup in 2004 in Canada, a competition played every two years since (no. 12). The women's national team, under the same umbrella organisation as the men's team, USA Baseball, continues to offer the most high-profile opportunity for women baseball players.[15]

*   *   *

It is easy for baseball and cricket to become isolated from each other. The concerns of each game are now so engrossing for administrators, fans and especially players. Today's top-level cricketers and baseball players share the lot of modern professionals, and the best of them enjoy lucrative endorsements by corporate sponsors. Baseball players market their skills through a complicated

12
USA jersey worn by Robin Wallace during Women's Baseball World Cup final, 8 August 2004
One of only a handful of women in baseball management, as general manager to several minor league men's teams, Robin Wallace was inducted into the National Women's Baseball Hall of Fame in 2002. She wore this jersey in the inaugural Women's Baseball World Cup in 2004 in Edmonton, Alberta, Canada. Like many players passionate about baseball and committed to the women's game, she has also been an active advocate, coach and administrator.

system of drafts, contracts, arbitration and free agency, and in a successful career have the opportunity to play for numerous major league teams. And each major league franchise also supports numerous minor league teams, providing playing opportunities for a domestic and international pool of talent.

Most top international cricketers are primarily contracted to play through the national body overseeing cricket in their home country. This body selects them for international representative matches, and with the permission of their board they are also allowed to enter into contracts with domestic teams in other countries – such as the county cricket clubs in England or the IPL teams. Each country also hosts layers of domestic competitions with players hoping to achieve selection to the national side – just as happens in baseball's minor leagues where players strive for major league opportunities.

It is unlikely any player will ever again play both cricket and baseball to anything like the level of some of the 19th-century Americans profiled in this book (although that tradition was continued until quite recently in Australia). Neither are we likely to engage in the passionate and fiercely patriotic debates about which sport is better. Still, a better understanding of modern and historic parallels and influences helps to overcome the tendency to isolation within one's own game, and will hopefully lead to a better appreciation of both.

Games played with bat and ball have much in common, and speculation about the origins of cricket and baseball, the premier bat and ball games of modern times, has occupied historians of both sports for centuries now. Much has been written – factual, speculative or just plain fanciful – and every new documentary shred is lovingly excavated and cherished. Interest in origins has recently enjoyed a considerable revival, especially among baseball historians, encouraged by a number of significant finds and by digitisation projects bringing 18th- and even 17th-century sources online.

William Redmore Bigg,
John Chandos Reade as a Boy
(see page 35)

The late 19th century was also a time of concentrated interest and writing about the origins of both cricket and baseball. The precursors of the game of baseball, as developed and played by Americans in the 19th century, started interesting baseball writers early. Initially many seemed happy to follow Henry Chadwick's lead pointing to the English game of rounders. That is, until the search for baseball's origins got sidetracked in the early 20th century by A. G. Spalding's patriotic desire to see the sport as a purely American invention, which resulted in the famous assertion that baseball was an American game invented in 1839 by Abner Doubleday, a famous Civil War general (see pages 174–76).

While baseball writers debated the nationality of their sport's progenitor, some cricket writers pondered over the linguistic origin of their sport's name. A few examples will suffice. Alfred T. Story in *The Strand Magazine* in 1895 followed the lead of philologist Professor William Skeat that cricket derived from the Old English word *crycc* or *cricc*. Arthur B. Reeve repeated this suggestion in the American sporting magazine *Outing* in 1910, but added the possibility that the French *croquet* might instead be the source.[1] This approach concentrates on the fact that both words, meaning stick or staff, refer to the bat as the distinctive cricket attribute and therefore must be the source of the modern word for the game. Charles Box suggested in 1877 that perhaps the stool being bowled at in early forms of the game was the key to the name and therefore put forth another popular option – 'Crickit', as he wrote it, deriving from the Flemish/Low German *krick-stoel*, for a low long stool.[2] This issue remains unresolved today and *The Wisden Dictionary of Cricket* cautions against arguing with the *Oxford English Dictionary*'s verdict of 'etymology uncertain'.[3] More recent scholars have focused on the Flemish word for hockey, *met de krik ketsen*, positing that *krik ketsen* was anglicised to 'cricket' in the 16th century.[4]

The cricket historian James Pycroft argued in 1851 for cricket's long antiquity, suggesting that before it was known as cricket it existed under other names: 'Club-ball' and 'Handyn and Handoute' in the 13th century, 'Creag' in the year 1300 and 'Cat and Dog' around 1700. In linking club-ball with cricket

Francis Hayman RA, *Cricket as Played in the Mary-le-bone Fields*, c.1744
This painting, traditionally believed to depict Marylebone Fields (now Regent's Park) in London, is one of cricket's most famous images. It was painted by Francis Hayman (1708–1776), who later became a founding member of the Royal Academy in 1768. It shows the early traits of the game of cricket – the curved bat, two-stump wicket, under-arm bowling and two umpires leaning on their bats. Scorers with their tally sticks sit in the foreground while the bowler is poised to release an underarm delivery.

Pycroft was following Joseph Strutt (who asserted in 1801 that cricket combined the earlier games of club-ball and stoolball) but other cricket historians have been less willing to make the leap that, as Pycroft wrote, 'cricket is identical with Club-ball'.[5] Robert Henderson, for one, pointed out that club-ball never referred to a specific game but rather a variety of ball games all played with some kind of club.[6] Still, cricket's great antiquity seems, to many, almost instinctive. When, where and from what it originated, however, have been far less clear. Alfred Story felt the infancy of the game 'is lost in obscurity', a sentiment echoed down the years and most recently by John Major, the former British Prime Minister, who wrote in his high-profile 2007 history of early cricket: 'the search for the birth of cricket has been as fruitless as the hunt for the Holy Grail: neither can be found'.[7]

What is beyond dispute by all cricket historians from the 19th century to today is the testimony of Mr John Derrick in a 1598 court case over land ownership. Nearly 60 years of age, he tells the court of his time as a 'scholler' of the free school of Guildford when 'hee and diverse of his fellows did runne and play there at creckett and other plaies'.[8] This otherwise unmemorable English gentleman gives cricket its oldest signpost: by calculating back in time to his

schooldays, we know the game was played by its current name by children around 1550. Perhaps, though, it was still just a children's playtime game, for there is no mention of it in the popular plays of Shakespeare, the writings of Jonson or Marlowe, or indeed in any surviving memoirs or letters of the time. Nor is it mentioned in the 1618 *Book of Sports*.[9] Scattered references give an insight into the early game, and some, such as the 1610 match between the men of North Downs and those of the Weald, give the first hints of an adult's game. The disapproval of the church and the penalties meted out by the courts, usually to village peasants caught playing on a Sunday, give us periodic documented records of the game. A curate, for example, was censured for playing cricket in 1629 'in very unseemly manner'. He defended his conduct by pointing out the 'repute and fashion' of his fellow players, suggesting a more widespread acceptance of the game.[10] This 17th-century cricket was a relatively simple and informal game, and had yet to spread beyond south-eastern England, cricket's ancestral cradle of Kent, Surrey and Sussex. Yet the essence of modern cricket was evident, so much so that even in the very first account of a 'great' cricket match, in the *Foreign Post* in 1697, 'they were eleven of a side' and playing for 'fifty guineas a piece'.[11] As the 18th century progressed, references to cricket begin to proliferate and the development of the game got well and truly underway (no. 13).

'There are few things more easy to be determined than that cricket is a game entirely and exclusively of English origin,' wrote Charles Box in 1877, echoing the sentiments of many.[12] And yet recent research has suggested an apparent concurrence of several Flemish features in early cricket: the Flemish name for their game of hockey, *met de krik ketsen*, played with a curved stick some believe similar to early cricket bats; the identification of John Derrick as a Flemish name; and the fact that the early distribution of cricket around its centres in Sevenoaks and Maidstone in Kent, the Guildford area in Surrey and Chichester in Sussex closely matched trade routes in southern England where Flemish migrants were active in the cloth trade. Could there be some connection between the 16th-century Flemish migration into this area of England and the evolution of cricket?[13] So far the evidence is inconclusive, and a cricket-like game has never been found on the continent.

*　　*　　*

In 1937 Robert Henderson published an article in the *Bulletin of the New York Public Library* containing clear documented evidence that a game called 'baseball' had been played for a hundred years before any supposed American 'invention' of the game. This article, together with his 1947 book *Ball, Bat and Bishop: The Origin of Ball Games*, clearly dismissed the popular story that Abner Doubleday had invented the game. It also prompted future baseball historians to seek the historical origins of the game beyond American shores, and a small but growing group of dedicated researchers began to search with renewed interest for the earliest references to a game called 'baseball'.

In 1993, Patrick Carroll, a member of the UK branch of the Society for American Baseball Research (SABR UK), put forward the proposition that any 'authoritative history of baseball' in England needed to start with a serious look at all the references pointing to a British origin of the game and that the researchers of SABR UK were well placed to undertake such an assignment.[14] The first task for Carroll was to untangle what he called the 'the rounders-as-chicken-baseball-as-egg theory'. Despite the many assertions, scholarly and otherwise, that baseball evolved from the 'old' English game, no one had yet proved the antiquity of rounders. Crucially, it turned out that the name 'rounders' dates only from the early 19th century, and what Carroll found was a confused semantic logic that 'baseball evolved from rounders, only rounders, at the time when baseball was evolving from it, wasn't called rounders, it was called baseball'.[15]

These first steps were picked up and significantly expanded by baseball historian David Block who, in a prodigious endeavour of scholarship, 'sought to identify and analyse every possible early ball game and pastime that might have a place in baseball's genealogy'.[16] He uncovered a German description of *das englische Base-ball* dating back to 1796 making an overt connection between the game and England (see below), and his ground-breaking book *Baseball before We Knew It* brought the story of baseball's beginnings to a broad audience. It is now widely acknowledged that baseball is not only of British origin but that the game had been called baseball, or at least 'base ball', since at least the middle of the 18th century. Some of this evidence was new and some had been known, but not emphasised, for many years. A concentrated effort to bring this story to the fore was further strengthened by an exciting new discovery in 2007 (no. 14).

> *After Dinner Went to Miss Jeale's to play at Base Ball, with her,*
> *the 3 Miss Whiteheads, Miss Billinghurst, Miss Molly Flutter,*
> *Mr. Chandler, Mr. Ford, H. Parsons & Jolly. Drank tea and stayed till 8.*
> William Bray, diary entry in Shere, Surrey, England, 1755

William Bray (1736–1832) was a solicitor and antiquarian who lived in the Surrey village of Shere and wrote the seminal history of the county. He was

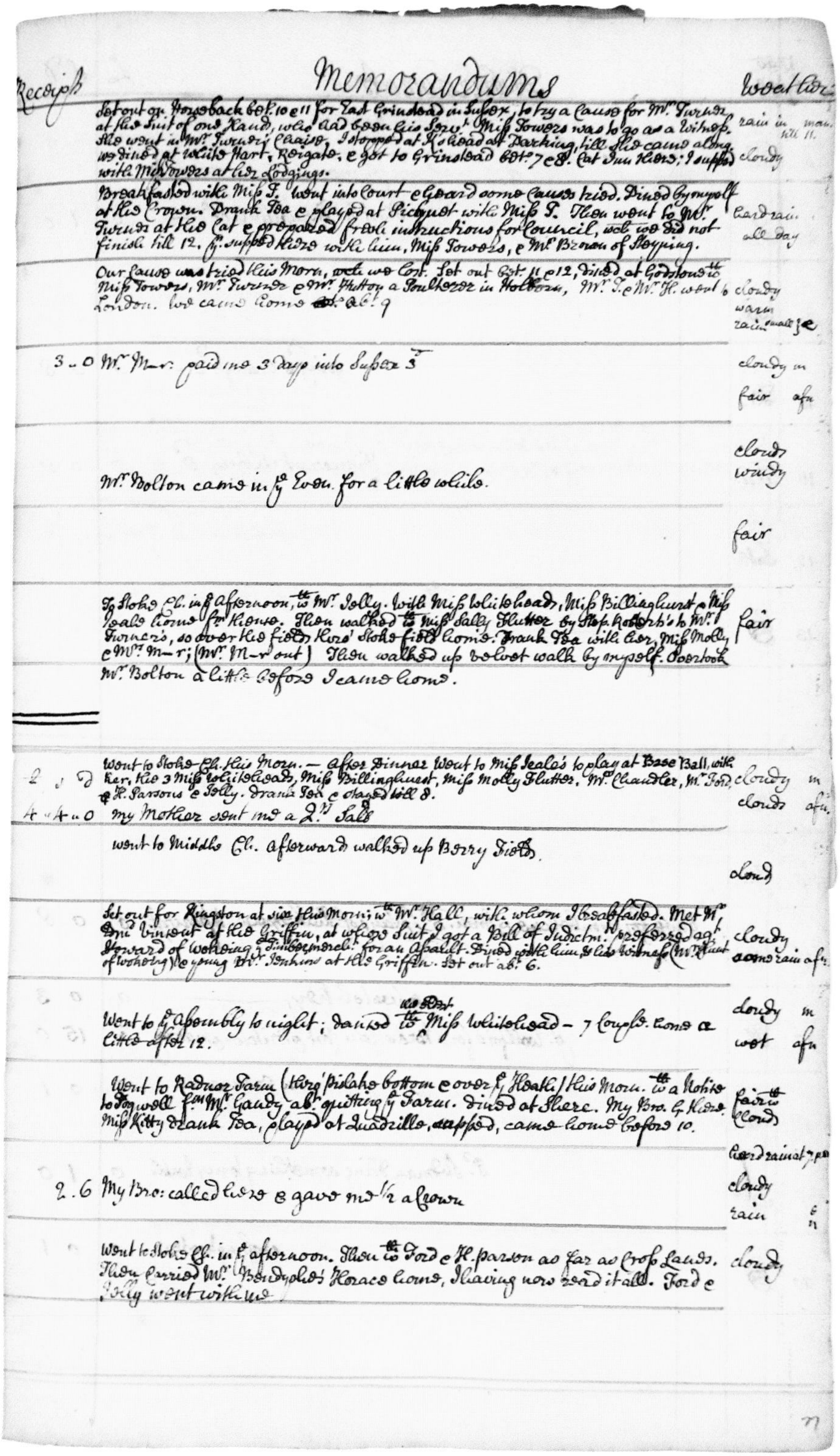
Receipts | Memorandums | Weather

Set out on Horseback bet. 10 & 11 for East Grinstead in Sussex, to try a Cause for Mr. Turner at the Suit of one Hand, who had been his Serv.t Miss Towers was to go as a Witness. She went in Mr. Turner's Chaise. I stopped at K's Head at Dorking, till she came along. We dined at White Hart, Reigate, & got to Grinstead bet. 7 & 8. Lay at Inn there; I supped with Miss Towers at her Lodgings. — rain in morn till 11. cloudy

Breakfasted with Miss T. Went into Court & heard some Causes tried. Dined by myself at the Crown. Drank Tea & played at Picquet with Miss T. Then went to Mr. Turner at the Cat & prepared fresh instructions for Council, wch we did not finish till 12. Supped there with him, Miss Towers, & Mr. Brown of Steyning. — hard rain all day

Our Cause was tried this Morn, wch we Lost. Set out bet. 11 & 12, dined at Godstone with Miss Towers, Mr. Turner & Mr. Hutton a Poulterer in Holborn, Mr. T. & Mr. H. went to London. We came home ab.t 9 — cloudy warm small rain

3 . 0 Mr. M—r: paid me 3 days into Sussex 3 — cloudy m. fair afn

Mr. Bolton came in y.e Even. for a little while. — cloudy windy

fair

To Stoke Ch. in y.e Afternoon, wth Mr. Jolly. With Miss Whitehead, Miss Billinghurst & Miss Seale home for there. Then walked wth Miss Sally Flutter by Step. Roberts's to Mr. Turner's, so over the fields there Stoke field home. Drank Tea with her, Miss Molly & Mr. M—r; (Mr. M—r out) Then walked up velvet walk by myself. Overtook Mr. Bolton a little before I came home. — fair

Went to Stoke Ch. this Morn. — After Dinner Went to Miss Seale's to play at Base Ball, with her, the 3 Miss Whiteheads, Miss Billinghurst, Miss Molly Flutter, Mr. Chandler, Mr. Ford, & H. Parsons & Jolly. Drank Tea & stayed till 8. — cloudy m. cloudy afn.

4 . 4 . 0 My Mother sent me a 2.d Sal[?]

Went to Middle Ch. afterward walked up Berry field. — cloudy

Set out for Kingston at six this Morn; wth Mr. Hall, with whom I breakfasted. Met Mr. Dm. Vincent at the Griffin, at whose Suit I got a Bill of Indictm.t preferred ag.t Steward of Woking & Timbermerch.t for an Assault. Dined with him & his Witness (Mr. Hunt of Woking) & young Mr. Jenkins at the Griffin. Set out ab.t 6. — cloudy some rain afn.

Went to y.e Assembly to night; danced wth Miss Whitehead — 7 Couple. Home a little after 12. — cloudy m. wet afn

Went to Radnor Farm (thro' Pitlake bottom & over y.e Heath) this Morn. wth a Notice to Sopwell fm Mr. Gandy ab.t quitting y.e Farm. Dined at there. My Bro. & there. Miss Kitty drank Tea, played at Quadrille, supped, came home before 10. — fair wth clouds

hard rain at 7 pm

2 . 6 My Bro: called here & gave me 1/2 a Crown — cloudy rain

Went to Stoke Ch. in y.e afternoon. Then wth Ford & H. Parson as far as Cross Lanes. Then carried Mr. Bendysh's Horace home, I having now read it all. Ford & Jolly went with me — cloudy

14
Diary of William Bray
The historic entry for 31 March 1755 appears halfway down the page, beginning 'Went to Stoke Ch. this Morn – After dinner…'

15–17

15–17

A Little Pretty Pocket-Book, Intended for the Instruction and Amusement of Little Master Tommy and Pretty Miss Polly, 1760 (10th edition)

15: page 43 (base-ball)
16: page 40 (cricket)
17: page 41 (stool-ball)

The earliest printed reference to 'base-ball' is found in this diminutive children's book printed by John Newbery in London, which depicts 32 different games and activities, each illustrated and described with a poem. Other games featured include cricket and 'stool-ball'. No copies of the 1744 edition seem to exist, nor of the eight subsequent editions. Single copies of later editions – the earliest in 1760 – exist in library collections. Pirated American editions were produced in 1762 in New York and in 1786 in Philadelphia, although neither edition survives. Isaiah Thomas published the first major American edition in Worcester, Massachusetts in 1787.

also a meticulous diarist and many volumes he kept over the course of his long life are now in the collection of the Surrey History Centre. Bray was a tireless chronicler of varied interests and his diaries have long been a treasure trove of everyday life for historians of 18th-century England. In 2007, a previously unrecognised reference to 'Base Ball' was discovered in the first volume of his diaries, written when Bray was still a young man.[17] Among his detailed daily entries is one on Easter Monday in 1755 when the 18-year-old Bray writes of a social gathering where he played 'base ball' with some friends, both men and women. Seven years before, a royal courtier Lady Hervey wrote a letter, dated 14 November 1748, describing the wintertime diversions of the family of the Prince of Wales: 'in a large room, they divert themselves at base-ball, a play all who are or have been, schoolboys are well acquainted with'. Taking part were 'the ladies, as well as the gentlemen', showing that by this time 'base ball' or 'base-ball' had evolved beyond a children's game into an acceptable adult diversion, played for social entertainment rather than serious competition.[18] This letter itself seems no longer to exist – we know of it only because it was published with others in 1821 – and this means Bray's diary is the oldest surviving handwritten reference to the game of baseball in England – or indeed, anywhere.

There are, however, even earlier printed sources. The first known printed reference to baseball is in John Newbery's children's book *A Little Pretty Pocket-Book, Intended for the Instruction and Amusement of Little Master Tommy and Pretty Miss Polly*, first published in London in 1744 (nos 15–18). This book is considered to be the first children's book specifically intended for entertainment. It is also the earliest known reference to baseball; however, it seems that no copies of the 1744 edition have survived, the earliest existing edition dating from 1760. Another book, *The Card*, this time published by John Newbery but written by John Kidgell, mentions 'Base-Ball' (describing it as 'an *infant* Game')

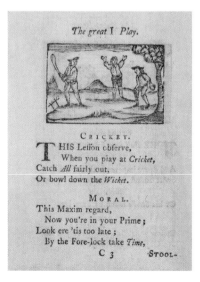

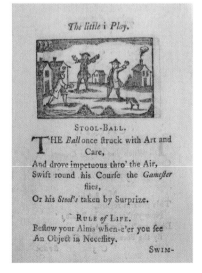

and was published at the end of 1754.[19]

The first published rules of baseball appeared in Germany in a book of games and sports by Johann Christoph Friedrich Gutsmuths in 1796. Gutsmuths describes two versions, *das englische Base-ball* and the related German game, *das deutsche Ballspiel.* The English game is described in detail and a diagram of the game is also included, suggesting that baseball was well known by the close of the 18th century. While many aspects of the game changed over the years, much is still recognisable like pitching, batting and base running (no. 19). Baseball made a cameo appearance in Jane Austen's *Northanger Abbey,* written between 1798 and 1799 although not published until 1818. Later it was also among the festivities on offer at the birthday of the Duchess of Kent in 1858.[20]

18
Handkerchief: The Pretty Pocket-Book Companion, mid-18th century
This handkerchief appears to be a companion to *A Little Pretty Pocket-Book* and probably dates from around the mid-1700s. Based on the book, it shows a vignette and poem for many of the activities featured in the book, including both baseball and cricket.

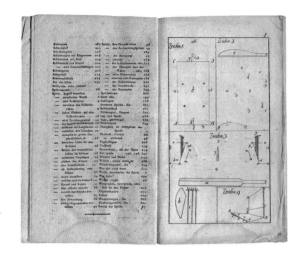

19

Johann Christoph Friedrich Gutsmuths, *Spiele zur Uebung und Erholung des Körpers und Geistes: für die Jugend, ihre Erzieher und alle freunde unschuldiger Jugendfreuden / gesammelt und praktisch bearbeitet von Gutsmuths,* **1802**

A clearly identified version of baseball is described in this German book by Gutsmuths (1759–1839), first published in 1796. The title translates as 'Games for the exercise and recreation of body and spirit for the youth and his educator and all friends of innocent joys of youth'. A diagram of the game is featured at top right (the illustration marked 2).

The ancestor games: what came before cricket and baseball?

These early baseball references join other bat and ball sports in England – the ancient games of stoolball, trapball and cricket, among others. Together these show us that by the middle of the 18th century, and arguably much earlier, there was a social tradition of play that included all of these sports bubbling along together.

One of Britain's longest surviving rural sports, stoolball (no. 20), is often credited as an ancestor of both cricket and baseball. David Block feels that 'no other single game contributed more to baseball's early development'.[21] The earliest confirmed written citation of stoolball dates to 1450, and stoolball was undoubtedly being played by young men and women together in the 16th and 17th centuries, customarily at Easter-time, and was strongly linked to fertility and courtship.[22] This tradition of Easter-time ball games was continued by William Bray and his friends playing baseball in 1755. Stories about milkmaids and their beaus playing with the milking stool as the wicket, allotting prizes of cakes, especially tansy cakes, and kisses to lucky winners, and literary references, too, all attest to the cultural importance of the game.

Stoolball can be played on almost any ground, level or not, and several variations were played throughout the late 19th century. The ball could be hit with the hand or with a bat to defend a stool, as the wicket is defended in cricket, and there could be multiple stools, like the bases in baseball. In today's version the game is still played by both sexes, although more women than men play competitively (there are ladies' matches and mixed matches). There are two 'stools', wooden boards on stakes, and the field is marked with a 90-yard-diameter boundary. As in cricket, teams are eleven-a-side, and there is a central pitch, in this case 16 yards long, with batters at either end. Bowling is underarm, and as in baseball the ball reaches the batsman without hitting the ground. The bowling crease is ten yards from the batsman's wicket, and the bat is made of willow and paddle-shaped, like in table tennis but with a long, sprung and spliced handle. Scoring and rules are similar to cricket, with some key differences including eight-ball overs and a body-before-wicket (bbw) rule in place of the leg-before-wicket (lbw) rule in cricket due to the markedly different size and shape of the wicket.

Stoolball was popular in the 19th century, especially with young women

20
Stoolball, *c*.1923
This ball was found in a biscuit tin in Plumpton, East Sussex, and dates to a few years after Major W. W. Grantham established the first national stoolball body.

21
Trap, late 17th century
22
Ball, possibly child-sized for cricket, c.1637
From Canterbury, Kent, this dark oak trap is shaped like a 17th-century Puritan shoe, with squared-off toe but with a pivoted, ladle-shaped tongue, the head of which fits into a circular depression at the heel, on which the ball is placed before play, as in this picture. It is not known if the ball shown here was ever used as a trap-ball; this one is recorded as being used for cricket around 1637 (although the date is disputed) and has a cricket-like seam, but is more the size of a stoolball or trapball.

around the Sussex area. While a number of variations of the sport appeared in the 18th century, along with reports of it being played in northern England, the 1840s saw rapid growth in East Sussex with clubs of women and girls competing over the summer months. Formalised rules followed, laid down in 1881 at Glynde in East Sussex. During World War I Major W. W. Grantham, a member of the Military Tribunal, saw stoolball as the perfect sport for the 'battered heroes of the war in our military hospitals' (his son had been badly wounded in France). Unlike tennis or cricket, it was not overly strenuous for wounded soldiers who had frequently lost limbs. A seminal match held that year at Sussex County Cricket Club's ground saw the soldiers 'damaged by wounds' defeat a team of lawyers 'damaged by age', including Major Grantham.[23] The sport's popularity was such that there were annual matches at Lord's from 1919 to 1927, and the Stoolball Association of Great Britain, formed in 1923, spread the game through schools and even to other parts of the Empire. By the 1930s there were a thousand teams in Sussex and south-east England.

More recently, the sport has gone from strength to strength since the National Stoolball Association took up the reins in 1979. While there remains a certain affectionate sentimentality towards the courting traditions of the game, the modern competition can be highly skilled and keenly fought. Formally rebranded as Stoolball England in 2008, this national body today runs a competition of over 200 clubs with over 5,000 active players largely concentrated in Kent, Surrey, Sussex and Hampshire, a part of England also renowned as the cradle of cricket.

Touch lightly the Trap,
And strike low the Ball;
Let none catch you,
And you'll beat them all

Thus was trapball described in *A Little Pretty Pocket-Book*, but the sport was already centuries old by the middle of the 18th century. References to it date back to the 1400s, and it survives to this day, but only in a few English pubs. The game, primarily a batting and fielding exercise, had a basic premise: place a small ball on the trap, use the lever to launch it into the air, and then hit it with a small bat, also called a trapstick (nos 21–22). Early sport historian Joseph Strutt described a regional variety played in the county of Essex that was played with a round bat, rather than one with a flat face, which hit the ball 'an astonishing distance'.[24] It had a few regional variations and it remained a simple but popular pastime for generations. The bat seems to have changed shape a number of times from paddle-shaped to one thin and round, to the cricket-influenced flat-faced bat seen in 18th-century paintings showing children with trapball equipment.[25] The flat-faced bats are typically like a small child-sized cricket bat and the balls are also small, with a distinctive figure-eight seam on the leather cover, similar to the modern baseball.[26]

The portrait reproduced here of John Chandos Reade (1785–1868), later the 7th Baronet of Barton, shows him holding a small trap bat and ball (no. 23). He stands next to a mechanised trap 'shoe', a new device brought into the game in the 18th century.[27]

23
William Redmore Bigg,
John Chandos Reade as a Boy
This portrait of a boy playing trapball is typical of William Redmore Bigg (1755–1828) who is noted for his rustic portraits, many showing children in sporting and rustic scenes.

Play! / Play ball!

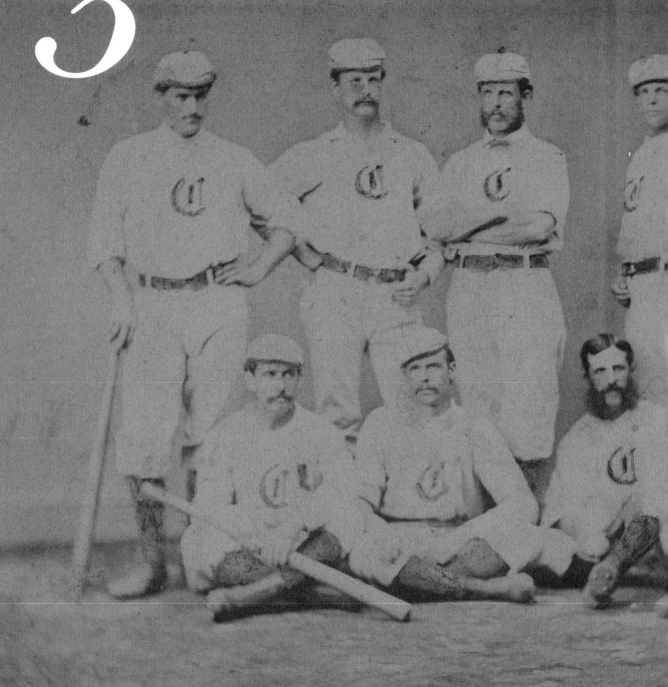

Old Red Stockings (Cin

The game of cricket is thoroughly British.
John Nyren, 1833

Cincinnati Red Stockings,
1869 (see page 43)

*[Baseball] is a game which is peculiarly suited to the
American temperament and disposition.*
Charles A. Peverelly, 1866

If a baseball fan sat down at an international cricket Test match with no preparation and no guidance, in all likelihood they would feel lost. And the same goes for the cricket tragic at a major league baseball game. Yet taken in small pieces, what someone knows from one of the sports can help him or her to understand the other. The comparisons can tell us much about both games.

A glimpse of the early games

In September 1743, the widely read *Gentlemen's Magazine* remarked rather sourly that 'noblemen, gentlemen and clergy' had made 'butchers, coblers [sic] or tinkers their companions in the game'. This oft-quoted observation signalled that cricket by the 1740s was no longer child's play but had become established across a wide range of English society, crossing class structures and played by adults. And while the above correspondent censured 'people of fashion' for drawing working people away from their employment to watch their games – 'to the ruin of their families' – his austere view must have held little sway as regular competitive cricket matches were increasingly reported and promoted in the press and attracted thousands of spectators.[1] This early form of cricket was remarkably similar in fundamentals of play to the later game, even though it was played with ancient-looking long, curved bats and underarm bowling, and the wicket behind the batsman was lower than today and consisted of two stumps (wooden sticks driven into the ground) rather than the modern three.

Only 50 years later, by the 1790s, many more elements of cricket had become recognisably similar to the modern game. The widely distributed Laws of Cricket regulated play and increasingly popular clubs played each other on a regular basis. Dress and equipment had become fairly standardised. On the field, the wickets were higher and had three stumps each rather than the original two, giving the bowler a more hittable target and therefore a more serious role in the game. Balls were still delivered underarm but no longer rolled along the ground; bowlers now delivered them in the air so that they bounced before reaching the batsman, the aim being to hit the batsman's stumps. The bats too were in their modern form, thicker and straight-edged with the distinctive flat face, allowing the batsman to either hit the ball or block it to protect his more vulnerable wicket. Two umpires, wearing coats and leaning on bats, controlled the game, and two scorers kept tally by notching runs onto sticks, as seen in the painting *The Game of Cricket* of about 1790 (no. 24).

Jump forward to the 1850s and an even more rapid transformation had brought baseball to a similar stage in its development. Over just a few decades in early 19th-century America, an assortment of closely related informal bat and ball games had been taken up by adults. These games often had different names in different areas and, with limited transportation and communication, little standardisation. They were fluid and flexible enough to allow for local variations in available fields and equipment, and in the number of players. Several were associated with one particular area. Round-town was common in rural Virginia, while New England had a game of its own commonly known as round ball, but which came to be known as the Massachusetts game. The game of town ball, on the other hand, sprang up in numerous large cities. In Philadelphia in the early 1830s one of America's pioneer ball-playing clubs, the Olympic Ball Club, was originally formed to play town ball. It seems likely that town ball was a generic, catch-all term for whatever variety of early baseball was played in any particular town.[2]

24
English School, *The Game of Cricket, c.*1790

A small number of clubs in the New York area took to baseball with particular seriousness of purpose. The Knickerbocker club formalised its own rules in 1845 that, with variations, were more widely adopted by other clubs in the 1850s. The end of the Civil War brought greater enthusiasm and standardisation into the game, continuing the earlier trend. From the late 1860s, baseball clubs grew more popular, and more numerous outside of the New York City hub, as the sport became increasingly structured and serious.

Two great New York area rivals, the Atlantics of Brooklyn and the Mutuals of New York played a tightly fought 'Grand Match for the Championship' in 1865, as captured in a popular print (no. 25). The field, equipment and position of the players depicted are all recognisably modern, but still some early features of the game remain: underarm pitching, gloveless play, bib-front uniform shirts, a single umpire off to the side, and standing spectators on the boundary of the field.

As cricket and baseball transformed from popular pastimes into codified and formalised games popular with prosperous gentlemen in urban environments, the dress of the players underwent a corresponding change. Early cricketers had mostly played in their everyday clothes. For gentlemen in the 18th century this meant white linen shirts and breeches, perhaps with coloured ribbons at the knee fasteners, and long stockings. Some clubs wore formal colours, like the light blue coats with black velvet trim of Hambledon

25
The American National Game of Base Ball: Grand Match for the Championship at the Elysian Fields, Hoboken, New Jersey, 1865 (lithograph of 1866)

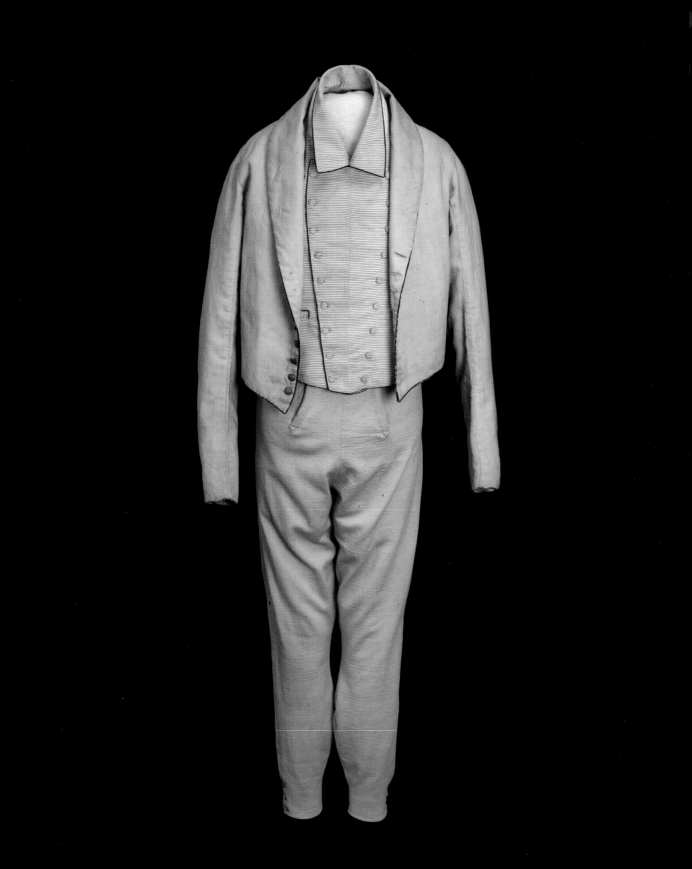

Club in Hampshire, the foremost club in England in the late 18th century. But by the late 1820s the now traditional white shirts and long trousers were generally worn at all levels of the game, from the village green to the great matches.[3] In the earliest surviving cricket outfit, from approximately 1821, the jacket and waistcoat are both short and close fitting, and the trousers are very narrow, especially at the ankle; all the clothes are white (no. 26).

Later, as can be seen in the 1868 photograph of Philadelphia's Merion Cricket Club (no. 27), the trousers widened, which allowed for thin, rudimentary padding underneath. Merion's players wore typical on-field clothing for any cricketers of the 1860s, standardised even on an international scale: a combination of plain, striped and polka-dot shirts, white trousers and boots. Some players wore bowties or other neckties, caps of assorted styles replaced earlier everyday headwear – like the top hats seen in *The Game of Cricket* (no. 24) – and most sported the elaborately embroidered belts with decorated brass buckles so popular at that time. The belts all but disappeared in the late 1870s and 1880s as cricketers adopted the practice of using their club ties to hold their trousers up. Their sudden fall in popularity could well be explained by W. G. Grace's caution that accidental contact of the bat with the buckle could be confused by the umpire as the sound of the ball hitting the bat, increasing the batsman's risk of being unfairly dismissed.[4]

One of baseball's best known early amateur clubs, the Knickerbocker Base Ball Club of New York City, introduced baseball's first official uniform in 1849, a plain white shirt worn over blue woollen pants with straw hats.[5] The bib-front or shield-front jersey, embroidered with the club's initials, was

26
Cricket Outfit worn by Henry Daw of Christchurch, *c.*1821
This cricket outfit was worn by Henry Daw of Christchurch in Dorset, on England's south coast. It has been dated to around 1821, making this the earliest known surviving cricket outfit, and a very early example of what was to become the standard cricket uniform.

27
Merion Cricket Club, Philadelphia, First Eleven, 1868
This Philadelphia team is mostly wearing typical on-field clothing for cricketers of the 1860s. Interestingly, two players on the left in the photograph wear the knicker-style pants later more commonly associated with baseball clubs but worn by American cricketers in the 1860s. This photograph was taken the year after the Cincinnati Red Stockings first adopted them and made them a central part of the baseball uniform (see no. 29).

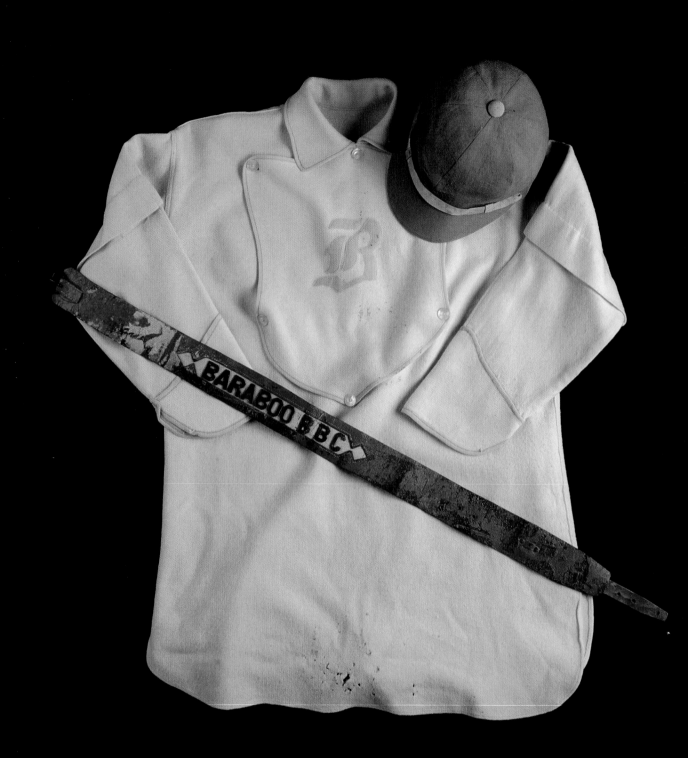

extremely popular in the 1860s and 1870s, reminiscent of volunteer fire company uniforms. Early clubs also frequently wore belts sewn in thick leather with their club name prominently visible at the front and fastened at the back. All of these features can be seen in the earliest known surviving baseball uniform, dating from about 1866 (no. 28). A few years later in 1868, the Cincinnati Red Stockings (no. 29) unveiled knicker-style pants, a fashion reminiscent of 18th-century gentlemen cricketers' pants but radically new for baseball's on-field uniform. These allowed for greater ease of movement and also showed off the Cincinnati signature red socks. Given the club's ambitious and hugely successful playing tour the following year, it is not surprising their unusual pants were soon copied and in fact they remain a part of baseball today – although far fewer players choose to wear them now.

28
Baseball jersey, cap and belt worn by LeGrand Lippitt from the Baraboo BBC, *c*.1866
This is the earliest surviving baseball uniform. It was worn by LeGrand Lippitt when he played for the Baraboo Base Ball Club of Baraboo, Wisconsin.

29
Cincinnati Red Stockings, 1869
This studio photograph was taken in Washington, DC by celebrated American photographer Mathew Brady.

Old Red Stockings (Cincinnati) 1869

Bats

It's hard work making batting look effortless.
David Gower, England cricketer, 1989[6]

The development of the cricket bat is a much longer story than that of the baseball bat, because the cricket bat started out in a very different form from the heavy straight bats used today. Depicted here is one of the earliest surviving cricket bats, dating to around the 1730s (no. 30). This bat is made from a single piece of wood and is lightweight and modest in size.[7] But it is its shape that is most striking, curved up at one end like a hockey stick. These early bats, described as being like 'a table-knife with a curve in the back', were designed to strike at the ball with what we would now consider to be a more baseball-like sweeping motion as it was delivered underarm to the batsman. As such the bat was well suited to the two-stump wickets at a time when defence of the players' wicket was not as paramount as it would become later in the 18th century.[8]

Cricket bats took on their familiar straight-sided rectangular shape in the 1770s as part of 'a total revolution' in the style of play.[9] A bouncier 'length' version of underarm bowling had evolved, and would be perfected by Hambledon's David Harris, that demanded a new, more defensive style of batting and a new bat. These straight, flat-sided bats were still made from a single piece of wood, and to the batsman's personal specifications, as well illustrated by John Ring's bat (no. 31), which is inscribed with his nickname, 'Little Joey'. In 1774 the width of the blade was limited to $4\frac{1}{4}$ inches (10.8 cm), and in 1835 the length was also limited to its current standard, no greater than 38 inches (96.5 cm).[10] While Ring's bat dates from 1792, it is still well within modern specifications. A right-handed batsman from Kent, Ring is sometimes cited as one of two players who first used their leg pads, rather than the bat, to keep the ball away from their stumps. This style of play brought about the leg-before-wicket (lbw) Law, where a player is given out if the umpire deems the ball would have hit the stumps when blocked by the pads. It is hard to know where this story came from, as Ring's playing career began after the law was introduced, but Ring is also famous for a less happy reason as one of the game's fatalities. He died seven years after using this bat, aged 42, the cause being a fever seemingly due to a broken nose sustained when he was hit in the face by a cricket ball delivered during a practice session by his brother.[11]

Around the late 1830s, a separate handle began to be inserted into the blade to allow more 'give' when striking the ball. By the time the great English cricketer, W. G. Grace, began his celebrated career in 1864, one that saw plenty

30–35
Three centuries of cricket bats. From left to right:
30
Cricket bat made from a single piece of wood, *c*.1730s
31
John Ring's cricket bat, inscribed 'Little Joey', 1792–93
32
W. G. Grace's cricket bat, *c*.1880
33
Spalding cricket bat signed by the Australian Eleven, 1921
34
Paul Collingwood's cricket bat, 2006
35
Mongoose cricket bat, 2009

36 (opposite right)
Wagon Tongue brand baseball bat, *c.*1892

The Wagon Tongue brand, manufactured by A. G. Spalding & Bros, was made from seasoned second-growth ash and was named after the older practice of making baseball bats from a covered wagon's tongue (the pole that connects the wagon's wheel base to the yoke of the horses or oxen).

37 (opposite left)
Barry Bonds's maple wood SAM BAT, 2001

Bonds hit a massive 451-foot home run with this bat on 7 June 2001, setting what was at the time the distance record at Pacific Bell Park in San Francisco. This was his 32nd homer for the season and 526th career home run. Six years later, on 7 August 2007, Bonds broke Hank Aaron's career home run record when he hit his 756th homer, an achievement clouded by allegations of steroid use.

of powerful hitting, this design was commonplace (no. 32). Grace is also said never to have used a new bat himself, but to have a young player, who could not hit hard, play with it to wear it in and acquire its 'face'.[12]

With few exceptions, willow has been the wood used to make cricket bats since the 1740s. A fast-growing and resilient but light wood, it is naturally soft and therefore treated to achieve the hardness needed for a cricket bat. The more durable, close-grained red willow was favoured by W. G. Grace and some of his contemporaries at the close of the 19th century, but soon after the softer white willow became more popular. A good example is the cricket bat signed by the Australian side that toured England in the summer of 1921, manufactured by A. G. Spalding & Bros at their Putney Wharf plant, London – part of Spalding's worldwide sporting goods empire (no. 33).

Cricket bats today, although still made from willow, with spliced handles, tend to be heavier and the maker's branding is more obvious than in the past, as can be seen from England batsman Paul Collingwood's Slazenger bat, with its distinctive scooping curve (no. 34), which he used to score his first two Test centuries, 134 runs against India and 186 against Pakistan, both in 2006. The handles are made from cane wrapped in twine but covered in rubber for better grip, and players no longer use twine and wire to mend a crack in the blade like W. G. Grace did with his bat.

Innovations continue as the game changes, as can be seen with the 'Mongoose' bat (no. 35), a style developed for aggressive batting with a long handle and shortened blade. This specialised bat, tested and approved at Lord's Cricket Ground in 2009, is designed for the increased power and speed called for in today's game. A few players, contracted as Mongoose company ambassadors, have used it at international level, including the Australian Matthew Hayden who switched to the Mongoose for the 2010 IPL after hitting balls at practice sessions with a baseball bat. The Mongoose 'gives you extra power when you are in an attacking position and wanting to dominate the bowlers,' said Hayden.[13]

Bats used in early baseball would have been handmade from available materials, rudimentary and certainly variable in length and size. As the game standardised in the 19th century the bats, while heavier, less tapered and longer than those of today, were otherwise remarkably similar in size and shape. The Spalding Wagon Tongue brand bat illustrated here, despite its nostalgic name, dates from the 1890s (no. 36). They were made with or without a knob, and the rules of 1857 determined that all bats be round in cross-section and no more than 2½ inches in width around the thickest part. Starting in 1868, bats could be no longer than 42 inches, but below this limit bat lengths varied considerably – this example is 35 inches long. Soon after this Wagon Tongue

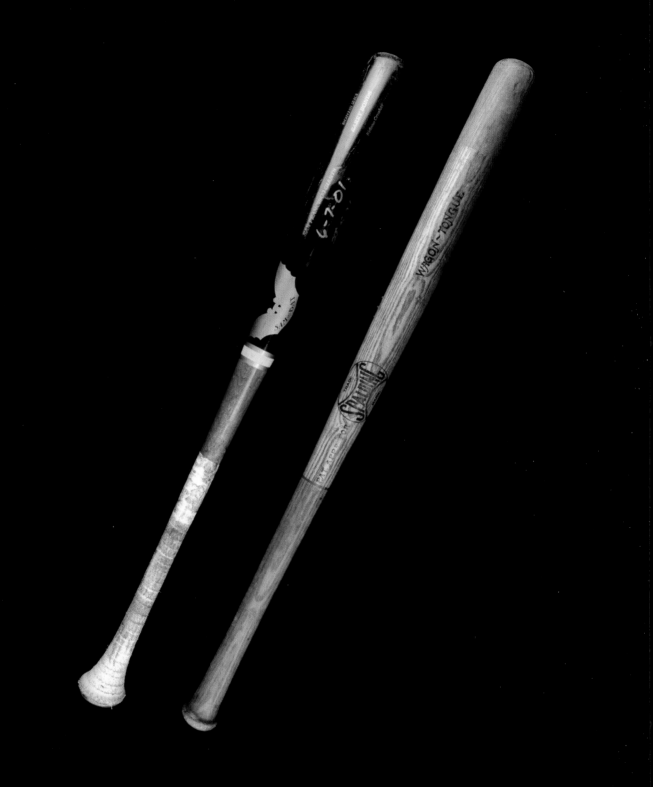

was made, the maximum width was increased to today's 2 ¾ inches.[14]

Until recently, baseball bats at major league level have all been made from ash wood, but Barry Bonds recently changed that when he became one of the first to use a bat made from the harder, more durable maple wood. His success set an example that other players soon followed. During the 2001 baseball season, he dramatically closed in on the single-season home run record of 70, set by Mark McGwire in the 1998 season, before surpassing it on 5 October 2001, and ended the season with a new record 73 homers, all achieved using a bat made from maple rather than the traditional ash (no. 37).

Unusual bats

The blade shall consist solely of wood.
Law 6.4.b of the Laws of Cricket

The bat shall be one piece of solid wood.
Rule 1.10.a of the Official Rules of Major League Baseball

Both baseball and cricket specify that bats used at the highest professional level must be made out of wood. And both have strict specifications on the allowable length and width to ensure all players are competing with equal equipment. This has not stopped many from trying to circumvent these regulations by covert means. Players have been known to hollow out the top of their baseball bat, fill it with cork or rubber balls and then cover the hole with a wooden plug in an attempt to hide their illegal 'corked' bat. Famously, the cricketer Thomas White of Reigate in the early 1770s appeared with a bat as wide as his stumps.

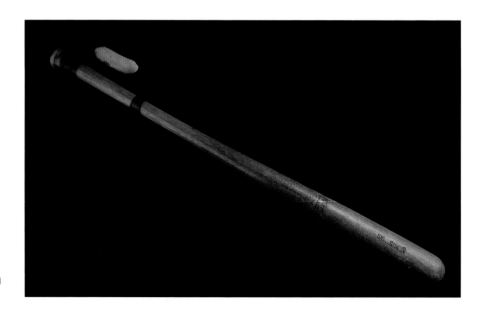

38
Syl Simon's modified baseball bat, *c*.1927

Two hundred years later Dennis Lillee attempted to use an aluminium bat during a Test match in Perth in 1979. Kookaburra bat makers supplied Australian Ricky Ponting with a wooden bat backed with graphite in 2006. All of these bats went against the standards of the day and were promptly judged illegal.[15]

Both sports have ruling bodies – the Office of the Commissioner of Baseball and Marylebone Cricket Club, respectively – to judge the legitimacy of any innovations to the bat. One unusual bat, officially allowed in baseball for a short time from 1885 to 1893, had a flat-sided face, like a cricket bat.[16] This was a specialist bat for bunting, used only when players wanted more control so as to perfectly place the ball close in the infield.

The two bats shown here have been modified, not to gain advantage but to allow two players missing fingers to be able to hold the bat. Syl Simon, whose Louisville slugger bat (no. 38) has been modified with a padded iron handle, was a professional player when, in the autumn of 1926, when he lost all but the little finger and part of his thumb on his left hand in a furniture factory accident. This bat allowed him to return to play minor league ball in 1927, until retiring in 1932.

The modified cricket bat shown alongside (no. 39) is much older, dating to the 1790s or early 1800s and was specially made for Robert Robinson, whose many nicknames included 'Long', 'Long Robin' or 'Long Bob', due to his great height at six foot one inch, and 'Three-Fingered Jack', due to his deformed right hand. Reports in the 19th century vary but it seems he was missing one or two fingers, lost either through fire when a boy, or due to the violence of a cricket ball. Robinson had an iron cuff fitted to his wrist with which he grasped the upper part of the special handle on his bat.[17] During his long cricketing career spanning from before 1792 until 1819 (when he retired, aged 54, just three years before his death), Robinson played at the top of the game and was for many years considered one of the best batsmen, and hardest hitters, in England.

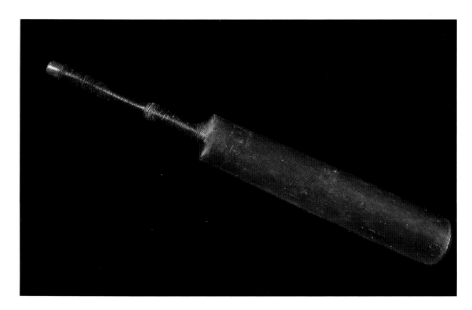

39
Robert 'Long' Robinson's modified cricket bat, *c.*1790–1819

A farmer's son, tall and powerfully built, his batting action was described as 'like a countryman mowing with a scythe'.[18] In the days before strictly regulated bats, his modified version caused him no problems, apart from one time when the width of his bat was questioned. Found to be too wide, Robinson was forced to watch angrily while his bat was whittled down with a penknife. 'I'll pay you out for spoiling my bat,' he cried, and went on to play one of his best innings, although no one seems to have recorded the score.[19]

Balls

The ball shall be a sphere formed by yarn wound around a small core of cork, rubber or similar material, covered with two strips of white horsehide or cowhide, tightly stitched together. It shall weigh not less than five nor more than 5¹/₄ ounces avoirdupois and measure not less than nine nor more than 9¹/₄ inches in circumference.
Rule 1.09 of the Official Rules of Major League Baseball

The ball, when new, shall weigh not less than 5¹/₂ ounces/155.9g, nor more than 5³/₄ ounces/163g, and shall measure not less than 8¹³/₁₆ inches/22.4 cm, nor more than 9 inches/22.9 cm in circumference.
Law 5.1 of the Laws of Cricket

40
Cricket ball from the match at Lord's in which William Ward hit 278 runs, July 1820

For balls the situation is reversed, for the oldest known cricket ball is remarkably similar to those of today, while the baseball progressed through a number of stages to reach the signature figure-eight stitching of today. The oldest known cricket ball dates only to 1820, hardly very old for such an ancient game (no. 40). This ball is the one William Ward smacked to all corners of Lord's Cricket Ground during a memorable four-day match in July 1820. At a time when large scores were rare, and the Lord's pitch was notoriously rocky and uneven, Ward made 278 runs, the highest score made in any class of cricket at that time. He batted through the first day – his 33rd birthday – and the second and into the third day, to create a ground record at Lord's that would stand for 105 years. It is no surprise that the ball – its cork centre wrapped in worsted wool covered with four sections of tanned hide – is somewhat lumpy and misshapen. That same year the English ball maker Duke & Son was granted a royal warrant to manufacture cricket balls, bringing to an end the tradition of players making balls purely for their own use.[20]

In baseball, the balls were also initially made by hand. Rubber from an old overshoe often made up the core, which was wrapped in woolen yarn and covered with an old piece of leather. If a small amount of rubber was used the ball would be 'dead'; using more rubber and tightly wound yarn made for a bouncier, 'lively' ball. As in cricket at that time, a single ball was used for the entire game, its size largely unregulated. Baseball's first convention in 1857 required that balls weighed between 6 and 6¼ ounces and measured between 10 and 10¼ inches in circumference. Baseballs were not manufactured on any kind of scale until the late 1850s. In fact, in the 1850s most balls in New York were made by just two men, Harvey Ross, a sail-maker and member of the Brooklyn Atlantic Base Ball Club, and John Van Horn, a cobbler and member of the Baltic Club in New York who supplied balls to the Knickerbocker club.[21]

An unusual ball from the earliest known All-Philadelphia baseball game, between the Mercantile and Continental Base Ball Clubs in 1860, reflects the difficulty teams had in securing baseballs at the time (no. 41). Somewhat more like a cricket ball than a baseball, its leather cover is in two halves – rather than the usual four pieces for a cricket ball, or one for a baseball at that time – and it is sewn with only a single seam, rather than cricket's more usual triple seam. It was made into a trophy after the game.

The game ball from the All-New York and All-Brooklyn 'picked nines' played on 17 August 1858 (no. 42) shows more typical 'lemon-peel' seam and dark leather of early baseballs. A different kind of early seam – today called an H-seam – can be seen on the trophy ball from the Brooklyn Excelsiors' 41–16

41
Trophy ball from an All-Philadelphia baseball game between the Mercantile and Continental clubs, 8 November 1860

victory over the Olympic club in Philadelphia (no. 43), painted gold after the game to commemorate the final game of the famed Excelsiors' nine-day tour in September 1866.[22]

Regular rule amendments continued to change the dimensions of baseballs from 1859 onwards, until finally in 1872 the ball had been reduced to its current standard of between 5 and 5¼ ounces and between 9 and 9¼ inches in circumference, the same standard set for cricket balls in 1838. Introduced in the late 1860s, the modern figure-eight seam was fully established by the mid-1870s, yet the centre was still made of vulcanised rubber (no. 44). Most balls were also white by this time, although in this same year baseball writer Henry Chadwick praised the short-lived Peck & Snyder 'Dead Red Ball', a red-coloured baseball, 'the color of cricket balls for fifty years past', on the grounds that the darker colour would not dazzle so much in the air and then later become soiled.[23] This was also the last year that a single ball was always used for the entire game, balls being costly and difficult to come by in large numbers. In 1876 umpires were allowed to replace a damaged ball or one that had been lost (adding a limit of five minutes to search in 1877).[24] A second ball made games quicker, but balls were still highly prized. Today the rapid turnover in balls is a hallmark of the modern game. This change is neatly illustrated by the ball from pitcher Randy Johnson's 300th winning game in 2009, which was used only briefly in the first inning (no. 45).

William Ward's famous cricket ball from 1820 was made in much the same way as balls are still made today. At 5¼ ounces it is slightly lighter than would be required for a modern cricket ball, but with a circumference of 9 inches it meets current requirements on dimensions. The ball stayed largely the same throughout the 19th century, even though bowling styles were revolutionised. During the underarm era, round-arm bowling gradually became more widely practised until MCC legalised it in 1828, after which time bowlers pushed their arms higher and higher until finally overarm bowling was allowed in 1864. Nevertheless the ball remained just as heavy and hard and batsmen had to adjust to faster and bouncier deliveries without much more protection than thin leg guards and tubular gloves until the 1860s, when more substantial protective equipment was adopted by batsmen.

Ward's 1820s cricket ball doesn't seem to have been coloured, although red was the popular choice for cricket balls as far back as we know. By 1843 the colour was widely known, as we can tell from a metaphor Charles Dickens used in *Martin Chuzzlewit*: 'green ledgers with red backs like strong cricket-balls beaten flat'.[25] With only some exceptions, including the unusual blue cricket ball made by Gamages for women's cricket in 1897 (no. 46), red remained the

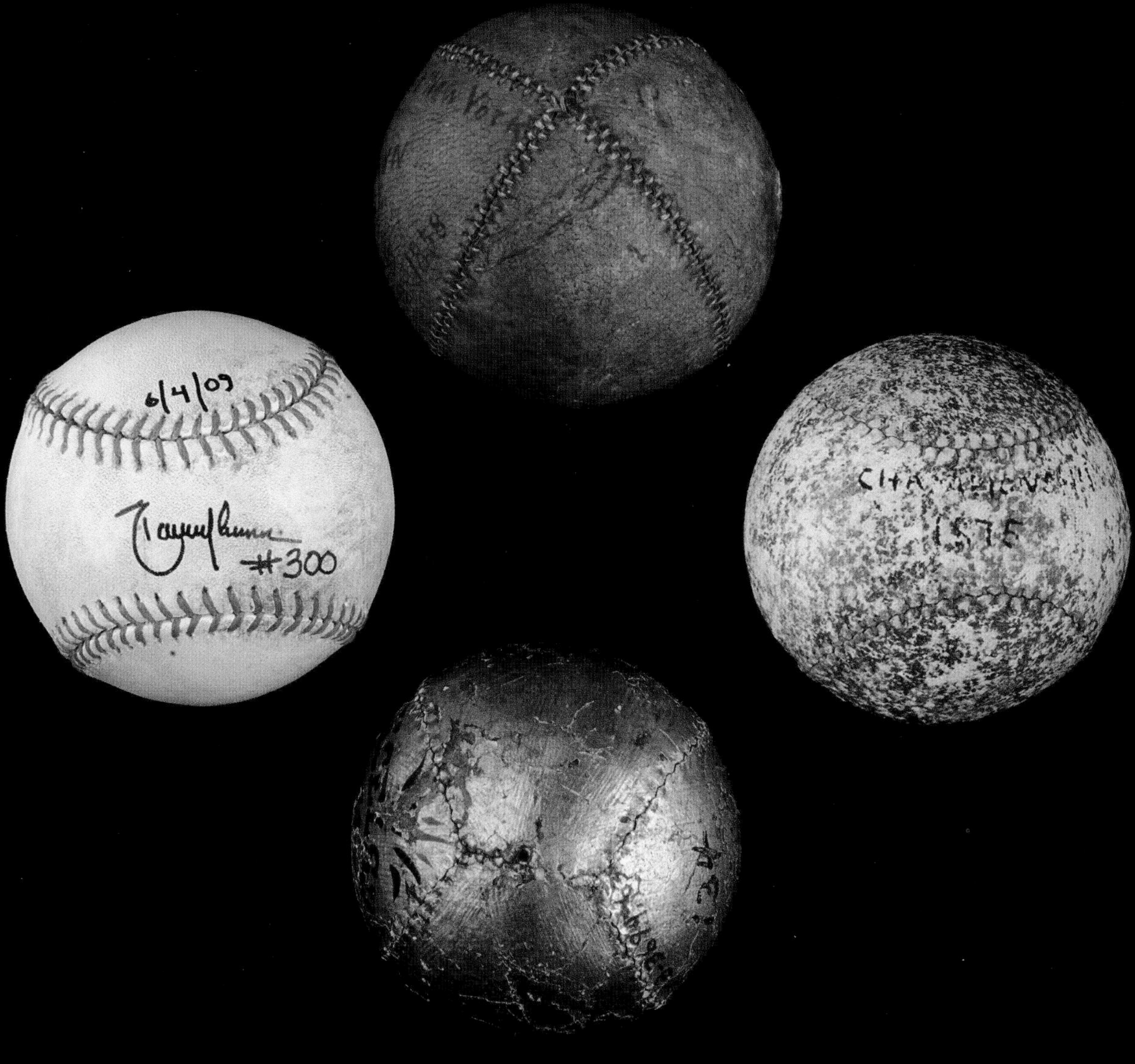
6/4/09
#300

46 (below)
Blue cricket ball made by Gamages for women's cricket, 1897

47–50 (opposite)
Four recent cricket balls. Clockwise from upper right:
47
Duke & Son Test match cricket ball, unused, 2009
48
Kookaburra Turf one-day match cricket ball, unused, 2009
49
Yellow cricket ball for indoor school cricket, a modified version of the game developed in Australia in the 1970s, 2009
50
Pink cricket ball made by Duke, trialled by MCC at Lord's on 21 April 2008

standard for cricket balls until the 1970s.

Today, there are two very different balls used in cricket: a red ball for Test cricket (no. 47) and a white ball for One Day Internationals (no. 48), although a yellow ball is also used specifically for indoor cricket (no. 49). In Test cricket the ball is replaced at the start of each new innings, and the fielding captain can request a new ball after a minimum of 80 six-ball overs. White balls were introduced with the advent of day–night games for their better visibility under floodlights and against coloured clothing, and they are now used for all limited-over matches including One Day Internationals and Twenty20 matches. Although manufactured the same, the red and white balls play differently. The white swings more at first and deteriorates more quickly. Since 2007 it has been mandatory to replace the white ball with a used, but clean, ball in the 35th over of each innings of a One Day International. Similarly, a lost, damaged or modified ball is replaced by the umpires with a used ball in similar condition to the one being replaced. Unlike in baseball, a ball hit into the stands cannot be claimed by a spectator as a souvenir, but must be returned to the field of play.

Experimental balls

As I recall it, they were regular hardballs that were dyed orange. And that was the problem, because it made it real difficult to pick up the seams on the ball. As a hitter, you look for the seams… With those orange-dyed balls, you couldn't see the seams – they were camouflaged by the dye – and that made it tough.
Joe Rudi, 1973, Oakland A's player

I can't imagine playing with a pink ball. If people had said when I started playing that we'd have pink balls I'd have said, 'No chance.' It's something we'll try and if they get a ball that stays the same colour, I'm all for it.
England bowler Darren Gough, November 2007

Cricket authorities and players have been frustrated that while the red cricket ball used in Test cricket is remarkably durable and can last 80 overs, the white ball often cannot last the 50 overs of the one-day format. The white titanium dioxide dye rubs off the leather, which scuffs and becomes stained with grass, leaving the ball hard to see and potentially

more dangerous. Experiments with an orange ball in 1989 were dropped because of the ball's poor visibility on television. Recent work by MCC in association with scientists at Imperial College, London has resulted in an experimental pink ball. The ball pictured here was part of an official trial at Lord's Cricket Ground on 21 April 2008. At that match, between MCC and Scotland, a Kookaburra brand pink ball was used when Scotland was batting, and this pink Duke & Son ball was used for MCC's innings (no. 50). Players in that match were generally happy with the ball, finding it easier to pick up against white seats, and, as can be seen, it certainly retained its colour after 50 overs. Trials are continuing (no. 51).

A fluorescent orange-dyed baseball was part of a spring training experiment in 1973 dreamed up by Charlie Finley, the flamboyant owner of the Oakland A's. But this wasn't the first time baseball experimented with different coloured balls. There was the 'Dead Red Ball' of the 1870s. And in 1938 a 'high visibility' yellow ball was trialled. This yellow ball was developed by New York colour engineer Frederic H. Rahr, who adopted the yellow colour universally

51
Pink and white cricket balls used in a trial by MCC at Lord's, alongside similar unused balls, 2008

used for safety markers. It was first used by university and amateur teams, who reportedly found it 'very useful' and then trialled it in only one major league game at Ebbets Field later that summer.[26] The verdict from the Brooklyn Dodgers and St Louis Cardinals was lukewarm at best. Dodgers president and baseball innovator Larry MacPhail had obtained permission for the trial and he signed the ball from that game, as did Fred Rahr and others (no. 52). The surface is worn in places where the yellow dye has come off, something several players complained about after the game, especially Dodgers pitcher Fred Fitzsimmons who found the ball 'a little harder to grip' as a result.[27] As with the pink cricket ball, both the yellow and orange baseballs were conceived of due to visibility concerns, but, unlike the pink ball, these baseballs lacked a rigorous scientific approach and meticulous testing and never made it past initial trials.

52
Yellow baseball used in the game between the Brooklyn Dodgers and St. Louis Cardinals, Ebbets Field, Brooklyn, 2 August 1938

The catcher, the wicket-keeper and the fielders

Batting helmets are hot and uncomfortable for keepers. A slight adaptation of the classic baseball catchers' mask would be perfect. More and more keepers will need to stand up to the stumps, even to quick bowlers, so technology will have to keep up.
Mark Boucher, wicket-keeper of South African national team, 2009

I played with a lot of injuries. I had six broken bones in each foot, a broken thumb, a split thumb, a broken little finger, a broken ankle… it's just a matter of getting out there… We played with groin injuries and hamstring injuries.
Johnny Bench, Cincinnati Reds catcher, 2000[28]

Bengie Molina of the San Francisco Giants is one of the famed Molina brothers, a trio of Puerto Rican-born catchers known for their defensive prowess. A Gold Glove winner in 2002 and 2003, Molina is a respected senior player who wears the newest equipment behind the plate, including a hockey-style mask and 'Knee-Savers' pads (nos 53–54). This equipment would be unrecognisable to a 19th-century catcher. Early catchers stood much further

53
Bengie Molina catches during a Giants v Astros game, 5 July 2009.

54
Catcher's gear worn by Bengie Molina, San Francisco Giants, 2009

behind the plate than now, a necessary choice given their lack of protection, but also a strategic one given that up until the 1880s a foul ball caught either on the bounce or on the fly was an out. The catcher in early baseball was one of the most important positions; indeed, a 19th-century writer declared, 'much of the success of a nine depends on the ability of the catcher'.[29]

There is some evidence that in the 1860s and 1870s catchers acted more as cricket wicket-keepers do today, varying their position to stand closer or further away as conditions of play dictated. Even with the advent of protective equipment, catchers would don or remove their equipment, moving closer or further back, until 1902 when they were required to remain behind the plate at all times.

Roger Bresnahan, elected to the Hall of Fame in 1945, played for the New York Giants from 1902 to 1908 (no. 55). In 1907 he became the first catcher to wear shinguards, his first set consisting of pads borrowed from cricket. Large and bulky, these did not initially find general favour, but were soon reduced in size. In 1908 he also improved the wire mask with rolls of leather around the face.

The wicket-keeper in cricket, like the baseball catcher, is essential to the game and must catch or stop any ball that the bowler has managed to bowl past the batsman. His name derives from this function; he 'keeps' the wicket. Early images of wicket-keepers from the 18th century show them crouched directly behind the wicket to scoop up the rolling deliveries of the bowler, but without

55
Roger Bresnahan, catcher for the New York Giants, c.1908

56
Philadelphian wicket-keeper Francis William Ralston, 1880s–90s

any protection at all. Initially this wasn't even a specialist position; rather, the bowlers took up position behind the stumps between their bowling overs. The importance of the role changed and by 1854 James Pycroft, in the second edition of his influential book *The Cricket Field*, advised university teams to 'choose first your bowlers and wicket-keeper and long stop; these men you must have, though not worth a run'.[30] The 'long stop' was a fielder positioned behind the keeper to intercept missed balls, essential in the days before prepared, flat pitches and skilled wicket-keepers, but defunct by the end of the 19th century. With the advent of specialist wicket-keepers, pioneered in the main by Australian Jack Blackham in the 1880s, this position assumed even greater importance. It also demanded more skill as the keeper strategically moved closer to or farther away from the wicket according to the speed of the bowling, and required increasingly athletic reflexes.

The greater pace and bounce of the bowler's deliveries, combined with the more active role of wicket-keepers, meant progressively more padding, bigger and better gloves and other protection. When Philadelphia's Francis William Ralston positioned himself behind the stumps in the 1880s and 1890s, we can see that leg guards and thin gloves were all that protected him from serious injury (no. 56). The modern wicket-keeper's kit, as shown in the 2002 photograph of Australian Test wicket-keeper Adam Gilchrist (no. 57), does not look so different from Ralston's but the compact, lightweight pads (outside and inside of the

57
Australian wicket-keeper Adam Gilchrist receives the ball from a fielder and breaks the wicket with it, trying to run out Craig White of England, but the batsman has made his ground.
1st Test match at Brisbane, November 2002

clothes) and gloves nevertheless provide far better protection, and keepers usually also wear a helmet when opting to stand close behind the batsman because of the reduced reaction time. Gilchrist has been very influential in the game in that his exceptional batting throughout his career changed world cricket's expectations of wicket-keepers and ushered in the modern era of wicket-keeper/batsman. He retired from most forms of the game in 2008, but continued to play in the IPL.

Cricketers have long admired, and borrowed from, baseball's fielding techniques. As far back as 1914, *The Times* in London questioned 'whether the finest fielders at cricket in England could ever match the speed and precision of a good [baseball] fielder stopping and returning a struck ball'. At the same time, baseball writer William Phelon asked, 'but how many of the jeering Americans have ever noted that the English fielders face a rocky ball without a glove?'[31] For much of the 20th century many Australian cricketers played baseball for part of the year and their improved fielding always gave them an edge. In 1926 they were described as able to 'throw like the big leaguers in America' and they were the first national side to contract a baseball coach for fielding, something increasingly common now in world cricket.[32]

Adjudicating the game: laws, rules and umpires

Cricket is a game that owes much of its unique appeal to the fact that it should be played not only within its Laws but also within the Spirit of the Game. Any action which is seen to abuse this spirit causes injury to the game itself.
Preamble to the Laws of Cricket

Baseball not only has maintained its position as the National Game of the United States, but also has become an International Game being played in more than 100 countries. The popularity of the game will grow only so long as its players, managers, coaches, umpires and administrative officers respect the discipline of its code of rules.
Foreword to the Official Rules of Major League Baseball[33]

Umpires have long been a central feature of both games, their roles cemented through evolving sets of rules and laws governing play. Umpires in both cricket and baseball today are expected to ensure the field is properly prepared and the correct equipment is used, to enforce the rules of play, adjudicate decisions and judge what is 'fair and unfair play'.

Cricket's tradition of two on-field umpires is a long one, being included in the oldest surviving Articles of Agreement for matches in 1727, as well as the first Laws of Cricket from 1744 (no. 58), which also confirmed their absolute authority: 'each Umpire is the sole Judge of all Nips and Catches; Inns and Outs; good or bad Runs… and his Determination shall be absolute.'[34] The first Knickerbocker rules of baseball date from 1845; they determined that rather than the two umpires used in cricket, there would for baseball be a single umpire who 'shall keep the game in a book provided for that purpose, and note all violations of the By-Laws and Rules during the time of exercise.'

Cricket still retains Law 27, which states that 'neither umpire shall give a batsman out, even though he may be out under the Laws, unless appealed to by the fielding side.' Early baseball initially borrowed this practice. In many

instances, the baseball umpire would not give a ruling except when appealed to with a call of 'judgment' or 'how's that?', the latter term likely adopted from cricket. Today cricketers still theatrically appeal with a throaty 'how's that?', but in baseball only a few remnant appeal categories remain where an umpire will not make a judgment unless asked: a batter hitting out of batting order, a runner failing to touch base on a long hit, a player leaving base too soon after the catch of a sacrifice fly, and the checked swing, which the catcher can appeal to the plate umpire as a strike.[35]

A baseball manager has scope within the rules to argue certain calls directly with the umpire during a game. In contrast a cricket umpire's decision, once made, has traditionally been final; however, in 2008 the Umpire Decision Review System, under which players can refer a limited number of decisions to the off-field third umpire for video review, was introduced to international matches on a trial basis. The system, still being refined, has been applied in selected series only and is not universally popular, but seems to be here to stay in one form or other. A similar system of player challenges has been introduced in tennis.

59
The Game at Cricket, as settled by the several cricket-clubs, particularly that of the Star and Garter in Pall Mall, **1755**

60
The Laws of Cricket, **2000 Code 3rd Edition, 2008**

In both sports, the game was standardised through the distribution of printed laws and rules. For cricket this first happened in 1755 with the publication of a small pamphlet, *The Game at Cricket*, the first unequivocal set of cricket laws issued as a discreet publication (no. 59). MCC, based at Lord's in London, has been the custodian of the Laws of Cricket since the club's formation in 1787 and continues to regularly review them and issue international updates on them (no. 60). The Knickerbocker Base Ball Club drew up 20 official rules of baseball for their club in 1845. First published in 1848 and reissued in multiple editions (no. 61), these rules, including such elements as three strikes to put a batter out, fair and foul territory and the elimination of hitting ('soaking') the runner with the ball, soon spread what became known as the New York game, the predecessor of the game of baseball as we know it today. Today Major League Baseball sets forth the Official Rules of the game at the beginning of each baseball season (no. 62).

Umpire responsibilities have always been onerous in both sports and their tasks evolve to keep pace with rapidly modernising games. Both major league baseball and international cricket now usually use four umpires for each game. In cricket, two of the umpires stand on the field of play and two are off-field. To ensure the highest standards and the most impartial adjudication, the ICC created in 2002 an elite panel of neutral umpires who are contracted full-time. They are assigned to matches by the ICC based on independence from the two countries competing in the match, performance, availability and workload.[36] For all Test matches, the two on-field umpires are drawn from the elite panel; in One Day Internationals one elite panel umpire is paired with a home umpire.

Since 2000 the Laws of Cricket have included a new preamble on the 'Spirit of Cricket' and this is now an important feature of the sport, providing guidelines on the behaviour expected of players on the field, as enforced by the fourth umpire, or match referee, who has the power to fine and suspend players for on-field incidents. But it is the work of the third umpire, or television umpire, that has been most revolutionary in recent years, called on by the on-field umpires to review video replays and the 'Hawk-Eye' ball-tracking computer system and decide on dismissals and boundaries.

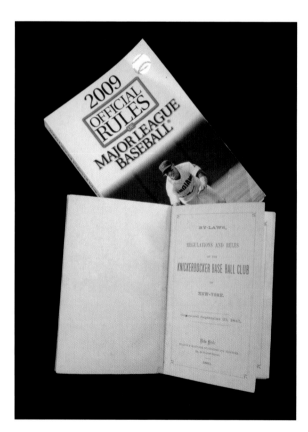

63
Cricket umpire's counting stones, n.d.
Cricket umpires choose many different devices for keeping track of the numbers of balls bowled in each over during play. In these counting stones, presented to the CC Morris collection in Philadelphia in 1976, the stones are arranged in size from smallest to largest. Such is the power of the umpire in cricket that even if he miscounts the number of deliveries in the over, his mistake stands.

64
Baseball umpire's indicator belonging to Bill Klem, 1906
This indicator, which allows the umpire to dial balls and strikes as they happen, belonged to the highly regarded umpire Bill Klem, who was elected to the National Baseball Hall of Fame by the Veterans Committee in 1953. Klem's long career lasted from 1905 to 1941, when he retired at 67 years of age. He also umpired the games between the Chicago White Sox and the New York Giants on the World Tour of 1913–1914 (see pages 101—03).

Major league baseball umpires generally work in crews of four (although there are six for the All-Star Game and the postseason), one of whom is the Crew Chief. The four umpires rotate places each game: home plate, first, second and third bases. Major league baseball made use of the new instant replay referral system to decide on home-run rulings for the first time in 2008.

A cricket innings is divided into overs, each over consisting of six balls delivered by a bowler from one end of the pitch to the batsman at the other end, who tries to defend the wicket by hitting the ball. One umpire stands at the bowler's end, looking towards the batsman, and the other stands about 25 yards away looking side-on at the batsman, at the 'square leg' position. After the over is complete, a second bowler then delivers another six balls from the other end. The bowling end then reverts back to the first end, and the first bowler may bowl again. The umpires' many duties include keeping track of the number of balls delivered in each over. To assist them with counting, umpires in all levels of the game make use of pebbles, coins or counting devices (no. 63).

In the game of baseball, the battle between pitcher and batter is, at its most basic level, divided into balls and strikes. A strike is called when the batter either swings at a pitch and misses, hits the ball into foul territory (with less than two strikes already called), or lets a fairly pitched ball through to the catcher. A ball is called for any pitch deemed to be outside the strike zone, as long as the batter has not swung at it. Three strikes and the batter is out; four balls and the batter can advance to first base; three outs and the half-inning is over. The umpire has to keep track of balls, strikes and outs. Just as in cricket, baseball umpires make use of various counting devices (no. 64).

The numbers game

In the earliest forms of both cricket and baseball, the ball was delivered up to the batter. Both the cricket bowler and baseball pitcher acted more like 'feeders' than the competitive players they soon became. In cricket, from the end of rolled deliveries in the mid-1700s until the 1870s, when prepared grounds gave batsmen some respite, bowlers owned the game. Low-scoring games were typically won or lost in two to three days as batsmen faced the perils of cricket pitches with rocks, dents, ridges and holes, all of which made the ball bounce in unpredictable ways. Runs were relatively rare and celebrated, while bowlers gathered in dismissals (much like baseball today). With the development of safer pitches, top-dressed and evenly mowed by specialist groundsmen, batsmen began to bat for longer innings and they used the friendlier conditions to begin the modern trend of amassing great scores. Progress in this direction was slow at first: William Ward's score of 278 runs in 1820 was a rare, lonely achievement (see no. 40, page 50) and no individual scores over 100 were recorded from 1829 to 1833.[37] When, over a century later, English batting great Len Hutton scored an impressive 364 at The Oval during the 1938 Ashes, this was still an exceptional feat. Of the 160 double centuries (scores of 200 and over) made by Test cricketers since 1877, 94 of those or 58.7% have been scored since 1 January 2000, albeit in an era of more frequent Test matches and much heavier bats.[38]

Conversely, baseball began as a batter's game. Underarm pitching, gloveless fielders and no rules that dictated called strikes made for high-scoring games in the 1850s and 1860s. Runs were par for the course, and put-outs celebrated as a testament to great skill. Unlike cricket, it was baseball batters who most benefited from the typically poor ground conditions of the early game, which hampered fielding. Thus a 53–11 victory by the Cincinnati Red Stockings in 1869 (see no. 151, pages 128–29) was not as extraordinary as it seems today. When the 'dead' ball, with its rubber core reduced to no more than one ounce, was adopted in 1870, scoring rates immediately declined, the batters further challenged by relaxed pitching restrictions, better field conditions and the introduction of fielding equipment.[39]

The main reason we can make such comparisons and track these changes over time is because of abiding passions in both cricket and baseball for the

65
Cricket at the Artillery Ground, London, 1752
This etching of an 18th-century game clearly shows a scorer using a notching stick and knife to score this single-wicket cricket match. At left it also features a good example of an early wicket, consisting of two stumps rather than the modern three. The bowler delivers the ball in the old underarm style.

66 (below left)
**Thomas Henwood, *The Scorer*,
1842**

67 (below right)
**Scorebook belonging to
William Davies, 1832–33**

68–71 (opposite)
**Cricket scorecards and
scorebooks down the ages**
68 (opposite bottom)
**Scorecard: *A list of the
gentlemen cricketers now
playing on Sevenoaks Vine:
His Grace the Duke of Dorset
against Sir Horace Mann,*
20 June 1781**
69 (opposite right)
**Scorecard for England v
Australia 2nd Ashes Test,
16–20 July 2009**
70 (opposite centre)
**Scorebook for Young America
Cricket Club Junior Eleven,
1888–89**
71 (opposite top)
**Scorebook for Merion Cricket
Club, open at the page for
the game against Mass Ave,
2 October 1993**

numbers of each game. Record-keeping obviously came to cricket first, and it was initially simple in its scope, indeed almost primitive by today's statistic-obsessed standards. Scorers would sit close to the action and keep a tally of the runs by notching them onto sticks (indeed, this is the origin of the term 'score'). An engraving in *New Universal Magazine* in 1752 shows a scorer at work during a single-wicket game in this way (no. 65). But such a simple system was ill-equipped for the demands of this important job, especially when a considerable wager was riding on the results. A more sophisticated method for scoring was soon developed, the scorer now recording all the details of players' performances in a standard cricket scorebook.

To this day the role of the official scorer remains central to the game, and that this has long been the case is well illustrated by Thomas Henwood's 1842 portrait in oil of William Davies (nos 66–67), the official scorer to the Sussex County Cricket Club and Lewes Priory Club. By the early 1800s, it had become common for the scorer to fill in his scorebook sitting at a table on the side of the field. Davies has with him on the table his wind-up tape measure, which he would have used to mark out the pitch and creases before the start of play, a job later handed over to the groundsman. A comfortable chair and flagon of claret make the task more enjoyable.

At major matches printed scorecards were soon made available for the public at the ground. These would be updated as the game progressed, as shown here on an early scorecard printed mid-game after the first innings had been played (no. 68). The results of the first innings, on 20 June 1781, are printed in the first column – The Duke's Men scored 158 to Sir Horace's Men's 136 – and

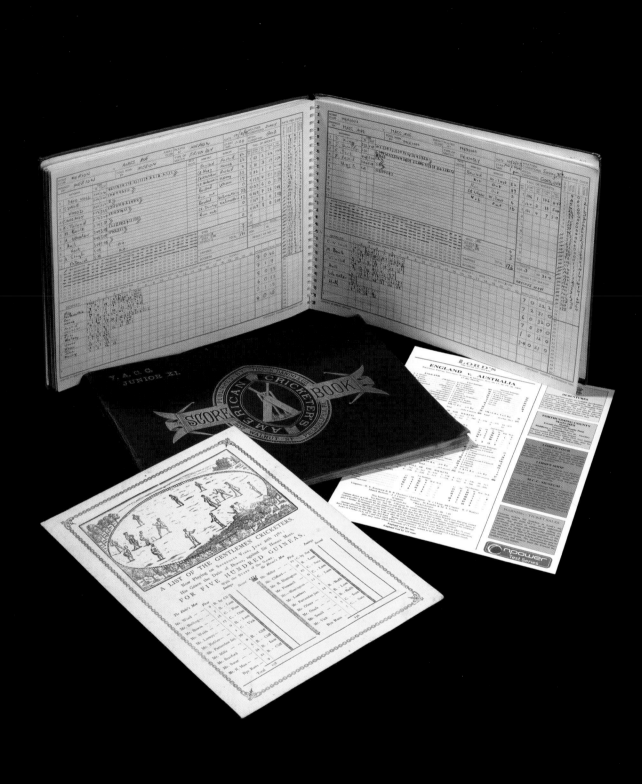

72–75
A collection of baseball scorecards
72 (bottom right)
The Enquirer: Amateur B. B. Score Card, *c.*1890
73 (bottom left)
Official Scorecard: Chicago League Ball Club, 15 July 1896
74 (centre)
Scorecard for Boston v Philadelphia, 14 October 1872
75 (top)
Scorecard for Boston Red Sox v Philadelphia Phillies, 13 June 2009

blank spaces are left to record the scores in the second innings. Such printed cards are still produced today and sold at the ground during a match (no. 69).

For the official scorer, and those enamoured of the true intricacies of the game, there are thick scorebooks with columns and boxes to record every ball and every run. These books, filled with season after season of matches, become treasured club records and the fact that two scorebooks created in Philadelphia a hundred years apart, like those of the Young America Cricket Club in 1888–89 (no. 70) and Merion Cricket Club in 1993 (no. 71), can be understood side-by-side by any cricket enthusiast says much about cricket's long-established universal scoring language.

Baseball shares cricket's fascination with quantifying and comparing performance. The scorecard is as important to baseball as it is to cricket, and, benefiting from cricket's legacy, the shift from notching stick to scorecard happened quite early in the game's history. Henry Chadwick's *Beadle's Dime Base-Ball Player* first published a scoring system in 1861 along with Chadwick's insistence that 'every club should have its regularly appointed scorer'.[40] And while his complex system didn't survive, the impetus nevertheless grew into the modern box score now widely used. Scorecards of different levels of complexity are available for fans to fill in at both amateur and professional games.

Two examples from the 1890s show mass-produced scorecards that fans could purchase for use at games. 'The Enquirer' (no. 72) depicts a lively amateur game in a rural setting on its front cover, while the Chicago League Ball Club scorecard (no. 73) presents a more official-looking image for the professional game, with Uncle Sam pointing the way to a city ballpark where 'our national game' is underway. Another example illustrated here is a very simple record of the players and score of a game between the Boston Red Stockings and Philadelphia Athletics in 1872 (no. 74), of particular interest as eleven of the 18 players toured England to play baseball two years later. This was not a regular season game but one played in a special tournament, which nicely mirrors the 2009 scorecard between the same two cities shown alongside (no. 75), recording an inter-league game, Boston and Philadelphia no longer being in the same league.

That two Red Sox fans – father and son David and Matthew Weinstein – travelled to Philadelphia, carefully scored this entire game and endured a lengthy rain delay is testament to the staying power of baseball fans. But it also points to the sheer pleasure that comes from taking part vicariously in the game by scoring every play. In both baseball and cricket the long tradition of scoring has opened up a whole world of statistical analysis that allows everyone an active role in the elite game. The convergence of hundreds of years of records and modern statistical databases with electronic communications means that the results of the serious work done by groups of statisticians painstakingly compiling game results, player averages in batting, bowling, pitching and fielding, the number of runs scored, plays made or wickets taken, are now freely available. These are now used by everyone from players, coaches and commentators to the millions of fans worldwide enjoying fantasy cricket and baseball every year.

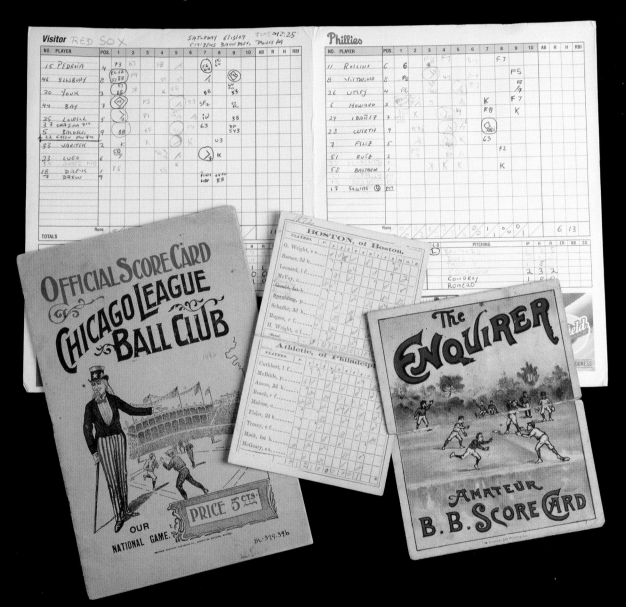

Henry Chadwick

English-born sportswriter Henry Chadwick (no. 76) is considered by some the most important figure in 19th century baseball. For over 50 years he brought vision, a new seriousness of purpose and a reformer's zeal to reporting and shaping the game in America. He came to the USA at age twelve, having spent his youth playing cricket, and his encyclopaedic knowledge and love for the English game would shape many aspects of baseball.

He began his reporting career in 1844 for Brooklyn's *Long Island Star*. According to his biographer Andrew Schiff, by the mid-1850s 'he had managed to integrate his love for cricket into his professional life, working as cricket writer for the *New York Times*.'[41] But after watching a 'particularly spirited' game of baseball between the Gotham and Eagle clubs at Elysian Fields in 1856, Chadwick came away a changed man. He saw for the first time that this game that he held in such low esteem was a fast and rugged game 'suited to the American temperament'. The next year Chadwick joined the popular weekly the *New York Clipper* and his enthusiastic reports of the New York game of baseball gained much wider circulation.

His influence went far beyond reporting the game. As a member of baseball rules committees, first for the National Association of Base Ball Players (NABBP) and later for the National League of Professional Base Ball Clubs, he advocated many reforms to make the young game of baseball more 'scientific' and 'manly'. A critical change – eliminating the then rule whereby a fielder could retire the batter by catching the ball after one bounce, in favour of cricket's established fly catch (catch on the full) – was a key to popularising the New York game around the nation. He also promoted overhand pitching, an action legalised for cricket bowlers in 1864 and baseball pitchers 20 years later, as 'favourable to strategic skill in delivery'.[42]

But he is best known for devising the box scoring system that, with a few improvements, is still in use today, and in the process laying the groundwork for baseball's rich statistical heritage. Although Chadwick never really played the game, he continually influenced it from 1860 onwards through his role as editor for *Beadle's Dime Base-Ball Player*, the quintessential baseball guide of its day,

76
Henry Chadwick, *c*.1880

and *Spalding's Official Base Ball Guide*. His imprint was left not only on on-field play but also through his advocacy for sobriety, morality and the healthy benefits of outdoor exercise. He has even been credited with pioneering sport as news.

Chadwick never lost interest in the game of his youth and was an active proponent of American cricket. He advocated the virtues of cricket as 'a field sport for gentlemen' in 1873 because it would never be 'subservient' to the evils of gambling, could be played into a 'much later period of life' than other ball games, and was flexible enough to provide a game for any number of players from two (in a single-wicket match) up to 33 (in a match of 22 versus eleven).[43] He was also a keen reformer of the game. Chadwick felt that 'unemployed people' in England with 'wealth at command' created for themselves a leisurely style of cricket that, in America, where 'the busy bees of the community find but little time to devote to recreation', appeared 'slow' and 'old fogyish' compared to the shorter game of baseball.[44] Yet he felt cricket's 'tedious delays' were not inherent in the game but grew out of English custom in violation of the rules of the game, which in themselves were in need of significant revision and did not 'reflect credit on the committee of the Marylebone Club'.[45] In his call to popularise the game in America, Chadwick took issue with 'the rules as they now read, both in regard to omissions and their indefinite wording'. His was a strong, self-confident (almost arrogant) stand that reflected his growing stature in American sport, his belief that all sports could be 'Americanised' and thus improved, and his pedantic nature.[46]

Chadwick truly believed in and strongly advocated baseball's ability as a noble civic institution to inspire the American youth to embrace outdoor exercise. His campaign against gambling earned him the reputation as baseball's conscience, and many of his moral reforms were successfully realised with the establishment in 1871 of the National Association of Professional Base Ball Players to clean up the game. When this became the National League in 1876, Chadwick's influence continued as editor of its official guide, *Spalding's Official Base Ball Guide*, distributed by his friend and protégé Albert Goodwill Spalding. At the height of his reporting career in 1866, Chadwick was lauded as 'reliable, impartial and talented', a man whose reporting on baseball, cricket and aquatics set a 'standard reputation and influence' among all who took an interest in 'American out-door pastimes'.[47]

Chadwick died at the age of 83 from pneumonia after catching a cold attending two opening-day games in April 1908. He was elected to the National Baseball Hall of Fame in 1938 and will always be remembered as the 'Father of Baseball'.

4 Empires and missions: spreading the game

English cricket's first foray onto the international stage came in 1859. This 'novel' and 'memorable exhibition' of twelve of the best professional players was celebrated by Frederick Lillywhite in his book *The English Cricketers Trip to Canada and the United States*, a volume prompted by 'an eager desire to promote and extend… that love for the noble game of Cricket'.[1] Playing tours of professional cricketers were popular in England, and North America was, at that time, a stronghold of the game outside of England. When Canadian and American cricketing interests combined to arrange a visit by English cricketers, it was a natural extension of the domestic touring tradition to take a team across the Atlantic. The players themselves were professionals on a tour of duty, and Lillywhite's account duly opens with a re-cap of their pay and expenses negotiations. And although this was a more adventurous undertaking than the usual domestic itinerary, none at the time could have guessed that they were laying the foundations for the great touring traditions that now form the bedrock of international cricket.

Fifteen years later occurred what was, superficially at least, baseball's equivalent, its first international playing tour, when the Boston Red Stockings and the Philadelphia Athletics visited England. As with the 1859 cricketers, the 1874 baseball tourists were some of the best professional players of their day, and this overseas trip was a logical extension of the playing tours then common between American baseball cities. But there the similarities end. For while Englishmen played cricket all over the world, thanks to the rapid spread of the British Empire, in the 1870s the American game of baseball was almost unknown outside its home country. Unlike the 1859 cricketing tour to North America, these players were not invited to play a local opposition; rather they came of their own volition and played exhibition games against each other to show 'Englishmen a practical illustration of the beauties claimed for the American game'.[2]

These initial tours were followed by others, and of course form only part of the much larger story of cricket and baseball's global expansion. In both sports, the first international tours were private, profit-oriented undertakings involving professional players. Only later did amateur and then national sides follow in their footsteps. A closer look at these early professional teams crossing the Atlantic in the decades around the turn of the 20th century – cricketers to America and baseball players to England – reveals the fledgling international development of each game while also shedding light on the ramifications for cricket in America and baseball in England. Why tours were undertaken and how the players and their respective games were received reflect much about the sporting landscape in each country, but also reveal deeper social, political and

The Chicago and All-American baseball teams in Egypt at the Sphinx, 9 February 1889 (see page 92)

cultural trends, painting a vivid picture of how two sports, so caught up in national identity, were presented around the world.

Early cricket in North America

Cricket had been on the American sporting scene for some time before the arrival of the first visiting English team. In colonial times cricket was informal and social, although more organised matches started receiving press interest by the mid-1700s, such as that 'play'd on our Common for a considerable Wager, by eleven Londoners, against eleven New Yorkers', in early May 1751.[3] This game, 'played according to the London Method', used the Laws of Cricket as first formalised in 1744, well before they were circulated in printed form in 1755, highlighting connections across the Atlantic, especially for those serious about their cricket. In 1779, the press announcement of 'A Cricket Match for Fifty-Guineas, between the Brooklyn Club and the Greenwich Club' reflected growing organisation, especially concentrated in the New York area. But another invitation to 'any gentleman who wish to partake of the amusement will please attend; there being a few wanting to complete the match' attests to a young pastime reaching out for new players.

In time clubs were formed, especially around the New York area, and by the 1820s the sport had spread to at least twelve states. Even so, the game of cricket could not be considered well established as an organised sport in America until the 1830s. Press patronage in the 1840s, especially in New York, helped promote cricket as 'fashionable' and 'much in vogue',[4] and from 1840 to 1855 cricket was America's leading ball game, reported more widely than any

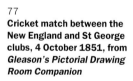
77
Cricket match between the New England and St George clubs, 4 October 1851, from *Gleason's Pictorial Drawing Room Companion*

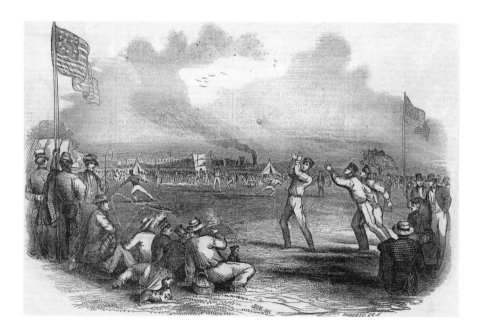

other sport apart from horse and harness racing. 'This invigorating and manly game promises to become exceedingly popular,' reported New York's *Spirit of the Times* in 1843, with new clubs 'springing up in all directions'.[5]

Many of the early American cricket clubs were formed by resident Englishmen in cities like New York, Brooklyn, Newark, Philadelphia and Boston, and places farther afield such as upper New York State, Chicago, Cincinnati, Delaware, South Carolina and Georgia. The establishment of the St George Cricket Club in New York, consolidated in 1839, and Philadelphia's Union Club, formed in 1843, mark the beginning of organised cricket. Yet American acceptance of the benefits of sport, exercise and leisure-time games was still in its infancy, so the game of cricket, while established and growing, nevertheless remained something of a novelty throughout most of the 1840s.[6]

The St George Cricket Club, established in 1838 by English migrants from Sheffield and Nottingham, helped to develop the game beyond parochial boundaries with interclub and even international matches (nos 77–78). It was originally called the New York Cricket Club but renamed on St George's Day, 23 April 1839.[7] By 1848 there were 67 members, and club membership grew to between 200 and 300 by 1866.[8] This club would prove to be long lasting and widely influential. St George not only spearheaded the general move towards organised and well-run sporting clubs in America, and helped to spread cricket clubs to other American cities, it also played a pivotal pioneering role in the first ever international cricket matches.

Fixtures against Canadian clubs, beginning in the 1840s, sparked real spectator enthusiasm. So much so that, after 5000 attended the 1845 club match between St George and Montreal, the *New York Mercury News* effused that 'seldom have we known a [cricket] match to create so much excitement'.

78
Cricket match between Canada and the United States, at Hoboken, 2–4 August 1858, from *Harper's Weekly* newspaper, 14 August 1858

England's Twelve Champion Cricketers, 2 October 1859
This photograph was taken on board the *Novia Scotian* at Liverpool on 7 September 1859 before the England team sailed for North America. Standing in the back from the left are Robert Carpenter, a fine batsman, William Caffyn, the wicket-keeper, and Tom Lockyer. Middle row: John Wisden, H. H. Stephenson, the captain George Parr, Jemmy Grundy, Julius Caesar, Tom Hayward, another great batsman, and John Jackson, one of the fastest bowlers in England. All-rounder Alfred Diver and John Lillywhite sit in the front. They are pictured here wearing the favoured cricket dress of long white trousers, belt with buckle, polka-dot shirt and tie.

When the Toronto and St George clubs decided to play a match that allowed the inclusion of players from other clubs, cricket's first ever true international match was in the making. On 24–26 September 1844 at the St George grounds in New York, a United States representative side played a Canadian one for a $1,000 wager, won by the Canadians, and so began what is by far the oldest international cricket series.[9]

While some American cricket clubs, most prominently the venerable St George, became increasingly Anglo-centric over time, others, especially clubs in Philadelphia, Brooklyn and Newark, promoted American control of the organisational structure of the game and encouraged more native-born and younger players. The New York Cricket Club, not to be confused with the early St George club before its name change, was founded in 1843 under the presidency of William Porter, editor of the city's *Spirit of the Times*. This club had a reputation for encouraging American participation in the sport both on and off the field. In part, this was a response to the exclusivity of its rival St George and the latter's focus on giving English players primacy on the field; in reality, though, it too ended up relying on English-born players to a great extent. Philadelphia was the only centre where American participation and control of the game came to full fruition, with long-lasting implications.

Professional cricket tours to North America

Rapid expansion in the 1850s meant that by the end of the decade 300 to 400 cricket clubs were active in at least 22 states. In 1855, the *New York Clipper* estimated that there were 5000 match-playing cricketers in all of the United States, a figure that must have quickly ballooned for by 1859 the *Spirit of the Times* estimated 6000 active cricketers lived within 100 miles of New York City alone, including Philadelphia.[10] The time was right for an English professional team to tour and rumours spread that just such a venture was planned. It was hoped that seeing the best cricketers in action would boost American cricket clubs, giving the sport a higher popular standing in the face of baseball's growing popularity. W. P. Pickering, a Cambridge Blue and member of Surrey County Cricket Club who had emigrated to Montreal, organised the funding and arrangements, with Robert Waller's support from the St George club, while Fred Lillywhite in England put together a crack team of professional players with the cooperation of cricketers George Parr from the All-England Eleven and John Wisden of the rival United All-England Eleven (nos 79–81; see also pages 117–19). At a time of intense Anglo-American rivalry, the announcement that the tourists would play matches against 22-strong Canadian or America teams in September and October of 1859, caused a sensation in New York, Philadelphia and many other cities.[11] In Philadelphia, many of the interclub matches for 1859 served as practice games in preparation for the single match against the Englishmen.[12]

Frederick Lillywhite organised many aspects of the tour and travelled with the players as reporter, publishing an account of the tour the following year – the first of the now popular genre of cricketers' tour diaries. He also brought his own printing-press and scoring tent with him and these travelled with the team, although not without incident. In unpredictable and often cold and wet autumn weather, Lillywhite's equipment caused problems on coaches and trains (nos 82–83). At one point the captain George Parr lost patience and the press was left behind, to catch up later with the tourists.[13] Once set up at the ground on match day, however, Lillywhite's scoring-tent was quite an

80
William Bromley III, *Portrait of George Parr, c.1850*
George Parr (1826–1891) of Nottinghamshire was the popular captain of the All-England Eleven, a professional all-star team that travelled around England playing local sides. A remarkable batsman – his big scores earned him the nickname 'Lion of the North' – Parr also excelled in the field and was a quick runner between the wickets.

81

William Bromley III, *Portrait of John Wisden*, *c*.1850
John Wisden (1826–1884), known to history as the founder of *Wisden Cricketers' Almanack* in 1864, was perhaps the finest all-rounder of his day and all but unplayable as a bowler in his prime. In 1859 Wisden was joint Secretary of the rival United All-England Eleven, and the touring side he and Parr put together was evenly chosen, six from All-England and six from United All-England.

attraction and introduced American crowds to printed cricket scorecards, updated by his own printing press as the game progressed.

The standout match of the tour was played on St George's ground at Elysian Fields, Hoboken, in front of 24,000 spectators over three days on 3–5 October 1859. After an easy victory in Montreal, George Parr's team humbled the American side, made up of players from the St George and other New York cricket clubs. Continuing a long cricketing tradition of allowing a weaker side a 'handicap' of more players, the American side, mostly amateurs, had 22 players to the English professionals' eleven. Even with double the number of batsmen and fielders, they still could barely hold their own against some of these giants of the game – ten of the 22 failed to score at all in the first innings, and two players shared the top score of six. It was a humiliating loss by an innings and 64 runs when it was all over, and sadly indicative of all the matches the English tourists played on a tour that some felt was a one-sided competition overshadowed by entrepreneurial business interests.

The growing realisation that sporting contests could be popular and even money-making events, a concept first grasped by 1840s cricketing entrepreneurs in England, was made abundantly clear for Americans by the 1859 tour. Towards the end of the tour the city of Rochester in upper New York state managed to secure an additional unscheduled match at considerable expense and in the face of initial resistance by English organisers. A great deal of money was spent on the cricket ground at Jones Square. Given Rochester's proximity to Canadian cricket fans, a combined USA and Canadian side was organised to meet the now famous English players. The local press got behind the campaign, proud to trumpet Rochester as 'one of the three cities of the US which came out to meet these champions of England in a noble game' and give local business a boost.[14] To take full advantage, the cricket ground was enclosed in order to charge admission – something the Rochester baseball ground would not copy for another nine years – and equipped with a refreshment stand.[15]

But the late October weather was inclement, and in what became known

The English Cricketers' Trip to Canada and the United States by Fred Lillywhite, 1860

Fred Lillywhite's engaging chronicle of the travelling conditions, social receptions, sightseeing events and matches was published in London the following year.

The Lillywhite family has been described as a cricketing dynasty. Fred was the third son of William Lillywhite, the unrivalled bowler known as the 'Nonpareil'. His older brother John was a batsman on the tour and later an umpire, while his cousin James later captained England. His younger brother Harry was already living in the USA when the cricketers visited, having been employed as a professional for the St George Cricket Club in New York since 1856. Harry later played for the New Brighton Cricket Club on Staten Island, and represented the United States against the 1859 tourists. He subsequently returned to England, possibly with his older brothers, staying there until returning to America in the 1880s. The Lillywhite brothers all went into business as sports outfitters and Fred had a long and varied career as a publisher, most notably of *The Guide to Cricketers* and *Scores and Biographies*.

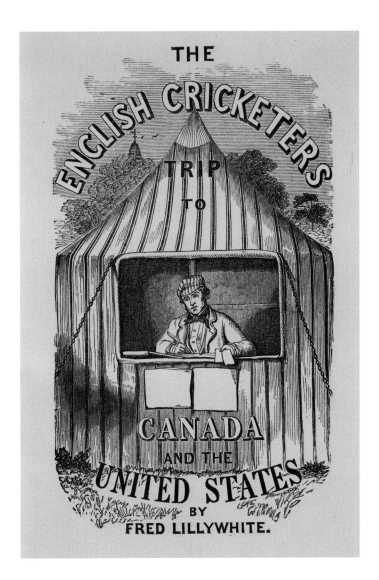

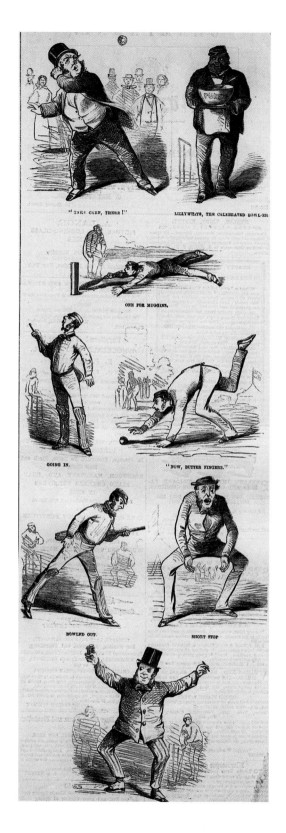

"TAKE CARE, THERE!"

LILLYWHITE, THE CELEBRATED BOWL-ER.

ONE FOR MUGGINS.

GOING IN.

"NOW, BUTTER FINGERS."

BOWLED OUT.

SHORT STOP.

as the 'Frosty Match' outfielders were reduced to wearing greatcoats and muffs. A fierce snowstorm stopped play on the second day, and, with no cricket possible, 'a game of baseball was got up among the [local] players of that game and a portion of the English party' at the nearby baseball ground. The local press reported that 'the English players appeared to be pleased with the game, of which they absolutely knew nothing', and approved of their play, judging that the English 'could handle the ball well, and might soon, by practice in rules become proficient'.[16] As for the English response to their first taste of baseball, Lillywhite simply notes they considered the early baseball rule allowing a batter to be out when the ball was caught either on the fly (without bouncing) or after a single bounce 'very childish'.[17]

The tour was adventurous and sometimes arduous for the players, who travelled over 7000 miles in two months by ship, coach and rail in conditions that at times could be 'both tedious and disagreeable'. One player, William Caffyn, vowed never to leave England again under any circumstances – 'no more water in order to play cricket matches'.[18] Yet they not only enhanced their reputations but also made a handsome windfall for their efforts.[19] And if the tour didn't quite live up to expectations, given the lopsided contests, it did make an impression on the American cricketing world and was one of the most widely publicised sporting events in antebellum America (no. 84).[20]

The most immediate impact of this first international tour was felt not in America, soon engulfed by the bitter fighting of the Civil War, but rather on the other side of the world. An Australian catering firm, Spiers and Pond, encouraged by the financial success of the 1859 tour, organised another professional side to brave the two-month journey to Melbourne in 1861. The tour was both popular and

84
Sketches by Our Artist on the Cricket Field, from ***Frank Leslie's Illustrated Newspaper***, **15 October 1859**

a stunning financial success. The English were greeted by huge crowds in Melbourne and Sydney, and generally enjoyed the same on-field dominance against Australian sides of 22 players. Two local sides, though, one in Sydney with only eleven players, did manage to beat the visitors. The success of these two touring ventures, only a few years apart, opened up new and lucrative opportunities for promoters and professional players leading to another tour of Australia and New Zealand in 1863–64 and a second tour to North America in 1868.

When Edgar Willsher's team of English professionals crossed the Atlantic in 1868, they found themselves in a vastly altered American sporting landscape. In the three years since the Civil War had ended, baseball's exploding popularity had swept the country, and cricket no longer enjoyed the same standing as during the 1850s, resulting in poor attendances for touring matches. It was a baseball game played between the English cricketers and the Union Base Ball Club of Morrisania that brought the biggest crowd to the St George ground in almost a decade – a situation only mildly alleviated by the pronouncement of the *New York Times* that the 'good old game of cricket has not been entirely given up in New York, and our old citizens still delight in this manly sport'.[21] Not surprisingly, given the continuing strength of the professional game in England, All-England easily swept through the cricket matches they played (nos 85–87). The most competitive game was at German-town Cricket Club against 22 amateurs of Philadelphia, and marked the beginnings of a post-war revival in that city that would culminate at the turn of the

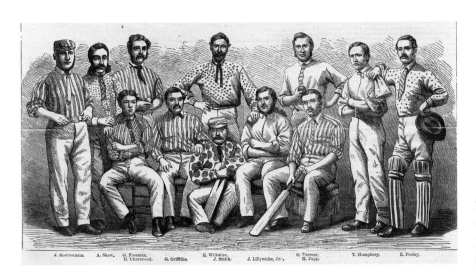

85
The International Cricket Match; The 'All-England Eleven' Cricketers and Their Umpire, from *Harper's Weekly,* **3 October 1868**

86 (opposite)
Cricket bat presented to George Wright, 1868

The English wicket-keeper, Ted Pooley, presented this cricket bat to George Wright – it is inscribed 'Pooley AEE to George Wright, 18 October 1868' – the day after the final match of the tour. Wright, on the cusp of his great baseball career in 1868, played in this match at Hoboken as a member of the American side. For the 21-year-old Wright, who had been playing as a professional cricketer since 1862, this must have been a great honour. As W. G. Grace later remembered, 'It was a great thing then to have a bat given you by one of the All-England players'.

87 (below)
Belt buckle inscribed with 'The Eleven', worn by Napoleon Bonaparte McLaughlin, c.1868

This belt buckle belonged to Napoleon Bonaparte McLaughlin. It appears to be a souvenir of the 1868 English touring cricketers. McLaughlin may have played cricket but he was definitely a member of the Knickerbocker Base Ball Club from 1855 to 1861, and tradition has it that he wore this belt while playing baseball. A captain in charge of the Union Army's 1st Massachusetts Infantry Regiment, whose progressively dwindling numbers saw action at the Battles of Fredericksburg and Gettysburg, McLaughlin eventually attained the rank of general.

century in the international success of the Gentlemen of Philadelphia (see chapter 7). This time the English tourists also took part in three baseball matches, all of which, in turn, were won by their American opponents. As it turned out, ball-playing skills were not as easily transferable as might be presumed. Just as the increasing amount of baseball played by some of the American cricketers did not really enhance their cricket skills, so the undoubted cricketing skills of the English did nothing to assist them on the baseball field.[22] Only a few Americans really excelled at both games.

With the success of these early international cricket ventures, soon gentlemen amateurs also joined the touring circuit – the first all-amateur side to North America was in 1872, and included the era's outstanding cricketer, W. G. Grace – before combined amateur and professional sides began to tour regularly to Australia and New Zealand and to North America through the 1870s and 1880s.[23] The competitive strength of the Australians was much greater than that of the Americans and so it was that the first international Test match, the ultimate 'test' of players' skills between two representative sides of eleven players each, took place in Melbourne in 1877 between Australia and England. International cricket tours were fully established as an essential element in the game by the end of the 1880s, when the first English cricketing tours to both South Africa and India took place, followed a few years later by the first tour to the West Indies. Jumpstarted by the 1859 pioneers, these tours not only drove the game to develop to higher standards but also provided a sense of cohesion and shared purpose, spiced with a sharp competitive edge, across the widely dispersed and culturally varied cricketing world.

The first international baseball tour

The numbers of Americans truly proficient at both baseball and cricket may have been small, but several of that elite group got the chance to try their hand at cricket on English (and Irish) soil in July and August 1874, when baseball's reigning champions, the Boston Red Stockings, combined with the 1871

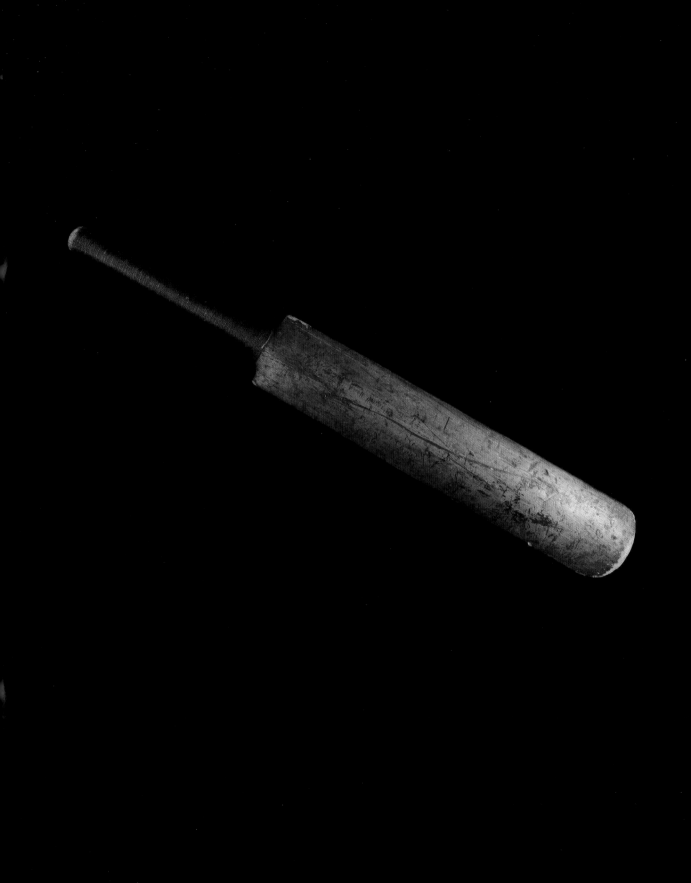

champions, the Philadelphia Athletics, on baseball's first international tour. This tour was the brainchild of English-born Harry Wright, who, after emigrating to New York with his parents as a child, had followed in his father's footsteps as a top American professional cricketer before switching to baseball. By 1874 he was one of the most influential baseball men of the 19th century, and this tour was in large part a very personal mission to showcase his adopted country's national pastime in his native land.

Albert Goodwill Spalding, the 23-year-old pitcher of Wright's Red Stockings, had been dispatched to England the winter before to negotiate the tour. To Henry Chadwick, Spalding was 'one of the most successful of the strategic class of pitchers… [whose] education and gentlemanly qualities place him above the generality of base-ball pitchers', but at the time he judged himself a 'mere stripling with very little experience in business or observation of society'.[24] Nevertheless, Spalding managed to enthuse Marylebone Cricket Club and secure the services of Charles W. Alcock, Secretary of the Surrey County Cricket Club. The very first game of American-style baseball in England was played in the depths of winter during these negotiations, on 27 February 1874. Alcock pitched for one side and Spalding for the other – two men who would both go on to make hugely significant contributions to their respective sports. Alcock's nine was victorious in the six-inning game.[25]

Spalding set up exhibition matches at Liverpool, Manchester, London, Richmond in Surrey, Sheffield and Dublin, but the driving force behind the tour was Harry Wright's desire of many years' standing to take the game of baseball to his 'Mother Country'.[26] Taking two of the best baseball teams on a major international tour had never been done before. And while English cricketing sides had toured North America, Australia and New Zealand, the American baseball players would be only the second sporting party ever to tour England. The first had been a team of Australian Aboriginal cricketers who visited in 1868 and played an arduous, although very successful, 47-match tour. It would be another four years before the Australian tour of 1878 established regular international cricket matches as part of the English season. So in 1874 the novelty of hosting an international sporting tour, combined with Britain's complete lack of understanding of the game of baseball itself, were major obstacles.

In fact, expectations for the tour itself diverged. To the British mind, since 'a base-ball match generally averages two hours', there was plenty of time for the tourists to 'show us how they can wield the willow on the other side of the Atlantic', especially as 'most of the best cricketers in America are also the leading baseball players'.[27] After three well-reported English cricket tours to the United States in 1859, 1868 and 1872, the English were very interested in seeing American prowess at cricket. The added entertainment of seeing baseball for the first time was a bonus. This wasn't what the Americans had in mind. They were thinking more along the lines of the *New York Times'* optimistic report 'that several English cricket clubs are organising and training nines to play against our champions [at baseball], and an exciting time is anticipated'.[28] Apparently, during initial negotiations Spalding had agreed to some cricket matches, but soon it all spiralled out of control. *The Sporting Gazette* announced the 'visit of American cricketers' and *Bell's Life in London* claimed that 'they will make cricket their chief aim in England' as well as giving exhibitions of baseball at each ground.[29] Spalding, admitting that the British public was 'thoroughly advised of the forthcoming cricket matches but only slightly informed about the exhibition ball games', later blamed the scant publicity organised by Charles Alcock, who, Spalding claimed, 'didn't know an earthly thing about baseball'.[30]

In all they would play seven cricket matches, each time against the odds, so that the entire party of 18 took to the field against a local eleven or twelve. 'They will make their first appearance in London at Lord's Grounds, on Bank Holiday, Monday, Aug 3,' reported the *New York Times*, 'when they will engage in the first game of base-ball between regularly organised professional clubs ever played in Great Britain.'[31] The atmosphere at Lord's was later described as 'more like a fete day than otherwise'.[32] This first match, played over two days, set the pattern. A baseball warm-up session started things off, delighting spectators with a display of throwing and catching, before play began for the day at 12.30 when twelve Gentlemen of the MCC and 18 of America met on the cricket pitch. MCC batted first, facing the bowling of Harry Wright and Dick McBride, until the sides retired for lunch at five past two. At this point, as the crowd watched with great interest, a diamond was marked out on the ground, and immediately the players trotted out for the exhibition baseball game (no. 88). McBride, having already bowled in the first innings of the cricket match, now pitched the entire nine-inning game for the Red Stockings, which they won 24–7 in two hours and ten minutes. The game struck many as 'a modernised, manly – and unquestionably an improved – edition of that most enjoyable old game of their boyhood, rounders'.[33]

After a short break, play resumed in the cricket match. The Americans, who had 'fielded very smartly and effectively' before lunch, were now, unsurprisingly, 'loose and ineffective'. Play was ended for the day and the Americans were then entertained at a dinner for 50 gentlemen hosted by the Marquis of Hamilton, the president of MCC. The following day, after a wet weather delay, the match resumed and the Americans went in to bat.

Base-ball in England: The Match on Lord's Cricket Grounds between the Red Stockings and the Athletics. **Coloured wood engraving from a sketch by Abner Crossman,** *Harper's Weekly,* **New York, 5 September 1874**

The print shows the first game of baseball played between professional clubs at Lord's Cricket Ground. Lord's second pavilion can be seen on the right. A Boston pennant flies from the roof of a building to the left and what appears to be a cricket sightscreen protects the spectators behind home plate.

Most went for big, hard shots, with Spalding, Andy Leonard and Cal McVey the best on the day. Despite rain and a soggy wicket, the Americans pulled off a thrilling finish, managing to scrape ahead by two runs before all 18 American batsmen were out. The matched was then called off on account of the weather after each side had completed one innings, giving the Americans their first cricketing victory of the tour, over the strongest cricket side they would face.[34]

In fact, with a number of experienced cricketers among the baseball players, including Dick McBride and Andy Leonard, and especially Harry and George Wright, the Americans won all the cricket matches on the tour, to some praise in the British press. But the fact that they faced average sides and were given 18 men meant 'little excitement was shown' by the British public over the Americans' victories.[35] By contrast, the baseball players were lauded in the American press for their 'extraordinary successes' on the cricket field against the 'strongest players from London, Sheffield, Manchester and Dublin', surely an exaggeration.[36] The *New York Times* made the highly improbable claim that 'with a little practice at the bat an eleven could be picked from the Boston and Athletic Ball Clubs that would test to the utmost the powers of the All England Eleven'.[37] Nevertheless, cricketing success went a long way at home to refute any lingering idea that cricket was more skilful than baseball: 'In all the baseball games in which the English professional cricketers took part during their visits to America from 1859 to 1880, they failed to begin to equal in their ball play the work done by the ball players in cricket in England.'[38]

Any idea that this tour would generate the kind of profit English players made from American interest in cricket was soon dashed. While crowds were at first 'attracted to the ground by the novelty of the amusement, and the animation which seems to characterise the game,' many seemed to share the feeling that 'baseball is merely a complicated form of rounders, and anyone can play at rounders'.[39] Even *Spalding's Official Base Ball Guide* noted that 'the Britishers did not take kindly to the game at all' and the tour was a financial failure.[40] All of this did nothing to deter later American touring enthusiasts from rewriting history, nostalgically reflecting on the 1874 ball players whose 'fine physical appearance and gentlemanly deportment while in England made a great impression on the English people'.[41]

Spalding's world tour of 1888–89

Fourteen years later American baseball embarked upon an even greater international mission. In October 1888, two teams of baseball players departed Chicago on a tour that would take them, and baseball, to Australia, visiting Hawaii and New Zealand on the way. This time Spalding conceived, organised and led the tour himself, which early on was expanded to include Ceylon (modern Sri Lanka), Egypt, parts of Europe and England, making it the first of its kind: a truly global world tour to bring baseball, and the America that it embodied, to all corners of the earth.[42]

Spalding's career had flourished since 1874 and he was now president of the Chicago White Stockings (the National League club today known as the Chicago Cubs) and head of his own thriving sporting-goods firm. In parallel, the game itself had grown and, as Spalding later wrote, 'had been advancing in popularity with such rapid strides… that I felt the time had come when this great pastime should be introduced wherever upon the globe conditions were favourable.'[43]

The reputation of Australians as lovers of all kinds of sport, who already played limited amateur baseball in the cities, and the sheer size and bold intentions of this 'mission of instruction' suggested there was a high chance of success (no. 89).[44] Spalding employed Leigh Lynch, a well-known professional theatre manager, to handle the engagements, and in Lynch, unlike his previous experiences with Alcock, Spalding found an enthusiastic baseball tour manager.

In addition to spreading American manliness and virtue through baseball, Spalding anticipated more pragmatic business outcomes as the take-up of baseball would naturally create new markets for his own sporting goods business.

Spalding's own White Stockings travelled on the tour and to oppose them he assembled an 'All-American' team, 'men of clean habits and attractive personality, men who would reflect credit on the country and the game'. Some players declined his offer, not wishing to travel or to be away during the off-season, or dropped out at the last moment. In the face of criticism, Spalding admitted that securing players was 'beset with many obstacles' but that overall 'capable men were available'.[45] Some family members and a group of journalists travelled with the touring party, as well as George Wright, the legendary batter and shortstop, who, now retired, acted as umpire for most of the baseball games. Clarence Duval, an African-American minstrel entertainer who had earlier served as the Chicago White Stockings' team mascot, was also signed on after the tourists, by remarkable coincidence, bumped into him in Omaha. By all accounts a talented entertainer and acrobat, he was duly dressed up and paraded around, an illustration of American prejudices in the Jim Crow era.[46]

Their first international game was played in Auckland, New Zealand (they had been unable to play in Hawaii as it was a Sunday), before arriving to warm public welcome in Sydney on 14 December 1888. They played exhibition baseball games in Sydney, Melbourne, Adelaide and Ballarat, buoyed, according to the *Spalding Base Ball Guide*, by the 'heartiness of the greeting, the boundless hospitality and the crowded attendance at their games'.[47] Newspaper man Harry Palmer claimed that 'our teams will stand ready to meet Australian cricket elevens or football teams at any city they visit',[48] but only one encounter took place in Sydney, where a shortened game of cricket was played between the Base Ball Eighteen and a Sydney Eleven on 18 December (no. 90). While some

89
Poster for *Spalding's Australian Base Ball Tour: Chicago vs All America*, 1888
The tour was initially advertised as 'Spalding's Australian Base Ball Tour' and this promotional poster, probably the only surviving copy, features baseball cards of the players Spalding had contracted for the trip. Two of his biggest signings shown here, Mike 'King' Kelly and 'Silent' Mike Tiernan, broke their contracts and refused to go at the last minute, much to Spalding's embarrassment. The poster, showing a game in progress and the *SS Alameda*, the ship that would take them to Australia, was sent out ahead of the baseball party to encourage public excitement about the games.

90
Chicago and All-American world tour teams, taken in Australia, December 1888
Taken in Australia in December 1888, this studio photograph shows the Chicago players in their light grey shirts and knee-breeches, black stockings and belts, with 'CHICAGO' in black letters on their jerseys, and the All-American players in their white shirts and knee breeches with blue stockings, and belts made of white duck with a silk American flag draped around and knotted at the hip. Each 'All-American' had the name of his home team in blue letters on his jersey. A. G. Spalding sits in the centre of the middle row, flanked by the two team captains. Seated on the far left is the tour 'mascot' Clarence Duval; seated in the centre is George Wright, with his cricket equipment; while on the far right is Harry Simpson, Spalding's personal secretary, who stayed behind in Australia to nurture baseball's development.

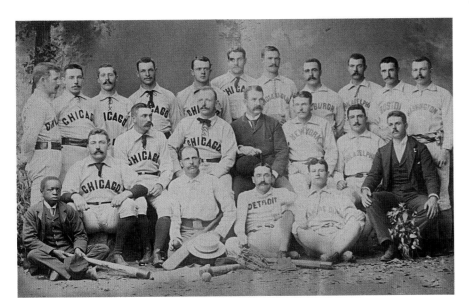

91
**The baseball tourists
in Egypt at the Sphinx,
9 February 1889**

players took the opportunity seriously, notably Adrian Constantine 'Cap' Anson, the player-manager of the White Stockings and one of baseball's first celebrity players, the disappointing gate receipts ensured no future cricket matches on this tour.[49]

The tourists set sail for Ceylon. After a brief stop there, playing just a single game, the party travelled on to Egypt, arriving in February 1889 in Cairo, where they stayed at the Orient Hotel. Always putting on a show, Spalding arranged a procession from the hotel to the Great Pyramids, the All-Americans on camels and the Chicagos on donkeys. A photograph was taken at the Sphinx (no. 91). Afterwards a flat stretch of ground, carefully oriented so that the Great Pyramid, Cheops, loomed in the distance, was prepared for the 30th game of the tour. It was umpired by Spalding himself and won after five innings by the All-Americans (nos 92–93). Free to look around after the game, the ball players showed remarkably little reverence for the monuments, attempting first a baseball throwing contest over Cheops and then directly at the right eye of the Sphinx.[50]

They finally arrived in England after games in Naples, Rome, Florence and Paris. Spalding felt 'the reception of our company in England was one of the great triumphs of the world tour,' thanks in large part to his own advance publicity.[51] He had learned a great deal from his earlier experience and carefully prepared the press to best position baseball. 'The Americans,' one planted story went, 'have no thought of competing for public favour with cricket, football, or others of our recognised sports.' The tour would only demonstrate the 'many good points of America's national game'.[52] He was less successful in avoiding some gentle British mockery, or comparisons to rounders. 'What a fuss people are making about base-ball,' ran a typical tongue-in-cheek column. 'When I was a boy at school we called it rounders, and didn't think anything of it.'[53]

Spalding joined forces once again with his old friend Charles Alcock, and the first game in England (the 35th of the whole tour) was hosted by Alcock's Surrey County Cricket Club. This game, held on 12 March 1889 at the famous Kennington Oval grounds in London (usually known simply as 'The Oval'), would be played in front of a VIP party bristling with nobility and dignitaries, several

92
Photograph of baseball match, Chicago v All-America, with Great Pyramid of Cheops in background, 9 February 1889

93
Baseball used for the match played next to the Great Pyramid of Cheops

cricketing heroes, including W. G. Grace and Ivo Bligh, and most critically the Prince of Wales (nos 94–95).

For the players, proceedings at The Oval kicked off with a rich and over-generous luncheon in their honour at the Surrey County Cricket Club tavern. Spalding, ever the baseball promoter, later wrote in *America's National Game* that their English hosts were invariably 'astonished' to see professional baseball players capable of the social and dress requirements of such occasions, compared to their professional cricketing cousins.[54] Although the menu, which included Gloucester salmon, aspic of lobster, pigeon pie, ox tongue and champagne jelly, was rather heavy for pre-game fare, a pleasant time was had by all (no. 96).[55] Anson recalled, 'We forgot entirely that we were lunching with lords and dukes. I never felt more thoroughly at ease in my life, and the rest of the boys seemed as much at home as I did.'

The day was damp and cold but a surprisingly large crowd had gathered, perhaps 6,000 in all, primarily to catch a glimpse of the future King Edward VII, for whom all play stopped and the players lined up in salute. In thick fog the game was hard to follow, the mist on the ground obscuring the ball, and the

The Chicago-All American Baseball Teams
at Kennington Oval, London, England,
where the first game in England was played by A.G. Spalding's World Baseball Tourists on March 1st 1889 in the presence of the Prince of Wales, Late King Edward VII.

Center - A.G. Spalding, George Wright
Bottom Row - Tom Daly, Tom Burns, Ed. Crane, W. Earle.
Second Row - Martin Sullivan, John K. Tener, Fred Pfeffer, Jimmy Fogarty, Ned Hanlon, Jim Manning, John Healy.
Top Row - S. Goodfriend, (correspondent) Capt. John M. Ward, Capt. A.C. Anson, Fred Carroll, Mark Baldwin, Tom Brown, George Wood.

The Visit of the American Baseball Clubs.

The Committee of the SURREY COUNTY CRICKET CLUB request the company at honour of _____

The Surrey Cricket Ground, Kennington Oval,
ON TUESDAY, MARCH 12, at 3.30 p.m.,
to see the first game of the American Baseball Players in London.

His Royal Highness the Prince of Wales has kindly consented to honour the American Baseball Players with his presence.

Please to present this Card at the Entrance to Ground and at the Pavilion

---

Surrey County Cricket Club
TAVERN,
KENNINGTON OVAL.

Reception Luncheon
of the
American Base Ball Players.

TOAST LIST.
THE QUEEN.
PRESIDENT OF THE UNITED STATES.
PRINCE AND PRINCESS OF WALES,
AND REST OF THE ROYAL FAMILY.
THE AMERICAN BASE BALL CLUBS.

March 12th, 1889.

unfamiliar rules and the frequent changes from batting to fielding baffled the uninitiated (no. 97).[56]

Spalding settled himself in the royal box on a spare chair he placed between the future monarch and his brother, leaving all aghast at this breach of royal protocol. The Prince of Wales, according to Spalding, became 'more and more impressed' and at one point slapped Spalding on the thigh. Emboldened, Spalding later touched His Royal Highness on the shoulder after an impressive slider into first base. Years later, he was still on the defensive: 'If I violated the code of court etiquette, I must plead that I was not at court, but at an American ball game. If I sat in the presence of Royalty, it is certain that the Royalty sat in mine. If I tapped the future King of Great Britain on the shoulder, it was nothing more offensive that a game of tag, for he had first slapped me on the leg.'[57]

Player Jimmy Ryan recorded in his tour diary: 'To-day we play our first game in England, at the Surrey Cricket grounds, Kennington Oval. The day was very foggy, but we entertained about 5000 people for a few hours. An elegant luncheon was served to us and after that an introduction to H.R.H. the Prince of Wales, who was present at the game and enjoyed it muchly.'[58]

Chicago eventually won the contest 7–4, after which the crowd received survey cards from the London edition of the *New York Herald* asking, 'Do you think baseball more scientific than cricket?' and, 'Do you think it will ever be adopted in England?' The Prince was shown the card by a reporter and, according to Spalding's later memory, wrote, 'I consider Base Ball an excellent game; but Cricket a better one.'[59] One spectator, the humourist O. P. Q. Philander Smiff, declared after the game that baseball was an acquired taste, like olives or caviar.[60]

The baseball tourists played their second match in fine weather at Lord's Cricket Ground. Spalding and George Wright had played there 15 years before as part of the 1874 tour, and, as an active cricketer still, another visit to this fabled ground must have been particularly pleasing for Wright. Among the large crowd, reportedly up to 8,000 spectators, were some of cricket's most influential figures. Lord Harris, past his prime as a player but at the height of his powers as a cricket administrator, was present, as were Lord Sheffield, Sir Spencer Ponsonby-Fane, MCC treasurer and a founding member of the famous amateur travelling club I Zingari, and the cricketers C. I. Thornton and G. F. Vernon. The game itself was an exciting one, won by the All-Americans after a thrilling finish.[61]

The third match was played the following day at the Crystal Palace ground (no. 98). It was won 5–3 by the All-Americans, despite the latter missing their captain, John Ward, who had sailed for New York that morning. Several thousand attended the game, held on the grounds named for the famous

94 (top)
The Chicago and All-American baseball teams at Kennington Oval, 1889

95 (bottom left)
Match invitation card to the Surrey County Cricket Club, 12 March 1889

96 (bottom right)
Toast card for the 'Reception Luncheon of the American Base Ball Players', 12 March 1889

nearby Crystal Palace, the building that had hosted the 1851 Great Exhibition in Hyde Park before being relocated here to south London. The grounds would be an important baseball venue for years to come. While the fielding, a highlight for British spectators, was not up to the standard of the two previous games, the crowd enjoyed the 'thoroughly interesting' eighth inning when All-American Ned Hanlon stole second base before his teammate Tom Brown hit the first home run in England 'amid great applause'.[62]

Next, the great cricketer W. G. Grace welcomed the players, arriving by train, to his hometown of Bristol. There, as captain of Gloucestershire County Cricket Club, he hosted a game played in fine but bitterly cold weather before several thousand spectators. Both teams rested their best pitchers and a game of vigorous batting ensued. The crowd initially appreciated the show, but after about an hour, almost half of those in attendance, having satisfied their curiosity, lost interest and left the ground.[63]

W. G. Grace and other members of Gloucestershire wanted to try their hand at batting, so the Chicago team stayed on the field after the game. Jimmy Ryan and Ed Crane pitched to the cricketers, and Crane later recalled, 'Grace missed 'em by about two feet. I gave him snakes, and in-curves, out-curves and twisters, all very slow, but he couldn't get the bat within a yard of them.'[64]

97
The American Baseball Players at Kennington Oval, from Illustrated London News, 23 March 1889
This engraving commemorates the game at The Oval, with portraits of the players running down both sides and inset full-length portraits of each captain. Typical baseball plays are depicted: everything from 'a strike', 'a hit' and 'a slide' to 'an error' and 'home sweet home'. The patronage of the Prince of Wales is commemorated. His son, George Frederick, would attend many future baseball games as King George V.

The following summer Grace wrote a column about baseball and cricket (reproduced on page 98) recalling the 'smartness of the fieldsmen, their catching and throwing being almost perfection'. Saying nothing of his own attempts at bat, he proclaimed the batting weak, at least to a cricketer, and felt, along with the crowd, 'disappointed that hitting the ball was the exception instead of the rule,' although conceding the lack of hitting was a tribute to pitching skill.[65] And this described what was, for baseball, a high-scoring game with weak pitching! His verdict on the day was the same, 'I should like to have been a pitcher when I was a young man,' adding, with typical Grace aplomb, 'I don't think anyone would have hit the ball.'

The final leg of the world tour was a whirlwind six games in six different British cities in just six days. The tourists began in Birmingham where the game was drawn in the tenth inning on account of darkness, the teams locked at four-all from the fourth inning. Such a dogged low-scoring affair in gathering darkness must have been a challenge for novice spectators, and the local press made little attempt at flattery: 'Base ball is a very nice game – something like rounders by demon players,' but judged it little understood by the crowd, who gossiped and only looked 'now and then at the game'.[66] Undaunted, the tourists continued on to Sheffield the next day for a short but hit-filled game at the

98
Artist unknown, *Game of the Chicago and All-America Teams, at Crystal Palace Grounds, London*, 1889

Cricket and Baseball by W. G. Grace, 1890

Cricket in Australia, as in England, is considered the national game; in America it has to contend against baseball. To realize the hold baseball has upon Americans we have only to watch one of the great matches. At every important match played the attendance is as large, if not larger, than at any first-class cricket match in England, and the fact is forced upon us that baseball, not cricket, is the national game there. Cricket clubs of importance are few in number in America; baseball clubs have a hold in every large town and city, and the doings of the professional players are followed with as much interest as the doings of every first-class professional cricketer in England.

99
W. G. Grace, 1874

I have been asked to account for the remarkable hold baseball has upon its followers, and to compare the two games of baseball and cricket. Frankly, I cannot. It would be presumption on my part to express an opinion on the merits of a game of which I have seen and know so little. My experience might be summed up in a visit to the Oval, and a visit to the County Ground, Ashley Hill, Bristol, when Mr Spalding's team gave their exhibitions. I was much impressed with the smartness of the fieldsmen, their catching and throwing being almost perfection. But the batting, to a cricketer, seemed rather a weak spot; and, with the crowd, I was disappointed that hitting the ball was the exception instead of the rule. Of course I am perfectly well aware that the pitcher is the most important member of the team, and that what I thought was a weakness in the hitting was really a tribute to his skill.

Our American friends say that a first-class match can be played in the course of a single afternoon, and that, being a busy, working nation, therein lies half of the charm of the game to them. They are certainly enthusiastic over it, and I know that but few Englishmen have yet realized the science and aptitude required to play it well; but I do not think it will ever take hold to any extent in England or Australia, where cricket is played to such perfection. And I hope its thousands of followers will pardon me when I say that I have too strong a love for the game with which I have been so closely associated for the last twenty-five years to wish that it should.

famous Bramall Lane ground, venue for both cricket and football (it was the home at the time of Yorkshire County Cricket Club), but the match was called off in the fifth inning on account of rain.[67] The weather was similar in Bradford the following day. On a day when 'not ten people would have started for the grounds' in America, almost 4,000 were delighted by the short but exciting display of smart fielding, clever catches and base stealing.[68]

Following a fixture in Glasgow, one of the tour's most exciting games took place at Old Trafford cricket ground in Manchester, in front of a small crowd. The next day the players headed to Liverpool, their final stop in England, where a very large, very animated crowd turned out at the Police Athletic Club grounds to see them. On that day for the first time English players would take on the Americans. This was the heartland of rounders, the indigenous British game popular in some areas as a competitive adult sport.[69] Spalding had agreed to a game of rounders after the obligatory, but shortened, baseball game between the Chicago and All-American teams. A picked eleven from the Crescent, Union, Cranmer, Crown and Derby clubs, all part of the Liverpool Rounders Association, took on a picked eleven of the American players, including the veteran George Wright and A. G. Spalding himself, at the English game.

The American press, interested in the game that baseball was so often measured against, predictably judged that 'so far as skill is concerned, any comparison with the American game is absurd'.[70] But the Liverpool players had the last laugh, coming out strongly as the Americans struggled with an unfamiliar field, differences in equipment and no foul territory (no. 100). Rounders, like cricket, is played across two innings, with each innings lasting until the full line-up is dismissed. Liverpool scored 16 runs in their first innings. All out for only eight runs in reply, the Americans had to immediately bat their second innings to try to build up a lead in the game, but managed only six more runs. The Liverpool side therefore won the match by an innings and two runs. To some in the American press, unfamiliar with the two-innings scoring method, this seemed a respectable 16–14 loss, but it was in fact a decisive victory for the English. (Spalding years later would 'forget' that the match was ever completed, claiming the English stopped the game when 'we were just getting the hang of it'.)[71] Next the Liverpool players tried the American game, with much less success, as the

100
Rounders ball used in a game in Liverpool between English and American players, 23 March 1889
This is the game ball from the rounders match between a Liverpool eleven and a picked eleven from the American baseball players. A rounders ball is much smaller than a baseball; the bat is shaped more like a cricket bat, but half the size. At that time the batter swung with one hand to hit the underarm-pitched ball, and a player running the bases could be out when hit by the ball. This feature of early baseball was eliminated by the Knicker-bockers in 1845. Rounders followed suit, also adopting two-handed hitting from base-ball following Spalding's visit.

Americans 'trifled at will with their opponents'. Showing off, they hit the pitching of champion Lancashire cricketer Frank Sugg for 16 runs in the first inning and two in the second, walloping their hosts 18–0 when the game was called off halfway through the third inning – an 'easy victory', but perhaps not one to encourage Liverpool ball players to switch sports.[72]

After a pleasant few days in Ireland, with games in Belfast and Dublin, and many players making side trips to visit relatives,[73] these 'athletic globe trotters' happily began their long trip home to New York City and a glittering reception.[74] The sumptuous welcome-home banquet, served 'In Nine Innings' at the famous *Delmonico's* restaurant, was attended by such luminaries as Mark Twain and the future president Theodore Roosevelt. Twain himself famously reflected on baseball as the 'very symbol, the outward and visible expression of the drive, and push, and rush, and struggle of the raging, tearing, booming nineteenth century'. The players, feted and lionised, were once again driven hard by Spalding to play barnstorming games all the way home to Chicago, to help recoup some of the substantial costs of the world tour. Spalding proclaimed the tour a success on every measure, telling reporters in New York, 'I have the proud consciousness of having established our game throughout the world, and feel certain that many countries will adopt baseball.'[75]

Spalding's legacy: the future of baseball in England

Today, Spalding's statement seems typical of the overblown bluster of a 19th-century showman, yet his tour did have some immediate baseball impact. In Australia, where the tour had been enthusiastically received and baseball played since the 1850s, Spalding arranged for his capable and enthusiastic secretary, Harry Simpson, to stay behind after the tour to nurture and promote the game. Simpson, a baseball and cricket player from Newark, New Jersey, had instant success in Melbourne and Sydney. Allied with investments from Spalding, Simpson's work led to the formation of fledgling organisations like the Victorian Baseball League competing for a 'Spalding trophy', and if not for Simpson's untimely death in 1891 from typhoid fever, aged 27, baseball might have had a very different future in Australia.

In England, Spalding's tour and a follow-up visit that same year by American college ball players who taught locals the game, gave momentum to the formal establishment of a professional league, modelled on the National League in America. The National League of Professional Base Ball Clubs of Great Britain was launched in 1890. With Spalding's financial support, it appeared that baseball could find a minor place in the British sporting scene at the end of the 19th century.

Apart from American residents and American companies operating in England, football clubs seemed most enthusiastic about baseball.[76] This first professional baseball league competed with four member clubs, three of them associated with football clubs – Preston North End, Aston Villa and Stoke – and a fourth independent club, Derby, founded by British industrialist Francis Ley (no. 101).[77] While this league collapsed after only one season (professional baseball would not return to England until the 1930s), amateur competition and intermittent organised baseball continued, strongest in north-east England and London (no. 102). By 1895, when England's first extra-innings baseball game was played at the Crystal Palace grounds, the National Baseball Association and the London Baseball Association had clubs in regular competition.[78] There was a visit by a Boston amateur baseball club, and some press enthusiasm about 'seriously contested' games attracting more English converts to the game every day.[79]

Twenty-five years later Spalding's opinion was still that 'base ball will be the international game'.[80] He was not alone in this view. Charles A. Comiskey, described as 'the Most Remarkable and Most Picturesque Figure in Base Ball', had long cherished a secret ambition to undertake a baseball world tour with his own club, the Chicago White Sox, an American League club that honoured the powerhouse Chicago club of the National League by co-opting that team's nickname.[81] John J. McGraw, the high-profile and outspoken manager of the New York Giants, was Comiskey's perfect partner in such a venture. They would undertake two international tours. The first, at the close of the 1913 baseball season, duplicated Spalding's world tour, but added Japan, China and the Philippines to the grand itinerary on top of Australia, Ceylon, Egypt, Italy, France and the United Kingdom.[82] Ten years later in 1924, Comiskey and McGraw once again took their players abroad, this time limiting them-selves to Europe and a more leisurely playing schedule.[83]

Both tours included some of the top players of their day, including

101

Derby Baseball Club, photograph by The Graphotone Co., Middlesex, 1890
Posed here in this well-known photograph with their president Francis Ley, a leading figure in British baseball, the Derby Nine sport the knicker pants popularised by the Cincinnati Red Stockings 20 years earlier and the sash tie belt popular with cricketers at this time. The club's ground was later taken over by Derby County Football Club, who retained its original name, the Baseball Ground, and used it as their home ground until 1997.

102

Ticket issued by the London Base-Ball Association, 1895
The London Base-Ball Association began in 1894 with five clubs: the J's, the Remingtons, the Electrics, Postmen and Thespians.

Larry Doyle, celebrated pitcher Christy Mathewson, Frankie Frisch, hard-hitting Giants right fielder Ross Youngs and outfielder Casey Stengel, centre fielder Sam Crawford (no. 103), Sam Rice, White Sox pitcher Urban 'Red' Faber and Boston Braves shortstop Dave Bancroft. Giants outfielder Jim Thorpe was a star drawcard during the tour after his sensational performance at the 1912 Olympics and his subsequent sensational disqualification and loss of his medals and records, after it was revealed he had violated amateur rules by accepting money to play baseball.

A highlight of the 1914 tour was an exhibition game played before King George V and his royal party at Stamford Bridge in London, the home ground of Chelsea Football Club. An estimated 37,000-strong crowd enjoyed an exciting eleventh-inning win for the White Sox in the final fixture of the four-month world tour (no. 104).[84] These tours were meant to showcase the great American game and 'spread the gospel of base ball among foreign nations'.[85]

103
Chicago tour jersey worn by Sam Crawford, 1913–14
The Chicago and New York teams on the tour included both regular roster players and stars invited from other clubs. One invited player was Detroit Tigers outfielder 'Wahoo' Sam Crawford who wore this jersey as part of the 1913–14 Chicago world tour team. Crawford was an outstanding player known for his powerful hitting. When he retired in 1917, he had amassed 309 career triples (some sources put his total at 312) – a record that still stands today.

104
Baseball used at Stamford Bridge, London, 26 February 1914
This is the baseball used in an exhibition game between the Chicago White Sox and the New York Giants at Stamford Bridge. The ball has been inscribed with details of the game, signed by players and officials, and then shellacked to preserve the surface, giving the ball a rich brown appearance.

105
Dinner programme for the banquet at the Biltmore Hotel, New York, 7 March 1914

And baseball had some enthusiastic champions in England, like Ben Toon of West Bromwich, who in January 1914 optimistically proclaimed a 'new Empire waiting to embrace baseball': he believed the sport would appeal to the football (soccer) fan, who, like his brother baseball fan, 'loves a scrappy, snappy game. He isn't always "gentlemanly". He likes clean sport but he does like a man who can give and take legitimate bumps. The vim of the game gets him going, and sometimes he forgets and cuts loose.'[86]

Returning to New York on 6 March 1914 at the end of their world tour, the players were greeted with a magnificent banquet for over 600 guests at the Biltmore Hotel (no. 105). Governor Tener of Pennsylvania, himself a member of Spalding's 1888–89 world tour, gave a rousing speech celebrating the deeds of the returning players, concluding that 'in every clime and country and under every sun Base Ball will be played… for wherever the game is implanted there will indelibly be associated with it the word "American" – the American game.'[87]

The 1924 tour also attracted plenty of high-profile attention. Once again the teams played in front of King George V at Stamford Bridge, and this time many commentators remarked on the chatter, yelling and unsolicited advice from players and American spectators during the game (nos 108–111). 'You cannot enjoy the great American game of baseball unless you are a "fan" which means you must encourage your own side with demonic yells,' wrote

106
Baseball match programme, United States v Canada at Lord's, 28 July 1917
107
Spectators at a baseball match at Lord's between Canadians and London Americans, 1917
The fledgling British baseball leagues did not survive the outbreak of World War I. The baseball played in England during the war years was between American and Canadian military personnel and these games attracted good crowds, many of them soldiers. *The Times* observed that 'many Londoners *heard* baseball for the first time' at Lord's when a notable series of benefit matches was played between American and Canadian teams in 1917 for widows and orphans of Canadians who fell in battle.

H. V. Morton in the *Daily Express* in 1924. George Bernard Shaw found it 'both surprising and delightful',[88] but P. G. H. Fender, a prominent Test cricketer of the time and otherwise admirer of baseball, felt that 'it is opposed to the whole spirit of English sport to have people "chipping" at one another, as the American baseballers do.'[89] Sir Arthur Conan Doyle, while agreeing 'that the continual ragging is from a British view-point a defect,' felt baseball was a developing young sport and that such elements would eventually 'pass away'.[90]

And yet, for all the hyperbole, the impact that the tours made was disappointing. 'Let us be honest with ourselves,' William Phelon wrote halfway through the 1913–14 tour, 'there aren't any new countries adopting baseball, not a darned one… you can't make Americans take up cricket, and you can't

108
New York Giants jersey worn by Casey Stengel, 1924
Casey Stengel, a colourful outfielder for the New York Giants, played on the 1924 Europe baseball tour. Later he built a somewhat mediocre reputation as a baseball manager before his glory days managing the New York Yankees from 1948 through 1960 with such superstars as Joe DiMaggio and Mickey Mantle. In his seventies he managed the bumbling but beloved new franchise, the New York Mets.

109
King George V meeting baseball players before the game at Stamford Bridge, 1924

110
Netting being erected in front of the stands at Stamford Bridge in preparation for baseball, 1924

111
Baseball at Chelsea **by Tom Webster, from the** *Daily Mail*, **25 October 1924**
This cartoon, from Ross Youngs's 1924 tour scrapbook, makes light of the noise generated during the 1924 game between the Chicago White Sox and the New York Giants at Stamford Bridge.

make other nations take up baseball… as to making other nations yell for baseball and turn out en masse with spike and glove – nix, nix, nothing doing.'[91] *Sporting Life* found the whole premise questionable: 'Of what practical use or value would be Asiatic or Antipodean conquests? And what care we for the good or ill opinion of our great democratic game in the class-ridden countries of old Europe?'[92]

The 1924 tour was equally harshly judged: 'And so ended a most ill-advised base ball tour,' intoned *The Reach Official American League Guide* of 1924–25, 'which was undertaken against the advice of the best friends of the promoters of the game; for which there was neither rhyme nor reason as there was no understanding of or demand for the game in Europe; and which did the game no good commensurate with the time, effort and money wasted.'

Baseball in England in the 1930s

But the effects of America's missionaries were not all in vain (nos 112–115). The English businessman John Moores, who had made his fortune from founding the Littlewood Football Pools, was enamoured with the American game. In June 1933 he met in his home town, Liverpool, with representatives of an English version of baseball, now known as British baseball or Welsh baseball but essentially the game previously known as rounders. In the 1890s, the Liverpool Rounders Association had been caught up in the wave of interest in baseball. Inspired perhaps by Spalding's 1889 visit and the compliments paid to the American athletes, the association had changed the name of its sport from rounders to baseball in 1892. The players may have felt baseball was a more

112
A posed action photograph of two baseball players at an empty Wembley Stadium, 14 June 1934

113 (above left)
The batter here, *c.* 1935, is Scottish footballer Alex Jackson, better known for scoring three times against England in Scotland's 5–1 win at Wembley in 1928.

114 (above right)
The last London baseball match of the 1936 season at an empty White City Stadium, 1 September 1936

115 (left)
Sam Hanna of the Pirates slides into third base as Roland Gladu of the Hammers applies the tag, West Ham stadium, London, 25 July 1937

appropriate name for their manly sport than rounders, more commonly associated with a children's game.[93]

At any rate, in 1933 Moores wanted them to go further and begin to play by American rules so as to join a new baseball league he intended to establish. Eighteen amateur clubs took up his offer and a new league took root in the Liverpool area in 1934. This was intended to be just a prelude, however, to Moores's real ambition of establishing professional baseball throughout England. His enthusiasm was as much for the game as it was for the business opportunities baseball offered his company, Littlewoods, since betting on the outcome of a baseball game would fit nicely into his successful empire based on football gambling. The North of England Baseball League started up in the Manchester area in 1935 with eight teams, using a combination of American and Canadian players and some English sportsmen – notably football players, including the great Everton and England striker Dixie Dean who played during football's close season. Jim Sullivan, rugby league star and top-class player of 'British' baseball, also played in this league for the Manchester North End Blue Sox.[94] Professional baseball expanded in 1936 with two new leagues, the Yorkshire League and the London Major Baseball League, all under the umbrella of the National Baseball Association.[95]

The northern stronghold

For two seasons the professional game seemed to flourish in England, although the players were generally Americans or Canadians, with few English on any teams. In London clubs like West Ham Hammers and their sister club the Pirates, the Romford Wasps, White City and the all-Mormon Catford Saints attracted pockets of spectators. It would be a short-lived experiment. By 1937, northern England was emerging as the sole stronghold of the game.

The National Baseball Association Challenge Cup was won in 1937 by Hull at that city's Craven Park in front of 11,000 cheering fans, who were so excited by their team's 5–1 victory over the Romford Wasps that they broke the barriers and invaded the field.[96] A working-class city on the north-east coast, founded on fishing and trade, Hull has remained a hub of British baseball to this day. By the 1938 baseball season, London had lost most of its top players to northern teams, and as a result never again fielded a professional competition.

Still, that same year, England hosted the first world amateur baseball championship, called the Amateur World Series. This international competition still runs, usually every year or every two years, and has been known as the

Baseball World Cup since 1988. Run by the International Baseball Federation (IBAF) it is still a largely amateur competition, and not to be confused with the World Baseball Classic. In 1938, only two teams took part: Great Britain and the USA. The Great Britain players were drawn from teams in the London and Yorkshire major leagues, many Canadian-born, while the Americans were talented high school and college-age players preparing for the 1940 Olympics (which were ultimately cancelled due to war). The tournament was played in August 1938 and Great Britain easily won four of the five games to become the first-ever baseball world champions (nos 116–117).

As part of a thriving Yorkshire baseball scene, Hull continued to back the sport enthusiastically. In 1938 the northern teams reorganised and Hull joined nine other strong teams with a new structure more akin to cricket's longstanding mixture of amateur and professional players (nos 118–120). Each team was allowed only three professionals, who, like their cricketing counterparts at the time, would train and develop local talent. This contrasted with the now-defunct London league that had fielded the best players available, inevitably from Canada and America.

116
The first game of the inaugural Amateur World Series baseball tournament between the USA and Great Britain, played in Liverpool, 13 August 1938
The five games in this series, played over seven days from 13 to 20 August in the north of England, were called 'Test Matches', borrowing the cricketing term for international contests.

117
The American baseball players look on as Great Britain win the match at Liverpool, 13 August 1938

118 (top left)
Hull v Halifax baseball programme, 3 August 1939
By 1938 only one 'professional' league remained in England, the Lancashire–Yorkshire Major League, with ten member clubs.

119 (top right)
Hull Giants v Leeds baseball programme, 4 June 1938
In 1938 a short-lived 'outlaw' league sprang up to challenge the three-professional limit. The International Professional Baseball League set up rival clubs in baseball centres – like the Hull Giants – but survived only a few weeks.

120 (middle)
Hull baseball team photograph (undated)

121–122 (below)
Hull Aces baseball jersey and batting helmet, 1980s
The Hull Aces were formed in the 1940s and have been a solid amateur baseball club active in local, national and even international competitions.

123 (below)
Baseball fielder's mitt, 1950s

The outbreak of hostilities in 1939 seriously slowed baseball's progress in England, as it had during World War I. In the war most baseball would be played by US and Canadian servicemen, and this influence extended well into the 1950s with the continued American military presence in Britain. Unlike in Japan, where baseball had flourished since the 1870s and acted as a lasting sporting tie between America and Japan despite war and occupation, by the late 1950s in England a close connection to America was seen as a hindrance to progress as the game was too identified with American culture and did not have enough home-grown attraction.[97] Even so, dedicated enthusiasts ensured that the sport survived, and it continues today in northern regions, including Hull (nos 121–123).

Baseball in Britain today

We fans who live outside the boundaries of the physical country of baseball, across large bodies of water, are the baseball exiles. We love our game in a way that most fans could not understand. We carry a diamond inside us.
Herman Irving, 1987[98]

Baseball remains an amateur sport in Great Britain. Its history has seen many ups and downs, but Josh Chetwynd, a player, commentator and writer on American baseball in England, has noted a resilience and an abiding optimism pervading many aspects of the game today. He has found a dedicated group of amateur players bringing their own British ethos to the game, and an enjoyable level of sportsmanship and teamwork (no. 124). While the players struggle to compete with the powerhouses of the international game, Chetwynd writes that, 'The esprit de corps I encountered on the first team I played for [in 1996] remains along with a tremendous enthusiasm for the game.'[99] One recent exhibition baseball game in Somerset in October 2008 pitted the Great Britain National Baseball Team against a cricket team called Banger's All Stars, as part of international cricketer Marcus Trescothick's benefit, and helped to increase the profile of the national team.[100] The Great Britain national team won silver at the 2007 European Baseball Championships, a result they are keen to match or exceed in 2010 in their campaign to secure a spot in the expanded World Baseball Classic competition for 2013.[101] The domestic amateur sport is also growing with 51 teams competing in four leagues in the British Baseball Federation (BBF) competition for 2010.[102]

Additionally, baseball on both sides of the Atlantic has a small but enthusiastic following in England, as can be seen by the various publications and interest groups active since the 1970s and the proliferation of websites today.

124
Great Britain national team baseball jersey worn by Josh Chetwynd, 2000

5 The scientific game: amateurs and professionals

The Knickerbocker Base Ball Club and Marylebone Cricket Club shaped and nurtured the development of their different sports in many ways, above all through their contributions to the rules and laws governing how each game must be played. One need only mention 'Knickerbocker' to baseball fans or 'MCC' to cricket fans to conjure up mental pictures of bygone visionary gentlemen, the founding fathers who turned informal games into national pastimes. They created respectable adult pastimes out of their sports by emphasising the 'manly', 'scientific' and morally uplifting aspects to their activities. But can a comparison of the two clubs, seen as bastions of the amateur 'gentlemanly' games, shed any light on the complex story of amateurism and professionalism that runs through the two sports?

At first glance it seems clear-cut. The Knickerbocker club's eventual demise in 1882 mirrors the general demise of amateur club baseball in the face of the unstoppable rise of professional baseball, which, in itself, marked a turning away from old-world social and economic structures in a modernising America. In contrast, and at the same time, MCC's continued and increasing control and stature reflected the strength of the amateur game in cricket with its attendant entrenched exclusivity, which, in itself, echoes a traditionalist, stratified English society. Seen in this light, baseball becomes a modern working-class pursuit and cricket an old-fashioned, elitist recreation.

The main problem with this conclusion – containing as it does some credible elements – is the assumption that baseball alone embraced professionalism while cricket held fast to its amateur traditions. It is true that amateurism had almost disappeared from organised baseball by the 1870s, but this had not happened in isolation from what was going on in cricket at the time. Indeed, 19th-century cricket had a strong element of professionalism, which was itself, in the American context, influencing baseball's own professional development. To understand fully the relative role of amateurs and professionals in baseball and cricket, including overlapping influences as well as deep differences, we need to go back to the 1860s, a critical decade in the modern development of both games.

English aristocrats, gentlemen and cricket clubs

By the 1860s, baseball and cricket were being celebrated as 'national sports' due to their general popularity, but organisationally both were unstable and haphazard. Marylebone Cricket Club, founded in London in 1787, grew directly out of the aristocratic and gentlemanly enthusiasm for cricket. By the early decades of the 1800s, the club was at the forefront of a shift in the control of

The All-England Eleven by Nicholas 'Felix' Wanostrocht (see page 117)

the game from individual wealthy patrons to cricket clubs. From the time MCC issued its own revision of the Laws of Cricket in 1788, it was firmly established as the sole guardian and arbiter of the laws, and its home, Lord's Cricket Ground, then located in Dorset Square – the first of the three grounds bearing the name of Thomas Lord – became the 'headquarters' of the game. That MCC could assume such authority over the Laws rested on the reputation and prestige of the men who were members.[1]

The club structure made the game more organised and less reliant on individual sponsors, and the popularity of clubs across the country increasingly encouraged a sense of regional cricket identity.[2] Clubs also made it possible for more and more enthusiasts to take up the game for, as John Nyren advocated in 1833, a complete game should comprise the full 22 players, eleven on each side, and for this purpose the prospective player 'must necessarily enrol himself as a member of some club'.[3] By the 1860s, membership in cricket clubs was at an unprecedented level and, as a prominent cricketer of the day observed, 'no other national sport is so extensively indulged in, or so universally practised by all ranks and grades of society'.[4]

This was an exciting time for cricket, and MCC was right at the heart of it. In 1866 the club was able to purchase the freehold on its third ground – still named after Thomas Lord, the first proprietor – and around the same time the club adopted its famous colours of red and yellow, still used today (nos 125–131). There were great matches at Lord's including the annual clashes of Oxford v Cambridge and of Gentlemen v Players. Celebrity players were feted in the press and the lively scene was formally documented by publications like *Lillywhite's Guide to Cricketers* and the new *Wisden Cricketers' Almanack*, which appeared for the first time in 1864 and is still published every year.

Yet even though cricket in England in the 1860s was thriving, it was also

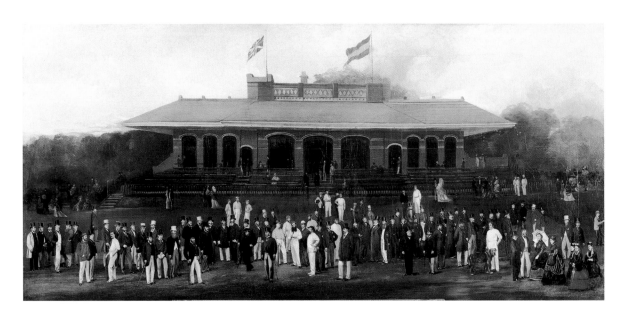

No. 475 MATCHES AT LORD'S, 1899.

May.
3 Anniv. Meeting & Dinner
3 M.C.C. & Ground v. Sussex
8 M.C.C. & G. v. Yorkshire
6 " v. Lancashire
11 " v. Derbyshire
15 " v. Leicestershire
18 Middlesex v. Somerset
(Benefit of W. Flowers)
25 " v. Gloucestershire
29 Middlesex v. Yorkshire

June.
1 M.C.C. & G. v. Kent
5 Middlesex v. Kent
15 England v. Australia
15 Middlesex v. Notts
19 M.C.C. & G. v. Camb. Univ.
29

July.
3 Oxford v. Cambridge

July—cont.
6 M.C.C. & G. v. Notts
10 Gentlemen v. Players
14 Eton v. Harrow
17 M.C.C. & G. v. Worcestershire
20 M.C.C. & G. v. Minor Counties
24 Gentlemen of M.C.C. v. Royal
    Artillery (Bands)
26 Gent. of M.C.C. v. Household
27 Middlesex v. Surrey (Brigade
31 M.C.C. & G. v. Australians

August.
3 Rugby v. Marlborough (Fields
5 M.C.C. & G. v. Lond. Playing
        v. Hertfordshire
        v. Wiltshire
14 Middlesex v. Lancashire
17 M.C.C. & G. v. Australians
        v. Staffordshire
24   v. Oxfordshire
28   v. Cambridgeshire
30   v. Nott Castle

John J. Weardon   Assist. Sec.

G. R. Burge.

Member's Name

Member's Signature   **NOT TRANSFERABLE.**

M.C.C.
MEMBER'S TICKET
1881

Fixtures at Lord's, 1926.
MAY.
6. Household Brigade v. Green Jackets
    2 days
15. M.C.C. v. Essex, 3 days
19. Middlesex v. Somerset, 3 days
22. M.C.C. v. Australians, 3 days
26. Middlesex v. Hampshire, 3 days
    Beaumont v. Oratory
    School, 1 day
29. M.C.C. v. R.E.
    (Band if possible)
    v. Australians, 3 days

June.
2. M.C.C. v. Wales, 3 days
5. England v. The Rest, 3 days
9. Middlesex v. Lancashire, 3 days
12. M.C.C. v. Warwickshire, 3 days
16. Middlesex v. Oxford University, 3 days
19. M.C.C. v. Yorkshire, 3 days
23. Middlesex v. R.A.F., 2 days
    (Band if possible)
26. London Clergy v. Southwark Clergy
30. England v. Australia, 3 days
    M.C.C. v. Cambridge University,
    3 days

Member's Name

Member's Signature

Fixtures at Lord's 1926.
JULY.
3. Oxford v. Cambridge, 3 days
10. Eton v. Harrow, 2 days
12. R.A. v. R.E., 2 days
    (Band if possible)
14. Gentlemen v. Players, 3 days
    Navy v. Army, 1 day
    (Band if possible)
21. M.C.C. v. Notts, 3 days
24. M.C.C. v. Lords and Commons, 1day
28. Clifton v. Tonbridge, 2 days
    Rugby v. Marlborough, 2 days
    Cheltenham v. Haileybury, 2 days

AUGUST.
2. Lord's Schools v. The Rest, 2 days
4. Public Schools v. The Army, 2 days
6. Young Amateurs v. The Young Pro-
    fessionals, 2 days
    Public Schools XI. v. Next XV, 2 days
11. Australians v. Public Schools XV.
    2 days
14. Boys' Match (under 16), 2 days
16. R.A.S.C. v. R.A.O.C. (Officers), 1 day
18. Middlesex v. Kent, 3 days
23. M.C.C. v. An Anglo-Argentine XI.
    3 days
28. Middlesex v. Gloucestershire, 3 days

SEPTEMBER.
1. Middlesex v. Surrey, 3 days
4. Middlesex v. Worcestershire, 3 days

Not Transferable.   Sec.

LIFE MEMBER.
No. 7

5119

130
MCC cap belonging to Brigadier General Edmond John Phipps-Hornby
Phipps-Hornby (1857–1947) was awarded the Victoria Cross when a major in the British Army with the Royal Horse Artillery for his action at Sanna's Post during the Boer War on 31 March 1900. He was an MCC member from 1886 until his death in 1947.

131
Rahul Dravid, Shaun Pollock and Anil Kumble wearing MCC ties, October 2008
Upon their election as MCC Honorary Life Members, these three modern stars of international cricket – Dravid and Kumble from India, and Pollock from South Africa – were presented with their MCC ties. The origin of MCC's colours is disputed, but according to one story the club switched its colours in the 1860s from light blue to the familiar red and yellow (or, affectionately, 'egg and bacon') as a way to thank one of its members, William Nicholson, for advancing the club the money it needed to purchase the freehold on Lord's Ground. Red and yellow were also the colours of Nicholson's Gin Company, of which he was the owner.

sharply divided. It had long been standard practice to pay cricketers to play in the English game. Dating back to the beginnings of formal matches in the first half of the 18th century, wealthy patrons arranged their own matches, and, with vast sums riding on the outcome, they often included good players as paid professionals to increase the playing strength of the side. Great early players such as 'Lumpy' Stevens in the 18th century and 'Silver Billy' Beldham in the late 18th and early 19th centuries were employees who played at the behest of their masters, the aristocratic 'amateurs'.[5] As a result, cricket was played by sides very mixed in their social standing and occupations. And while these paid players were valued for their skills, and often quite well known, this did not earn them any social recognition. Professionalism has always been a part of organised cricket, and the distinction between gentlemen amateurs and paid professionals went right through English society.

With the end of the Napoleonic Wars in 1815 and the resulting surge in interest in the game, cricket clubs offered sources of employment for professional cricketers playing in the grand matches and also acting as groundsmen, coaches and practice bowlers for club members. Alongside cricket's growing popularity came increasing emphasis on the perceived moral benefits of the game, its elegant and manly features, the advantages offered to health and discipline, and its 'scientific nature'. Accordingly, for a gentleman amateur to be proficient at such a 'highly scientific game', much time and attention were required, making it almost impossible to do without professionals whose services in instruction to all county cricket clubs of distinction 'cannot be too highly appreciated by aspiring cricketers', as a leading amateur of the time, Nicholas 'Felix' Wanostrocht, commented.[6]

Yet life was hard for the working-class professional cricketer whose income was seasonal, who had to pay all travel and expenses, and who had no protection against career-ending injuries. Many had numerous jobs throughout

Swinging Away: How Cricket and Baseball Connect

the year and struggled to get by. An opportunity presented itself in the 1840s, when, in 1845, a group of eminent gentlemen players joined together and formed an itinerant club called I Zingari, using the growing railway network to play matches around the country. Although I Zingari was a purely amateur team, their success came to the attention of a great professional spin bowler of the time, William Clarke. He noted the increasing number of enclosed grounds charging admission, the popularity of cricket and the growing celebrity status of the top professionals, and thought he might be able to make some money.

The All-England Eleven and the heyday of the professional game

The All-England Eleven professional touring team was established by Clarke in 1846 and made up of some of the most famous names in the sport (nos 132–134). Originally a bricklayer, Clarke became a professional cricketer, and through his second marriage was able to buy the land in Nottingham next to his wife's public house, where he made good money staging cricket matches on what would become the famous Trent Bridge Test match ground. One of those matches in September 1846 brought together a combined side that he called the All-England Eleven, a name that had already been used for over a century to refer to sides put together with players from disparate parts of the country. Offering better wages than the counties, and taking advantage of the expanding

132
Nicholas 'Felix' Wanostrocht,
The All-England Eleven, **1847**
Dressed in white shirts with red polka dots, white trousers and top hats, the All-England Eleven drew huge crowds as they toured around the country. The artist, Felix (1804–1876), was himself one of the side's two nominally amateur members, and included himself in this picture, seventh from right.

railway network, Clarke showcased the best cricketing talent in style, playing against local sides that fielded between twelve and 22 players. With refreshment marquees and brisk betting on the outcome, these matches were all about entertainment and profit. The team was very popular from the 1850s to the 1870s, and marked the rise of crowd-drawing, working-class professional cricket stars. Sometimes over 30 matches were played in a summer, with Clarke raking in the proceeds and paying his stars just enough to ensure their loyalty, although his mercenary and dictatorial behaviour caused considerable friction. Their success guaranteed many imitators, such as the United All-England Eleven (set up in part by John Wisden, after a falling-out with Clarke), the New All-England Eleven and Fred Caesar's New All-England Eleven. And it seemed for a short while in the 1860s and early 1870s that the professional game might just take off, run by professionals for the benefit of professionals.

These itinerant teams accelerated the development of cricket throughout England, and, with a strong focus on financial success, provided opportunities for professional cricketers on a scale unheard of in the earlier aristocratic game. The most talented players could market their skills and have their success translate into both financial and social improvement.[7] The most lucrative opportunities were in the All-England tours to North America and Australia

133
English School (19th century), Staffordshire pottery figures of George Parr, Julius Caesar and a batsman and wicket-keeper, *c.* 1860
These ceramic figures represent, from left to right, George Parr (see page 79), an unidentified batsman and wicket-keeper, and Julius Caesar, the latter a leading professional from 1849 to 1867 who turned out primarily for Surrey. Both Parr and Caesar played for the All-England Eleven.

134
Illustration from scrapbook by Felix of the All-England Eleven touring matches, 1850–51
This scrapbook was kept by the cricketer Felix while on the All-England Eleven tours around England. While expanding railway networks made extensive travel possible, the tours were still arduous for the players. The scrapbook includes examples of the trials of travelling for matches; this illustration is titled 'The journey from Spalding to Wisbech'.

(see pages 79–83), but there were also match fees, coaching and ground jobs – even overseas, as the game spread – and bonus payments.

Even so, far too many players still ended their days ill, alcoholic or destitute.[8] And the rival professional touring sides frequently feuded over disputes, refusing to play one another on occasion. While the advent of strong professional sides had shifted the focus of cricket from southern to northern England, the strong regional affiliations also caused friction. For a time in the mid-1860s, some players from the North refused to play in matches with certain players from the South until, as W. G. Grace, no fan of the professional player, later recalled, their 'jealousies and constant bickerings began to tire their supporters'.[9] When, as sometimes happened, professional cricketers boycotted big matches such as North v South and Gentlemen v Players, their presence was sorely missed.

It was, however, the success of the professional touring sides and the interest they generated in the game that brought about their end, rather than the players' failure to get along. As cricket became more popular, the county cricket clubs – all run by amateur committees – came to the fore and this opened up lucrative employment and playing opportunities for the professionals, since all the county sides mixed amateur and professional players. As county professionals, they no longer controlled the organisation of their sport but were employees of the clubs, seen almost like any other contracted labour in industrialising England.[10] The All-England Eleven played their last match in 1878 as an era passed in favour of the rising county cricket competition.

Early ladies' cricket

135 (below)
English School (18th century),
Cricket Match Played by the
Countess of Derby and Other
***Ladies,* 1779**
Lady Elizabeth Hamilton,
the Countess of Derby, is
seen here with other ladies
playing a match at the Oaks,
in Surrey, the rural retreat of
the Countess.

136 (opposite)
White Heather Cricket Club
blazer worn by Countess
Brassey, President of the
White Heather Club, 1910

137 (opposite)
Scorebook and scrapbook of
the White Heather Cricket
Club, 18 July 1888 to
30 May 1933

Although hardly on a level with men's cricket, women had participated in amateur cricket since the 18th century. The Countess of Derby (no. 135) was especially renowned as a player (and as a lover to the 3rd Duke of Dorset, who played for Kent and England and was a prominent aristocratic cricket entrepreneur in the 1870s). The first club for women, the White Heather Club at Nun Appleton, Yorkshire, was formed in 1887 by eight noblewomen, boasting a distinguished and enthusiastic membership for over 46 years (nos 136–137).

When James Lillywhite's *Cricketers' Annual* announced in 1890 the formation of two professional women's teams, it noted that this should come as no surprise to readers due to the many 'cricket matches during the past season in which ladies took part'. The Original English Lady Cricketers, split into two teams – the 'Reds' and the 'Blues' – played exhibition matches to big crowds (nos 138–139). Their first game, held in Liverpool, drew 15,000 spectators and they were a great success until their manager absconded with the profits. The English Cricket and Athletic Association Limited proclaimed the object of the exercise was to prove 'the suitability of the National Game as a pastime for the fair sex in preference to Lawn Tennis and other less scientific games'.[11]

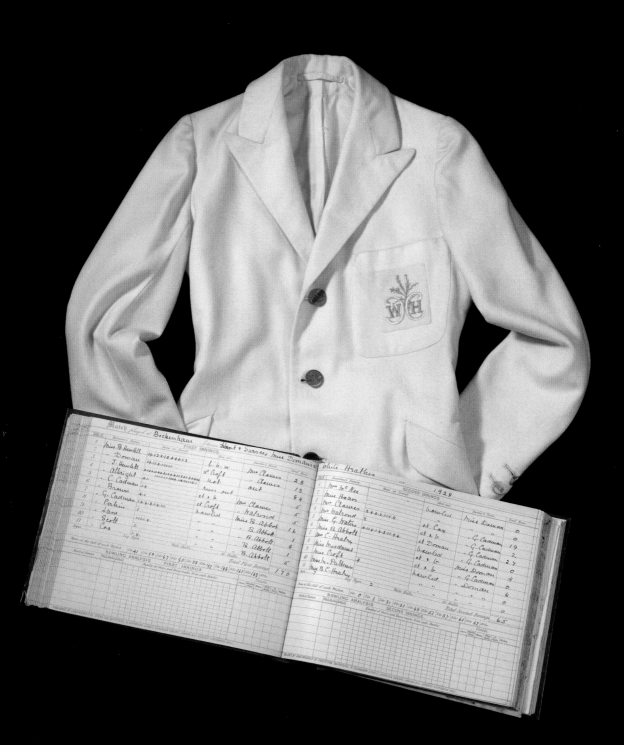

138

Uniform worn by Molly Beckenham of The Original English Lady Cricketers, 1890

The lady cricketers were accompanied by a chaperone and manager, and also, out of a sense of decorum, played under pseudonyms. Each was given sixpence a day expense money and provided with uniforms, red for one team, blue for the other. This two-piece costume was originally worn by Molly Beckenham – presumably her playing pseudonym – who played for 'the Reds'.

139

Poster for The Original English Lady Cricketers, 1890

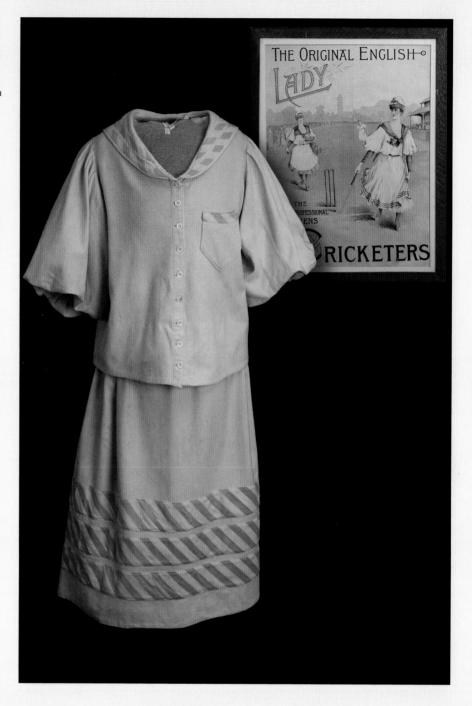

Gentlemen amateurs and baseball clubs

The Knickerbocker Base Ball Club of New York in many ways followed in MCC's footsteps. This group of like-minded urban businessmen gathered for exercise in 1842 and adopted the Knickerbocker name (a now archaic nickname for a New Yorker) in 1845. Like MCC, they revised existing rules and re-issued them under their own name. Their by-laws and regulations, formal on-field uniforms and detailed record-keeping (perhaps modelled on established New York cricket clubs) brought business-like, adult-world regulation to what had been an informal pastime.[12] And it is in this regard that they can be considered pioneers of the later regulated game. But they were not the first baseball club – a widely held view outside of baseball scholarship - and many of the rules of baseball they would follow were already widely practised in the New York area. The Gotham and Eagle clubs had formed before them, as had the New York Ball Club, an offshoot of the Gothams, and the Magnolia Ball Club of 1843. And before them all, since the early 1830s, was the Olympic Club of Philadelphia, albeit playing by very different rules.

The Knickerbocker club first wrote down their rules of baseball in 1845, and then from 1848 onwards they printed them under the title *By-laws, Regulations and Rules.* This first printing and further subsequent editions appeared just when revolutions in communication, transportation and technology were radically transforming how and where Americans lived. The Knickerbockers' game, by fortuitous timing, became the 'New York' game that was taken with people as they moved around the USA with greater ease. Over the next 20 years other forms of baseball were gradually superseded, as clubs adopted the 'New York' game and the amateur game flourished. The Knickerbockers, Peter Morris reminds us, were really 'just a group of young men who were out to have fun and get some exercise'. Still they brought uniformity to the game and a few of their rules were revolutionary – the elimination of 'soaking', for example. So they remain the game's first authority, who by their seriousness of purpose became the benchmark for all who came after.[13]

While American culture had yet to embrace fully the benefits of exercise and organised sport, the New York of the Knickerbocker Base Ball Club nevertheless turns out to be a far more interesting sporting place than was once thought. As we have seen, the 1830s and 1840s saw a boom in the establishment of cricket clubs in America (see pages 76–78). If the formation of the St George Cricket Club in New York in 1839 and Philadelphia's Union Club in 1843 mark the true beginnings of organised cricket in America, then the Knickerbockers' decision to formally organise in 1845 was part of a wider trend in sport.

By the 1850s, New York was the hub of amateur baseball with the Knickerbocker, Gotham and Eagle clubs joined by other clubs including the Excelsiors of Brooklyn and the Mutuals of New York (nos 140–144). There were many interclub matches throughout the decade, one of which between the Knickerbocker and Excelsior clubs in 1858 was captured in a remarkable photograph (no. 145). The earliest surviving on-field baseball picture, this photograph also points to another feature of the early game for one of the Knickerbockers posing for the camera is Harry Wright, who was at the same time a prominent member of the St George Cricket Club.

There is no doubt that cricketers and baseball players intermingled from the 1850s through to the early 1900s, although this was most prominent in the 1850s and 1860s. Harry Wright is a good example. English-born, he was the son of a professional cricketer from Sheffield, Sam Wright, who emigrated with his family to New York in 1837.[14] Sam was an active cricketer in the 1840s during Harry's childhood, employed as one of up to six professionals by St George, and he represented the USA in the first-ever international cricket match, the 1844 game against Canada held at St George's ground (see pages 77–78). Harry followed in his father's footsteps, playing competitive cricket by the age of 21 before joining St George in 1857 as a bowler and assistant professional (no. 146). The next year he made his own international cricket debut, again playing for the USA against Canada, and that same year he also became a member of the Knickerbocker Base Ball Club.

It is interesting that the Knickerbockers were happy to have a cricket professional playing in their ranks, and this questions their stodgy, exclusively amateur-at-all-costs reputation. Perhaps they weren't, at least at first, the sticklers we have taken them to be. Then again, nor was the St George Cricket Club at this early point the exclusive bastion of gentlemen's cricket that they

140 (opposite, top right)
Commemorative silver ball and miniature bats, 1879
Presented to Samuel H. Kissam by a fellow member to mark 25 years as a member of the Knickerbockers. The club gradually stopped playing baseball and disbanded in 1882.

141 (opposite, lower middle)
Trophy ball won on 29 September 1859, Excelsior BBC of Brooklyn defeating Gotham BBC of Hoboken, New Jersey

142 (opposite, upper left)
Belt worn by Jonas A. Polmatier, catcher of Eagle Base Ball Club of Florence, Massachusetts, 1868

143 (opposite)
Ribbons: Creighton of Norfolk, Virginia, late 1860s; Williston of East Hampton, Massachusetts, c.1867; Pastime of Richmond, Virginia, late 1860s/early 1870s
These rare silk ribbons were generally exchanged before or after a game as a goodwill gesture.

144 (opposite)
***Baseball Polka* sheet music, 1867**

145 (below)
The Knickerbockers (left) and the Excelsiors of Brooklyn, 2 August 1859
Harry Wright is sixth from left.

later became. While cricket in America could be said to have grown out of the aristocratic game in colonial times, the sport really came into its own in the age of the club. And in fact the English club structure, with gentlemen amateurs and paid professionals, was adopted wholeheartedly by American cricket clubs from the late 1830s. By 1848, St George employed six professionals, and its 67 general members were far from the upper echelon of New York society, being primarily from the middle class; 20 per cent were skilled craftsmen.[15] Many of St George's founding players came from northern England, places like Sheffield in Yorkshire. Sheffield and its rival town Nottingham had a long tradition of playing cricket but lacked the wealthy aristocratic traditions of the south.

Many of their early matches were self-funded, and the players were mainly lower-middle-class shop-keepers or publicans, tradesmen, such as framework knitters, or in the building industry.[16] Sam Wright, like many talented players from around Sheffield, had sought a professional position with cricket clubs there, and did the same in America after he arrived.

So if St George did have more working-class cricketing roots, at least early on, then the complexion of 1850s New York cricket looks somewhat different, less elitist than its later reputation would suggest. And if Harry Wright could be both a professional cricketer for St George and an amateur baseball gentleman with the Knickerbockers, then a picture of blurred boundaries begins to emerge.

He wasn't the only one either. Jim Creighton, baseball's first superstar, was a remarkable, inventive pitcher in the early 1860s for the Brooklyn Excelsiors, whose covert payments to Creighton also make it likely that he was baseball's first 'professional'. And he was also one of New York's premier cricketers, playing for the American Cricket Club and St George. The month before his death, he represented the USA in a cricket match at Hoboken against Military Officers of Canada, capturing five wickets for 16 runs. In October 1862 Creighton died, at the age of 21, from a strangulated hernia, perhaps aggravated while batting for the Excelsiors in his final baseball game.[17]

Professionals were certainly embraced by most cricket clubs, and players moved between the two bat-and-ball games, bringing features of cricket, the older game, to baseball. It is interesting to note that 30 years later Charles E. Clay, in *Outing* magazine, described St George as one of the earliest clubs in New York whose members, mostly resident Englishmen, 'devoted themselves to the pursuit of base-ball and the maintenance of the game of cricket'.[18]

In most of America, sport – baseball, cricket or otherwise – was brought to a near-standstill by the outbreak of hostilities in the Civil War. At the same time, English professional touring sides were taking the cricketing world by storm, and the amateur-run county cricket structure was growing at pace in England. For Harry Wright and other resident Englishmen, the war had surprisingly little impact (no. 147). Ineligible to enlist as non-citizens and relatively protected from the action in New York, they continued to play cricket and baseball, although on a reduced scale. After the Civil War, much as happened with English cricket after the Napoleonic Wars, interest in sport once again exploded – but by now the fashion had turned in baseball's favour.

147
New York Eleven (All New York). Photography studio of John W. Hurn, 1865
This very rare photograph features the All New York cricketers for the Grand Match against All Philadelphia played at Camden Grounds on 19–20 June 1865. The whole team is present except for Pratt from the Long Island club. Also included is the New York scorer Richardson and Umpire Wight (also recorded as White). The prominent New York cricket clubs St George, New York and Newark each had players on this representative side. Harry Wright is shown (far right kneeling) during his time as the professional for St George. The amateur–professional divide that American cricket inherited from England is clearly illustrated, with the four professionals in working-class clothes sitting in front and the amateur club members behind.

148 (top left)
**Cincinnati Red Stockings,
1869**

149 (top right)
**Baseball from the Cincinnati
Red Stockings' 1869 season**

150 (centre)
**Sheet music cover for three
compositions written in honour
of the 1869 Cincinnati Red
Stockings**
With sheet music cover art
featuring images of each
player, including brothers Harry
and George Wright, the *Red
Stockings Polka*, *Schottisch*
and *March* were dedicated
'to the Ladies of Cincinnati'.

151 (bottom left)
**Ticket to Union Grounds,
1 July 1869**
The price of this ticket was 50
cents. Earlier the same day, the
Cincinnati team had returned to
the city from a month-long tour
of the east, met by much pomp
and circumstance. The team
played against a picked nine
in a homecoming celebration,
during which they were presented with a giant wooden trophy
bat (see no. 154). The Red
Stockings won the match
53–11. Later in the evening,
members of the team enjoyed a
banquet attended by important
members of the Cincinnati
community and the press.

152 (lower left)
**Boston Red Stocking pin,
1871**

153 (bottom right)
**Levi Meyerle's National
Association contract with
Chicago for 1874 season,
signed 7 August 1873**

The rise of professionalism: Harry Wright and the Cincinnati Red Stockings

In 1865, Harry Wright left New York for Cincinnati where, for $1200 a year, he became the top professional – instructor and bowler – for the Union Cricket Club.[19] He didn't sever his relationship with St George Cricket Club, appearing for them twice more in 1868 and 1872 to play touring English sides.[20] As in New York, he joined the local baseball club that shared the Union Club's grounds, of which he soon assumed the captaincy. At this time baseball was still officially amateur, although a significant number of clubs covertly employed profes- sionals. Wright began a gradual transformation that would turn this amateur club in Cincinnati, whose members enjoyed the game but were of only mediocre playing ability, into the mighty Cincinnati Red Stockings Base Ball Club, a top- flight team of imported professional players.

In 1869, when the National Association of Base Ball Players reluctantly bowed to the inevitable and officially recognised professionally paid players, Cincinnati became the most dominant of about a dozen clubs to play openly as professionals. Wright was a man of high integrity who saw nothing wrong with earning a living through playing ball, but disliked sly under-the-table payments. The Red Stockings' undefeated record in 1869 and, under Wright's leadership, gentlemanly conduct led to short-lived hopes that the professional era could overcome the unsavoury encroachments of gambling and bad behaviour, as well as retain many of the characteristics of the era when clubs were ostensibly amateur. As such, Wright and the Red Stockings themselves played a pivotal role in ushering in a new era of professional baseball.

And they were a national sensation. In their first season as professionals they undertook an ambitious tour, taking advantage of the then largest and most modern railroad system in the world and their newest feature, dining and sleeping cars.[21] Travelling 12,000 miles, the Red Stockings finished the season with 57 wins and no losses against top-level teams, including elite East Coast clubs (nos 148–151).[22] The winning streak extended into the 1870 season and ended after 81 games in a thrilling eleventh-inning loss to the Brooklyn Atlantics. This was a low-scoring game that almost finished with the score tied 5–5 after nine innings, as the rules at that time allowed captains to agree to a draw. Instead they played on into the eleventh inning, the Brooklyn fans in the stands and Cincinnati fans in their hundreds around newspaper offices following every play until the Atlantics finally pulled ahead.[23]

Harry Wright had carefully assembled and nurtured his team, some of the best players of the day. Among them was his younger brother George, by

Old Red Stockings Cincinnati 1869
Won all games played season 1869

The Red Stockings

POLKA
4

SCHOTTISCHE
4

MARCH
4

New York, J.L. PETERS,   J.L. PETERS & CO. St Louis
599 Broadway   212 North 5th Street

Cincinnati   Boston
J.J. Dohmeyer & Co.   White, Smith & Perry

"RED STOCKINGS"
At Home.
Union Grounds, — July 1st, 1869.
COMPLIMENTARY GAME.
FIRST NINE.

that time captain, star hitter and shortstop for the powerful Washington Nationals. At age 22 George Wright became the highest-paid American baseball player, and he did not disappoint, recording an outstanding batting average of .518 in his first season with the Cincinnati Red Stockings, blasting 59 home runs in 52 games. Others Harry Wright brought into the club, like Cal McVey and Asa Brainard, also blossomed into top-flight talent.

Yet all was not smooth sailing in Cincinnati, where the club's directors and members still tried to hold fast to their previous ethos as an amateur club. Across the Atlantic, English county cricket clubs were growing in strength based on a similar model of amateur administration and professional players, but in Cincinnati resentments that imported professionals now took all the playing spots bubbled to the surface when the club lost a few games in 1870. The situation was not improved by the less than gentlemanly conduct of a few of the players. As a result, Cincinnati announced they would not retain any professional players for 1871 and members would return to playing a wholly amateur game.[24]

Amid a great deal of debate in the press, Harry Wright and most of his star professionals moved to Boston, taking with them the club's nickname and innovative red stockings and knickers pants, becoming, in 1871, the Boston Red Stockings. The team joined the newly formed National Association of Professional Base Ball Players for the 1871 season and continued their winning ways, taking the new National Association championship four years running from 1872 to 1875 (nos 152–153). The pattern was now set. Players in the National Association played on negotiated contracts, their teams were affiliated with an organising body, the season culminated in a championship, and clubs attracted fans and paying spectators keen to see their local team play well at home and on the road. Professionalism in baseball was here to stay.

154
Illustration in *Harper's Weekly*, 24 July 1869, showing presentation of a Champion Bat to the 'Red Stocking' Base-Ball Club, Cincinnati, Ohio, on its return home
Members of the Red Stocking baseball team and their distinguished guests are shown standing around a baseball bat 27 feet in length, presented to the team after amassing a 21–0 record (see also no. 151).

Young Ladies' Base Ball Club No. 1

A dubious character, going by the name of W. S. Franklin managed several troupes of young female baseball players in the 1880s. This cabinet card shows his Young Ladies' Base Ball Club in 1890, at a time when even the most accomplished women's baseball teams struggled to gain respect (no. 155). Within a year Franklin was arrested and imprisoned for the abduction of a 15-year-old girl whom he recruited to his travelling team and passed off as his niece. He had previously escaped prosecution for numerous similar arrests. While press reports noted in passing the competitiveness of the team, they mainly focused on the 'bright and buxom ladies' playing men's teams. *Sporting Life* in particular disapproved of Franklin and his teams, asserting 'WOMAN is nowhere on earth more out of place than on a base ball diamond'.[25]

Players wore striped dresses belted at the waist, polka-dot scarves around their necks, dark stockings, ankle-high laced leather shoes and matching striped baseball caps. One baseball scholar believes some of these players were 'toppers', men disguised as women to increase the team's competitiveness.[26]

155
Cabinet card photograph of Young Ladies' Base Ball Club No. 1, *c.*1890

George Wright

George Wright was one of the greatest baseball players of his time, with wonderful batting and fielding skills and an acrobat's flair. He was one of the first stars of the professional game, as part of the trailblazing 1869 Cincinnati Red Stockings and the championship Boston team in the 1870s.

George had grown up deeply immersed in the game of cricket, recalling, many years later, his first lessons with his father under the grape arbour at the rear of the family home in Hoboken. His older brother Harry – twelve years his senior – and his father both played as professionals for St George Cricket Club in New York. George followed in their footsteps, and, in his first appearance for the junior side at 13, made his first sporting profit when the club president gave him a silver quarter dollar for each of the five batsmen he dismissed.[27] His professional career with St George began in 1862, when he was only 16. Two years later, he played his first recorded baseball game with the Gotham Base Ball Club of New York. Like his brother, George continued to play both baseball and cricket throughout the 1860s, for St George, Philadelphia, the American Cricket Club and for the USA in international matches, before concentrating on his baseball career in the 1870s. It was considered at the time that the Wright brothers' proficiency at cricket and ability to apply the 'headwork' from cricket to baseball, was a critical factor in their success. Both are credited with many innovations to the early game of baseball.

George concentrated on his baseball career in the 1870s, culminating in a memorable championship season in 1879 with the Providence Grays. He retired from competitive baseball in his mid-thirties, playing his final game on 2 October 1882, and focused on his sporting goods business, Wright & Ditson, in Boston. He played pioneering roles in the development of lawn tennis and golf in America and also returned to his first game, assuming the captaincy of Boston's Longwood Cricket Club (nos 156–159). From the time George Wright joined the club until the turn of the century Longwood would be the pre-eminent New England cricket club, both competitively and in terms of wealth and facilities.

In 1883 he played in a cricket match for the USA against the Gentlemen of Philadelphia that was ranked as a first-class match, thereby making his debut at the top level of the game (equivalent to the major leagues in baseball). This makes him the first and only person to play both sports at the highest level. George represented the USA at cricket in 1886, 1888 and 1890, and finally in 1893 when he played for Massachusetts against the touring Australians. George himself insisted that, in comparison to baseball, 'there is really more science and enjoyment for the player in cricket. There are a hundred points in batting that one has to bear in mind, and the avoidance of a difficulty, or the accomplishment of a pet stroke give more pleasure to the player.'[28]

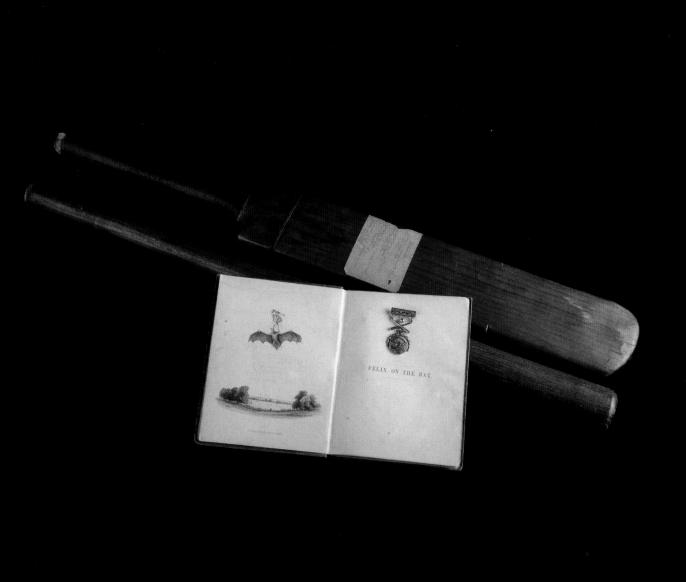

FELIX ON THE BAT

6 What Americans really think about cricket

You can't make Americans take up cricket…
William Phelon, 1914[1]

USA team blazer and
matching cap, 1968
(see pages 170–71)

'We, fast people of America,' wrote Henry Chadwick, the great sports reformer, in 1868, 'call cricket slow and tedious; while the leisurely, take-your-time-my-boy people of England think our game of base ball too fast.'[2] Time has always been an issue for cricket in America, from the young English aristocrat in America who wanted to learn baseball in 1911 because cricket was 'too slow', to a New York sports writer in 1932 who humorously described the game as 'played on the instalment plan'.[3] For Chadwick, the answer was to be found in interclub play – that is, between cricket and baseball clubs. First tried almost by accident – in 1859 the touring English cricketers played a pick-up game of baseball in Rochester, New York when snowy weather cancelled cricket (see pages 80–82) – match-up games in either sport featuring cricketers and baseball players provided a bit of spice and interest.

As we have seen, there were many examples of cricket and baseball clubs sharing grounds, and even players, as far back as the 1840s. One example, the Union Star of Brooklyn, was a cricket club founded in 1844 by English immigrants whose members also took part in a number of early baseball games. They played an unconventional kind of cricket, more accommodating of American players and purposefully free of the English class constraints of New York's St George Cricket Club.[4]

But it was clubs like the American Cricket Club founded in 1860 by Harry Wright, James Creighton, Asa Brainard, John Whiting and Thomas Dakin that Chadwick wanted to encourage.[5] Composed of baseball players with strong cricketing backgrounds, these teams aimed to infuse 'an American spirit' into the game.[6] The American spirit so wanting in cricket was mostly about punctuality and promptness. Matches that started an hour or even two late, players who dawdled to the wicket when it was their turn to bat, and the frequent interruptions for tea and lunch – these all-too-common features of cricket drove some busy Americans to distraction. Or to baseball, as was often the case. So inviting baseball players to play cricket, it was felt, would eliminate tardiness and preventable delays on the cricket field and thus increase the general popularity of this deserving and 'noble game'.[7]

The idea was not new, for the *Spirit of the Times* had lamented as early as 1839, 'What can be done to naturalise this beautiful game in America?' The short-lived American Cricket Club would be one of many attempts to 'reform' cricket to suit the American temperament. And the injection of baseball players into cricket in the 1860s did speed up the game. In one match in Long Island in

1861, pitting Englishmen against Americans, the strict time guidelines look very modern – scheduled start at 10am sharp, two minutes between batsmen, ten minutes between innings and 30 minutes for lunch. The success of these kinds of matches brought calls for closer affiliations between cricket and baseball clubs, increased opportunities for younger and more novice players, and restrictions on players appearing for multiple clubs. Henry Chadwick advocated adhering to English rules, not English custom, and some players even formed the short-lived American Cricketers' Convention to try to implement these changes fully.

Other, more experimental efforts were less successful. A new game called 'American cricket' was invented in Philadelphia in 1870 in a failed attempt to merge baseball and cricket. This was to be played on a triangular field with one wicket and two bases.[8] In another, rather bizarre example, the Staten Island Cricket Club undertook a baseball versus cricket experiment on 20 July 1884. A cricket match was played between club members wherein the first eleven used baseball bats and played against an eleven picked from the rest of the club who used cricket bats.[9] Finally, in 1890, prominent Philadelphian cricketer John Thayer proposed a whole new code of rules that would adopt, among other radical changes, baseball's 'three out, all out' rule with each side retiring after three wickets had fallen. By alternating batting and fielding, with no more than four minutes between 'turns', the game would, he proposed, be more interesting. The overs would consist of ten balls and each side would have up to 'six turns' at bat but the game would end at a pre-agreed time even if all six turns had not been taken. Even with Chadwick's support, these suggested changes did not transform the game as Thayer had hoped.[10]

The professional baseball players' success on the cricket pitch during the 1874 tour of England bolstered American ideas that baseball players could excel at both sports. In 1879, when Richard Daft brought a professional English cricket team to North America, the press emphasised the merits of American baseball players as cricketers. One correspondent went so far as to claim that 22 baseball players would fare better at cricket than the same number of American cricketers against the touring Englishmen, who were all seasoned professionals. But when Daft's eleven took on 18 baseball players in a cricket match at Brooklyn on 15 October 1879, even the experienced cricketers among them like George and Sam Wright and Joe Sprague could not save the baseball players from a resounding defeat by an innings and 18 runs.

The long-time editor of the *American Cricketer* magazine, Jerome Flannery, felt the American temperament was 'opposed' to the time required for a full match, and the American athlete too focused on 'activity' for the pace of the game. He spearheaded an effort to introduce a shorter version of the game in the 1890s, and by 1901 most matches were conducted in the space of an afternoon. It still seemed to Flannery a lost cause. With a much smaller 'leisure class' than in England, the business life of American players would forever impede their participation in the amateur game.[11]

By the 1890s, promoters began to emphasise differences, distancing baseball and cricket from one another like teenage siblings. Much of this settled on national identity and national character, for all the attempts to Americanise cricket had met with a conservative resistance to any change to the culture and English character of cricket. The year before, the 'Man About Town' columnist in *Country Gentleman* conjectured that if cricket were not 'so English you know' then the king of games might have reigned supreme on both sides of the Atlantic.[12] But even after almost 30 years of close association, many in the 1890s would agree with sentiments expressed in 1859 that 'cricket is not an American, but an English game, and therefore... only Englishmen play it here'.[13] Of course this was not strictly true, as the number of Americans playing high-level competitive cricket in Philadelphia, Newark, Albany and elsewhere attested. Even that most famous symbol of baseball, A. G. Spalding, not only donated the trophy for the Chicago Cricket Association in 1889 but was himself a member of the Chicago Cricket Club.[14] Looking back in 1890, Henry Chadwick recalled all the cricket ideas that he 'ingrafted' to the benefit of baseball during the period 30 years earlier when he was 'engaged in the evolution of our now national game of baseball'. And it seems baseball was indeed the overall beneficiary of those years of close association, through its access to the established grounds of the cricket clubs – and indeed their players, most famously Harry and George Wright who moved into baseball from cricket.

American commentators made much of cricket's presumed snobbery. 'Cricket... will do for college nobs and parlour dudes, but baseball is the dandy for the young American tough and every day boy,' was the verdict of the *Washington Post* in 1882.[15] The *New York Times* in 1903 was especially damning of cricket's prescription that 'no player – i.e. professional – is supposed to be a gentleman; his is merely "the ground" or part of it, a clod.'[16] This perception of the refined and elitist nature of cricket was only strengthened by American sporting clubs transforming themselves into exclusive and wealthy country clubs. At the forefront in the 1880s were the Staten Island Cricket and Base Ball Club and the Philadelphia and Germantown Cricket Clubs, embracing a mix of social sports (cricket, baseball, lawn tennis, lacrosse, association football, athletics and rowing) and social pleasures, including mixed-sex dining, dancing, winter skating and sledging, and musical evenings in the clubhouse.[17]

After 1900, the two games were truly distinct. Although pockets of American cricket enthusiasts were passionate for their sport, many Americans knew little about cricket and were therefore all the more perplexed by its attraction. 'Almost any game will prove slow to those who do not understand its science,' observed Thomas Wharton in 1892.[18]

The Australian cricketer Don Bradman, renowned to this day as one of the sport's greatest ever batsmen, toured North America with an all-star Australian cricket side in 1932. One highlight for him was meeting his baseball counterpart, Babe Ruth, in the stands at Yankee Stadium (no. 160). As Bradman later recalled, 'I was privileged to sit with Babe Ruth… [but] I had the utmost difficulty explaining cricket to him and can still hear the bewilderment in his slow American drawl as he said, "You mean to tell me you don't have to run when you hit the ball?"'[19]

'Americans don't bother to understand cricket,' wrote American sports correspondent Cliff Gewecke in 1968, feeling that Americans see it only as 'slow, dull, long-lasting' while ignoring its many nuances, strategies and exercising, even dangerous plays.[20] 'If you understand the intricacies of the game,' said Dr Anthony Ernest, a Californian cardiologist and cricket enthusiast in 1988, 'it's not boring. You have to understand what's going on out there between the bowler and the batsman. It's an ongoing battle.'[21]

'We're always getting articles about tea and crumpets,' observed one American cricketer in 1968. 'Big deal! What's the difference between our break for tea and your intermission for hot dogs and peanuts?'[22] Of course, American teasing of cricket goes back a long way. An article from a Chicago paper sent

160
The Don meets the Babe, 1932
The great Australian cricketer Don Bradman shakes hands with baseball legend Babe Ruth at Yankee Stadium, New York, 20 July 1932, during a cricket tour of North America by a team of Australian stars.

Swinging Away: How Cricket and Baseball Connect

into the London *Sporting Times* described a game between a representative Chicago side and the 1896 Australians: 'The sport is monotonous but gives plenty of exercise to the legs… cricket is a great game – for Englishmen, dead men or other phlegmatic and stoical people.'[23] 'Well,' observed one London taxi driver dryly after his first baseball game at Dodger Stadium in Los Angeles in 1964, 'in cricket, your agony takes longer.'[24]

Yet more seriously, Jerome Flannery's ideas in 1901 that cricket taught 'patience, unselfishness and self-control' were echoed by one American journalist in 1926 who saw the 'leisureliness' of cricket as the secret to its success as the flag-bearer for modern sportsmanship when the 'spirit of comradeship and fair play is more than victory'.[25] The same opinion was expressed again in 1964 by a columnist who found cricket in Los Angeles the perfect example of a sport 'in which the outcome is much less important than how it is played'.[26] The president of the Southern California Cricket Association concurred in 1988: 'you need application, dedication and discipline. If you don't have that, you won't be successful in cricket or in life.'[27]

Now that cricket has introduced shorter, quicker forms of the game that are played with aggressive batting and snappy fielding – a Twenty20 contest is shorter than most major league baseball games – cricket's inherent attributes are appealing to a new generation of American players. As Alfred Reeves, one of the shining lights in Philadelphia's recent cricketing revival, said in 2006, 'Cricket is the only sport in the world that has gentlemanly conduct written into the laws. Part of my gospel is: it's the game first; then it's the team; then it's the player.'[28] And it may be this sporting camaraderie that is bringing some Americans back to cricket – a game fast-growing among immigrants from the many cricket-playing nations. For some, like Zoeb Zavery from Kenya, playing with the Tri-City Cricket Club in Schenectady, New York, cricket continues a tradition he began as a boy.[29] Most American cricket clubs are a true melting pot, mixing players from almost every cricket-playing nation. For some of these cricketers, like the founders of the Pittsburgh Cricket Association, their own personal attachment to cricket sits alongside a pride in re-establishing the sport played by the Pittsburgh Cricket Club since 1883.[30] But for others, it is that extra something in the game itself, the mix of tradition, strategy, decorum and team spirit that draws them to cricket. A recent American convert to the game, Chris Spaeth, was looking for a 'sporting element' he couldn't find anywhere else, 'so I found my way to cricket.'[31] In Joseph O'Neill's bestselling novel *Netherland*, his narrator considers New York cricket to be not just 'a patch of America sprinkled with the foreign-born strangely at play' but also a vision of men in white 'imagining an environment of justice'.[32]

Babe Ruth tries cricket

161 (below left)
Babe Ruth with Australian cricketer Alan Fairfax in the nets at Thames House, London, 9 February 1935 (see also page 2)

162 (below right)
Babe Ruth signs autographs for two bellboys on the roof of the Savoy Hotel, London, 8 February 1935

163 (opposite bottom)
Burriss Jenkins, 'H'a'yah Kid! The Babe is 40 years old'

164 (opposite top)
Babe Ruth's Louisville Slugger baseball bat, 1935
Babe Ruth, the most internationally recognised baseball player, finished his professional baseball career after his return from London, not as a Yankee but with the Boston Braves. He made the final hit of his professional career with this bat on 25 May 1935 in the seventh inning of a game against the Pittsburgh Pirates. It was his third home run of the game, and incredibly long, clearing the double-deck stands in right field. It was said at the time to be the longest drive ever made at Pittsburgh's Forbes Field. The Pirates' pitcher Guy Bush said, 'I never saw a ball hit so hard before or since. He was fat and old, but he still had that great swing… I can't forget that last [home run]. It's probably still going.'

I could make one of the world's greatest batsmen out of him.
Alan Fairfax, 1935

At the end of the 1934 baseball season Babe Ruth announced, 'I'm definitely through as a regular player.' He wanted to retire as a player and manage the Yankees. Unable to realise this ambition, he took his wife and step-daughter on a barnstorming tour of Japan with other American League all-star players. After a successful playing tour, the Ruth family enjoyed a holiday in Paris (where Ruth was disappointed to find himself unrecognised) and London, during which he marked his 40th birthday. And it was in London in February 1935 that he famously tried cricket (nos 161–163).

Ruth was openly dismissive of the low salaries paid to English sportsmen, but open-minded about the games themselves. He enjoyed a particularly 'lusty lesson' with the Australian former Test cricketer Alan Fairfax in the indoor batting nets under Thames House in London. He first attempted the unfamiliar cricket batting stance before reverting to the more comfortable baseball posture, all the while smashing the offerings of two fast bowlers. 'Sure I could smack that [ball] all right – how could I help it when you have a great wide board to swing?' he eagerly told reporters afterwards. At the end of the session, with his bat in a 'deplorable state', he declared cricket to be 'a better game than I thought but I think I will stick to baseball' (no. 164).

7 Amateurism lives on in American cricket

The advent of professionalism in baseball brought with it a concern that players, now that they were paid for their services, would be corrupted by the influence of the many gamblers circling the game. An Australian observer in 1878 found American baseball controlled by 'a low class' whose gambling on the game was 'very objectionable', and there were many examples in organised baseball to support these apprehensions.[1] Gambling – at games, around the game at saloons, billiard halls and elsewhere – meant that baseball faced much the same situation as cricket had in England 50 years earlier.

The Newhall brothers
from Philadelphia, 1886
(see page 146)

In the early 19th century, cricket authorities struggled with a gambling culture dating back to at least the mid-1700s. It had been common to play most games for a stake, and the temptation of 'blacklegs', or gamblers offering money to throw a match, was often irresistible for poor itinerant cricketers. Slowly, beginning in the 1820s, professional gamblers were removed from grounds and, led by MCC, the threat of gambling was brought under control. Fifty years after one of cricket's great professionals, William Lambert, was banned for allegedly throwing a match, cricket's reputation was so far rehabilitated that it was seen in America in the 1870s as the true gentleman's amateur game. Cricket provided a shining example for those who felt the future of respectable ball sports was under threat. No place was this more true than in Philadelphia. Isaac Sharpless, president of Philadelphia's Quaker Haverford College, spoke for many when he wrote in the late 1880s: 'the noble game of baseball… has degenerated into a victim of gamblers and a trysting-place for all kinds of immorality… Cricket alone seems to remain on the high ground.'[2]

Compared to New York, cricket came late to Philadelphia, introduced by English residents in the 1830s. Even in the 1840s, when there was a growing club structure in the city, basic equipment like bats and balls had to be purchased in New York City.[3] The players at these clubs were a mix of university students, business gentlemen and working-class immigrants. The Wister family, who became a prominent American influence in early Philadelphian cricket, provides a good illustration of this mix. Brothers John and William Rotch Wister, like other youngsters in Philadelphia, played town ball for the Germantown Academy before trying cricket for the first time in 1842. They played with English weavers from a local mill, who, William later recalled, admired their ball-handling skills, learned from playing town ball. When the prominent Union Club was established, young William occasionally joined them for matches against New York's St George and Brooklyn's Union Star clubs. He joined a mixed membership combining English cricketers from Nottingham with upper-class English and American gentlemen, and other American enthusiasts, including baseball players. Two active club officers,

English importer Robert Waller, previously of St George in New York, and University of Pennsylvania professor Dr John K. Mitchell, recognised the need to encourage younger Americans and urged William Wister to set up a Junior Cricket Club with his fellow University of Pennsylvania students, all American-born players from middle- and upper-class Philadelphian backgrounds.[4]

Robert Waller envisioned that such a mixed membership, while desirable, would be strictly controlled by a St George-type leadership of gentlemen over the predominantly English working-class membership. This was initially attractive to some of Philadelphia's leading figures but proved volatile. The English players resorted to familiar old-country north/south dissensions and their occasionally violent bickering reduced the club, and the fledgling sport's reputation, in the eyes of the already sceptical public. The Union Club folded by

the end of the 1840s with Waller's return to New York, but the experience inspired a small group of enthusiastic American players to pursue a different course of action. When William Rotch Wister and a number of his former university club players, along with some who had played baseball, came together to form the Philadelphia Cricket Club on 10 February 1854, a new and distinctly Philadelphian cricket was born.[5] This was marked first and foremost by reliance upon the English community for competitive guidance, but there remained a clear resolve not to cede organisational control out of American hands. Such determination was not seen in New York, and its long-reaching implications in Philadelphia first emerged during the 1850s.[6]

Many founding members of the Philadelphia Cricket Club were lawyers, and the upper-class former university players gave the club an initial aristocratic flavour with a mix of middle-class and some working-class players. The Philadelphia CC was quickly followed by the Germantown Cricket Club, set up by younger relatives and friends of the senior players. Germantown would become a powerhouse club of the city, a strong local rival to Philadelphia and other inter-city clubs, and the host of many future international matches. Youth and a strong American independence, such distinctive features of Philadelphian cricket, marked the Germantown club from the beginning. In 1856, Germantown not only challenged their elders at the Philadelphia club, but were 'presumptuous' enough to beat them.[7]

The Young America Cricket Club was started by still younger friends and relatives of Germantown players who had been denied membership for being under the age of 16 (nos 165–166). The story goes that they were so jealous of their older friends and relatives in the Germantown club, and so incensed at not being allowed to play, that they staged an infamous 'Apple Riot' one day while Germantown played a match by pegging players on the field with apples from a neighbouring orchard. Whatever the truth of this tale, the Young America Cricket Club (YACC) was officially formed on 19 November 1855, assisted again by William Rotch Wister, who hosted their foundation meeting

165 (opposite)
Young America Cricket Club, 1868
The proud first eleven of the Young America Cricket Club pose in full uniform, including the popular embroidered belts and caps of the period. This studio portrait captures some of the best young players in Philadelphia, including five from the Newhall family. Seven of this eleven – George, Daniel, Charles and Robert Newhall, A. P. Bussier, W. B. Johns and R. L. Baird – all played in a tightly fought contest against Edgar Willsher's touring All-England Eleven in 1868. The elaborately carved frame features cricket stumps, balls and crossed bats, and a military oak leaf and branch decorative outline – a style commemorating the Civil War, just three years past.

166 (below)
Embroidered belt with decorative brass buckle, worn by Edward M. Davis Jr, *c.*1860s (front and reverse views)
A very rare American example of the embroidered belts, popular from the late 1850s to the 1870s as an essential part of cricketers' apparel. The owner of this belt, which is beautifully embroidered with 'YACC' for the Young America Cricket Club, was president of the club in 1866.

at his home and whose sons made up some of the club's new members. The Newhall brothers, later among the most famous Philadelphian cricketers, were conspicuous early members and helped to establish this club as a commanding organisation (no. 167).

The YACC's American-born membership, spirit of independence and refusal to employ professionals infused a long tradition of amateur cricket in the city. Appropriately, Benjamin Franklin's famous copy of the Laws of Cricket, brought back from Europe, is said to have been presented to the YACC in 1867 (although its present whereabouts are unknown).[8] Their reputation became legendary, as John Lester remembered almost a century later: 'They were a cocky, irreverent, contentious lot, quick to turn on anyone who seemed to invade their rights. They loved to win, and to mount the victim and crow.'[9]

As these players were too young in 1861 'to join the colours', they kept cricket going in Philadelphia during the Civil War. They were a popular side, their matches were well attended, and they were considered strong enough to take on any amateur side in the country. Tragically for the history of this important club, their clubhouse at Turnpike Bridge, Germantown burnt down in 1870 along with all club records (no. 168). The YACC amalgamated with Germantown CC in 1889, allowing the two clubs to combine resources and purchase their own grounds on Manheim Street for $90,000.[10]

From the very beginning of club cricket in Philadelphia, 'American' was a key distinction. The Philadelphia Cricket Club, for example, distinguished their American eleven as opposed to their general first eleven as early as 1856. Richard Ashhurst recalled in 1901 that the Philadelphia club membership was a combination of Englishmen 'beginning to advance in years' and younger Americans, 'enthusiastic lovers of the game'.[11]

The first all-American cricket match was played in August 1854 at Hoboken between a New York side, including many students from the Free Academy, and the Newark Club, one of the first to encourage American-born players. The fame of such encounters brought the Philadelphia and Newark clubs together in both competition and in spirit, although the Philadelphians initially benefited from continuing to hone their skills against more experienced English-resident cricketers. It wasn't until 1858 that an American eleven took on an English-born side on equal terms. Foreshadowing the future, the victorious Americans were all from Philadelphia.[12]

167
George, Charlie, Dan and Robert Newhall, 1886
These brothers played for YACC, especially in its early years, and the Gentlemen of Philadelphia in international matches. Robert captained the Gentlemen of Philadelphia two years earlier on the first American cricket tour of England; his brother Charlie was also there, but Dan missed out when he could not obtain leave from work. The large Newhall family, with ten cricketing sons, was the backbone of Philadelphian cricket, with these four among the city's best players for over 20 years – Charlie with the ball and the others with the bat.

When the All-England Eleven toured North America in 1859, the match at Philadelphia was the most closely contested of the tour. Afterwards the teams combined for an eleven-a-side match combining five English players with six Philadelphians on each side, which proved another valuable experience. This tour marked the beginning of Philadelphian dominance, dethroning St George from their self-appointed place at the top of American cricket. All visiting international sides made Philadelphia a mandatory stop, especially after the Civil War, when cricket resumed there more vigorously than elsewhere.

The most dramatic match was against the 1878 Australians, who were returning from their first tour of England. For the first time the Philadelphians, perhaps overconfidently, played with eleven players, not 18 or 22, against the Australian eleven. The match ended in an exciting draw and demonstrated to a thrilled home audience the abilities of their local cricketers. It marked a turning point in Philadelphian cricket, making front-page news and attracting 15,000 spectators on the third day, according to the *American Cricketer*. The fact that Australians found the umpiring biased – they dramatically stormed off the field in protest on the third day – and American cricket in general somewhat unorthodox seemed beside the point. This was a memorable first-class debut for the Philadelphian cricketers, especially Robert Newhall who performed well with the bat against the fast-bowling Australians. It not only boosted their confidence and enthusiasm but became part of the city's 'cricketing heritage', retold for decades to come.[13]

168
Young America cricket ground, Turnpike Bridge, 4 July 1867
Club members pose in front of the YACC clubhouse during Fourth of July celebrations. These grounds at Turnpike Bridge, Germantown, north-west Philadelphia, were used for practice every weekday through the months of May to October.

The Gentlemen of Philadelphia

....

*It would add a new thrill to life if England's cricket supremacy were
seriously challenged by the United States.*
B. A. Clarke, 1897[14]

From the 1870s onwards Philadelphia was the highlight of most English and
Australian cricket tours to North America, and, although minor blue-collar
clubs were still active in the city, the top level of the sport had shifted to more
exclusive and prosperous country clubs, increasingly dominated by the upper
class. Some of the five major clubs in Philadelphia even declined to hire a professional bowler and coach, as was common practice in other American and
English clubs.[15]

      The first all-amateur cricket side to tour North America, in 1872, led
by the urbane MCC Secretary, R. A. Fitzgerald, and including the young star
W. G. Grace, failed to capture a wide following in America but excited genuine
interest in Philadelphia. An 'immense crowd' gathered at the Germantown
ground to see the 22 American players chosen from the Philadelphian clubs
(professionals and Englishmen were specifically excluded) put up a good fight
against the might of the English.[16] For Fitzgerald, Philadelphia was 'distinguished above its fellows' both on and off the field. The city's well appointed
cricket pavilions and stately private homes would be frequently put to use entertaining visiting cricketers up until the early 20th century.[17] Some quarters of
the American press lauded the example set by these English amateur sportsmen
who had achieved 'a point of excellence in their national game which, in our
national game of base ball is only attained by high-paid professionals'.[18] Still,
the next two English sides to visit, in 1879 and 1881, were entirely professional
and it wasn't until 1885 that another all-amateur side came to Philadelphia.

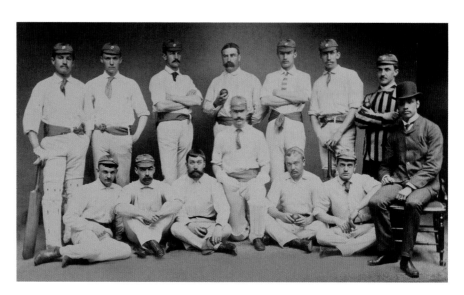

169
**The Gentlemen of Philadelphia
on their first tour of England,
1884**
Back row: John B. Thayer, Jr,
William Brockie, Jr, E. Walter
Clark, Charles A. Newhall,
Howard MacNutt, Joseph A.
Scott, William C. Lowry.
Front row: William C. Morgan, Jr,
Robert S. Newhall (captain),
Francis E. Brewster, Hazen
Brown (kneeling, wearing
wicket-keeping gear),
Sutherland Law, David P.
Stoever, T. Robins, Jr (scorer).

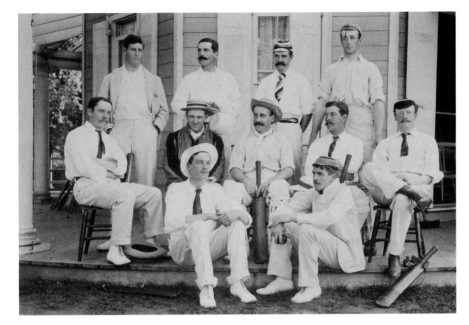

Lord Hawke's Eleven, North American tour, 1891
Taken at Germantown Cricket Club, where Lord Hawke's team played their two games in Philadelphia. The Gentlemen of Philadelphia won the first match and the tourists won the second.
Back row: S. M. J. Woods, G. W. Hillyard, K. McAlpine, G. W. Rickets. Middle row: J. H. J. Hornsby, H. T. Hewett, Lord Hawke, C. W. Wright, Lord Throwley. Front row: Hon. H. Milles, C. Wreford-Brown.

Nevertheless, cricket in Philadelphia was still a long way away from the true international level the clubs aspired to, and many believed that the only way to bring the improvement needed was to take a side to England. The Gentlemen of Philadelphia were put together for just this purpose. Like Philadelphian cricket itself, the Gentlemen of Philadelphia flourished only briefly on the international stage. Their pioneering tours in 1884 and 1889 provided educational groundwork and showed how the best English and Irish cricket was played and conducted (no. 169). They represented not only the best amateur club cricketers in the city but also its proud American cricketing heritage. Indeed, the 1884 tour to England was the first-ever international cricket tour of an American side outside Canada. They played 18 matches, all against amateur sides.

E. J. Saunders organised the 1885 English amateur tour of America in large part because of the 1884 tour to England by the Gentlemen of Philadelphia. Saunders was surprised to lose to the Philadelphians, the first English side in the United States to do so, but returned the following year in 1886 to exact revenge. Like Fitzgerald's amateurs 13 years before, Saunders's players were surprised by the big spectator turnout at the matches in Philadelphia, including a pleasingly large number of women.[19]

The 1890s saw the most significant English and Australian sides to visit

Philadelphia. The well-known Yorkshire captain Lord Hawke led two tours to North America, in 1891 (see no. 170) and in 1894, the latter at the invitation of the Germantown and Merion clubs of Philadelphia. The first tour solidified Philadelphia's reputation as the only American city where cricket was played as seriously as baseball in the post-Civil War era, and the locals' performance far outshone that of their rivals in New York, Baltimore, Boston and Chicago. The performance of the other American sides was handicapped by their overblown respect for the skill of the English players, of whom only five had appeared regularly in first-class matches that season. Yet the tour, as well as the new Inter-City League, did bring cricket to more prominence in several American urban centres, and Lord Hawke found the overall level of play improved by the time of his second tour (nos 171–175).

A top Australian eleven played a series of American matches in 1893 on their return journey home from a summer in England, as they had commonly done following each English tour since 1878. This time they were unprepared for the skill and class of players they met in Philadelphia, who, according to the Australian captain Jack Blackham, could be considered 'with England's best'.[20] Once again the Australians provided a benchmark for Philadelphian

171
J. B. King of the Gentlemen of Philadelphia bowling to Lord Hawke at Merion Cricket Ground, Haverford, 21 September 1894, from *Lord Hawke's XI: America and Canada 1894* **scrapbook**

cricketers by being sensationally beaten at the Belmont Cricket Club grounds, thereafter known as 'Lucky Belmont'. This win and another against the 1896 Australians bolstered calls for the Gentlemen of Philadelphia to play first-class matches on their next tour to England, and in 1897 just such a venture was undertaken.

By the time of this, their third and most ambitious tour, the Gentlemen of Philadelphia were poised at a critical juncture in the development of international cricketing tours, aiming to join Australia and South Africa in challenging at the highest level. Philadelphian cricket had been bolstered by both a robust domestic competition between the major clubs and 25 years of international cricketing visitors.

The Associated Cricket Clubs of Philadelphia raised the $8000 required to finance the tour and selected the strongest side from the relatively small pool of around 250 top club cricketers in Philadelphia (no. 176). Ambitiously, the organising committee declined to play just amateur teams but insisted on meeting full-strength county sides. Earlier calls for this tour to take a fully representative American side were ignored as logistically difficult, but apart from a few of the best players from New York, Boston and Chicago – many of

172
General view of Merion Cricket Ground during Philadelphia's 1st innings, 22 September 1894, with Englishman William Whitwell bowling to Philadelphia's John Muir. From *Lord Hawke's XI: America and Canada 1894* **scrapbook**

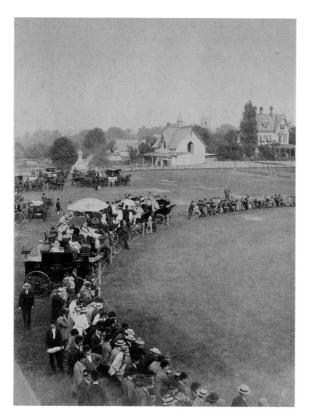

173 (above)
'The Coach Corner', Merion Cricket Ground, Haverford, September 1894, from *Lord Hawke's XI: America and Canada 1894* **scrapbook**

174 (above right)
Scoreboard showing end of Philadelphia's 1st innings, Merion Cricket Ground, Haverford, 22 September 1894, from *Lord Hawke's XI: America and Canada 1894* **scrapbook**

175 (right)
Invitations and menus, from *Lord Hawke's XI: America and Canada 1894* **scrapbook**

them English – the Philadelphians were arguably the best American players anyway.[21] However, despite the build-up and innate Philadelphian confidence, the consensus verdict on the tour was that the 'Quaker cricketers' were not yet up to first-class standard after all. English first-class county teams all included many professionals, sometimes outnumbering the amateurs, and it was the professionals who did most of the bowling. Only the tour games against Oxford and Cambridge matched amateurs against amateurs. The Americans lacked the versatility to adjust to unfamiliar batting surfaces – a long-standing weakness – and were handicapped by the American practice of playing time-shortened games, as most of their domestic matches lasted fewer than six hours. The toil of playing cricket day after day soon told on the American players.

Nevertheless, the tour was not without success. The Philadelphians did win the match against Sussex County Cricket Club on June 17–19 by eight wickets. Sussex collapsed in their first innings for 46 when John Barton ('Bart') King took seven wickets for 13. Moreover, the precedent of first-class cricket had been established. Most players felt taking on full-strength sides had been to their long-term benefit, and it was a mark of their keenness that they grasped this opportunity for improvement so enthusiastically. In particular, Bart King refined his bowling style on this tour to substantial future success, as did Percy Clark, while the batsmen Frederick Bates, John Lester,

176
Gentlemen of Philadelphia, 1897
A team photograph of the 1897 Gentlemen of Philadelphia before leaving for their ambitious third tour of England. Back row: Percy H. Clark, Edward M. Cregar, M. C. Work (manager), Harry C. Thayer, Francis H. Bohlen, Frederick H. Bates, Herbert L. Clark, John A. Lester. Middle row: Henry P. Bailey, Francis W. Ralston, J. Barton King, George S. Patterson (captain), H. Crawford Coates. Front, seated: Lynford Biddle, Arthur M. Wood.

177
W. G. Grace with G. S. Patterson during the 1897 tour of the Gentlemen of Philadelphia to England, 1897
Patterson, captain of the Gentlemen of Philadelphia on the tour and one of the top American batsmen of his day, poses with Grace, the greatest cricketer of the 19th century.

Pelham Warner's Eleven at Belmont Cricket Club, 1897

As with most cricket tours to North America, Philadelphia was the cricketing highlight of this visit. The match against the Gentlemen of Philadelphia at Belmont CC on 24, 25 and 27 September, where this team photograph was taken, was won by the Philadelphians by four wickets thanks to the strong bowling of Bart King, who, having just returned from the tour in England, had refined his bowling attack and captured nine wickets in this match for 25 runs. In addition, Warner played a match against the Philadelphia Colts, 22 young players who, signalling the health of the game in Philadelphia, had been eager for many years to match their skills against a visiting eleven.

Arthur Wood and captain George Stuart ('G. S.') Patterson also showed great improvement (no. 177).[22]

The 1897 tour set the stage for an exciting five years of Philadelphian cricket. The Gentlemen of Philadelphia were now established as a first-class team, and, perhaps even more importantly, they were also now fully accepted as part of the international cricketing fraternity. The wealth and standing of Philadelphia's elite, many of whom were members of the major cricket clubs, had been evident to visiting cricketers all along. By 1894, Philadelphia was issuing its own invitations, and Lord Hawke's tour of that year, lavishly sponsored by the Merion and Germantown clubs, was marked by relatively poor games but magnificent hospitality.[23] In 1897, while the Gentlemen of Philadelphia were still in England, their clubs at home were busy organising a visit by a young Pelham Warner (later England captain) to bring an eleven on tour (no. 178). From that year until 1901, the Philadelphia clubs organised an amateur English side to visit almost every year, bringing some of the best cricketers to North America in the process (nos 179–181).

The pinnacle for the Gentlemen of Philadelphia was undoubtedly their fourth tour to England in 1903. This was a reasonably experienced side, captained by John Lester who, with seven others, had gained so much from the

179 (above)
Prince Ranjitsinhji's Eleven at Merion Cricket Club, 1899
The great Ranjitsinhji, or 'Ranji', was an Indian prince who played cricket in England from his university days at Cambridge and then for Sussex and England from the early 1890s until he returned to India in 1904, ultimately to fulfil his duties as Maharaja Jam Saheb of Nawanagar. One of the finest and most exciting batsmen, he was noted for his mastery of stroke-play and is said to have invented shots commonplace today including the leg glance and the late cut. The team he brought in September and October 1899 was the strongest batting side to come to North America.

180 (right)
Match poster, Ranjitsinhji's Eleven at Merion Cricket Club, 1899
This poster advertises the second match of the tour, played at Merion CC on 29–30 September and 2 October 1899. Some considered it a Test match, but the Philadelphians were hopelessly outclassed. Ranji's team, boasting some of the best English batsmen (MacLaren hit 149 in 200 minutes, and Jessop 64 in 35), won by an innings and 173 runs. Press reports felt this foreshadowed a serious decline in Philadelphian cricket, but Philadelphia's John Lester considered it impossible that a single city, anywhere in the world, could match them.

181 (below)
Ranjitsinhji posing for George Beldam's camera, c.1904

INTERNATIONAL

CRICKET

MATCH

PRINCE RANJITSINHJI'S
ELEVEN
VS.
GENTLEMEN OF PHILADELPHIA

At HAVERFORD, Pa.
MERION CRICKET CLUB GROUNDS,
Sept. 29, 30, and Oct. 2, 1899

ON THOSE DATES THE

PENNSYLVANIA R. R. CO.
WILL SELL
EXCURSION TICKETS

From Wilmington, Paoli, Media, West Chester, Newtown Square, Phœnixville, Chestnut Hill, Trenton, Burlington, Mt. Holly, Haddonfield, Woodbury, and intermediate stations, to Haverford and return, including admission to the grounds, good on day of issue only,

AT REDUCED RATES

Ample train accommodations will be provided in each direction.

J. B. HUTCHINSON,   J. R. WOOD,   GEO. W. BOYD,
General Manager.   Gen'l Pass'r Agent.   Ass't Gen'l Pass'r Agent.

Allen, Lane & Scott, Printers, 1211-13 Clover Street, Philadelphia.

1897 tour. Lester was English by birth and had learned his cricket in Yorkshire before attending Haverford College in Philadelphia, where he was captain of the cricket eleven. Described as an 'excellent judge of the game', he was nonetheless the second choice for captain, appointed only after G. S. Patterson had to pull out of the tour.

They left home with the 'high hopes of their supporters' but without quite the same unshakeable confidence of the 1897 Gentlemen of Philadelphia, wondering if they would be up to such a high standard of opposition without their normal captain.[24] All but two of their 17 matches were against first-class opposition, and the results showed that the Gentlemen of Philadelphia had achieved the right to be considered their equals (nos 182–185).

Lester was the team's top scorer with the bat, and three of the five players making their first international tour, C. Christopher Morris, Nelson Graves and Frederic Sharpless, also batted well. But it was above all the improved attack, through the bowling of Bart King and Percy Clark, complemented by Lester's medium pace and Ed Cregar's slow bowling, and allied to good performances in wicket-keeping and fielding, that secured the final scorecard of seven wins, six losses and three draws (one match was cancelled due to rain). Bart King cemented his position as not only a top-class bowler but as an all-rounder: in the victory over Surrey he scored 98 and 113 not out, as well as taking six wickets.[25] The wicket-keeper Joseph Scattergood was sent home after being injured early in the tour, but Thomas Jordan was an able replacement. Two of the squad even made respectable places in the English averages for the entire season: King was tenth in the bowling tables and Lester 13th in the batting.[26]

The highest individual score on the tour was C. C. Morris's 164 against Nottinghamshire (no. 186).[27] Still a student at Haverford College and only 20 years of age, Morris showed signs of his future as a big match player. He went on to enjoy the longest international career of any American cricketer, remembered by *The American Cricketer* in 1927 as 'an attractive bat to watch, scoring quickly, hitting freely and yet possessing a thorough knowledge of the game'.[28]

This tour also highlighted to the American press the uniqueness of 19th-century Philadelphia cricket. The *New York Times* noted their success with pride, for 'a Philadelphian is an American', but cautioned against the idea that the Gentlemen of Philadelphia could ever take on an All-England side as the Australians had, noting that many English counties had larger populations than Philadelphia. Still, discounting this 'fond imagination' did not take away from the reward due to the Philadelphian devotion to the game.[29]

182
Bat, signed by the 1903 Gentlemen of Philadelphia
All members of the 1903 touring team signed this bat, apart from Frederick H. Bates, Reynolds D. Brown and Philip N. Le Roy.

183
Gentlemen of Philadelphia blazer worn by Captain John Lester, 1903
John Lester wore this blazer when he captained the side in 1903. He also played on the 1897 tour to England, when this style of blazer was first introduced, although a striped design was also worn then. In keeping with the blazer's pocket emblem, 'Philadelphia Maneto', meaning 'Let Brotherly Love Continue', Lester's leadership ensured a harmonious and happy tour.

184
Cap, Gentlemen of Philadelphia, *c*.1903

After such a good showing by Philadelphia in 1903, their fifth tour in 1908 marked the beginning of a decline from which the city's cricket never recovered. It was a great regret that the team wasn't stronger, because swing bowler Bart King at age 35 put in a remarkable personal performance on that tour. His figures included 87 wickets at an average of a mere 11.01, topping the English bowling averages for the year. Indeed no English bowler improved on King's figures for 50 years, until Les Jackson achieved an average of 10.99 in 1958. King was assisted by the Australian spin bowler, H. V. Hordern, who was studying at the University of Pennsylvania (and was known for his well-disguised 'googly' delivery). Little else of note was achieved by the other players, all veterans from earlier tours. The public showed little interest in the matches, many of which were affected by rain, and the Americans struggled on soft wickets. The overall results of the tour were, in C. C. Morris's opinion, 'only fair'.[30]

185 (photograph right)
Gentlemen of Philadelphia in England, 1903
Sailing from New York on 27 May, the team consisted of John A. Lester (captain), Frederick H. Bates, Francis H. Bohlen, Reynold D. Brown, Percy H. Clark, Edward M. Cregar, Nelson Z. Graves, Harold A. Haines, Thomas C. Jordan, J. Barton King, Philip N. LeRoy, C. Christopher Morris, Joseph H. Scattergood, Frederic C. Sharpless and Arthur M. Wood.

186
Bat used by C. C. Morris, 1903
One of five players making their first international tour, C. Christopher Morris proved his value as a batsman by scoring 164 against Nottinghamshire at Trent Bridge, in a match Philadelphia won by 185 runs. This is the bat he used in that innings.

Bart King

With his long bounding run up to the wicket, the ball gripped in both hands high above the head in the manner of the baseball pitcher in the final stride, he was a terrifying sight to batsmen.

Ralph Barker nominating Bart King as one of the *Ten Great Bowlers*, 1967

The one weakness in the 1884 and 1889 Philadelphia sides to tour England was common in cricket around the world at that time – the lack of first-rate amateur bowlers, a job that often required a professional. But with the 1897 international debut of John Barton King the glory days of Philadelphian cricket really arrived. As a bowler, Bart King stands alone in the history of American cricket, and he remains the only American to take all ten wickets in a first-class innings.

King started playing cricket as a teenager with the Tioga Cricket Club after initially playing baseball. Later, fellow Gentlemen of Philadelphia bowler Ed Craeger recalled enticing King away from baseball: 'The boys of Tioga were all for baseball, but we never lost an opportunity of talking cricket to them… Bart was the bright and particular star of this aggregation.'[31] Largely self-trained, King's unusual bowling style (no. 187) owed much to pitching experience, as did his trademark ability to swing a cricket ball much like a curveball in baseball, a delivery he called 'anglers'. King discovered that he needed a relaxed body, a release of the ball from full height straight above his head, careful wrist and finger control and seam placement. King felt the 'principle of surprise' meant that the 'perfected angler' had best effect when used in combination with more stock-in-trade deliveries.[32]

Swing bowling was of course not new to cricket, but King was the first to achieve – after much experimentation – a late, sharp and very pronounced swerve, in either direction, that was so effective it was soon copied. So much so, that the art of swing bowling was seen as a particular strength of American cricket and some attribute the techniques used to this day to King's pioneering techniques.[33]

Born in 1873, Bart King was from relatively humble middle-class origins, unlike many of his moneyed teammates from the Philadelphian upper class.

187
J. Bart King bowling
King's unusual action, raising both hands above his head holding the ball back behind his head, was a legacy of his early years as a baseball pitcher in Philadelphia.

He left his early employment in his father's linen and yard goods company for a career in insurance – a flexible situation apparently set up for him by his team-mates to allow him the time to devote to the game. His position as a gentleman player was never threatened, as it was common at this time for clubs to be more socially accepting of quality amateur bowlers.[34] In 1896 he joined the more socially accessible Belmont Cricket Club, located in a middle-class suburb in west Philadelphia, and played with them for most of his career, joining the Philadelphia Cricket Club for his final seasons from 1912 to 1916.

He was an affable, colourful character, never short of an anecdote or quip, who, according to one audience member during a hilarious 90-minute after-dinner address in 1908, 'told his impossible tales with such an air of conviction' that no one knew when to take him seriously.[35] Along with a taste for practical jokes, he had, as described by John Lester, 'the physical equipment that a fast bowler covets' – he was six foot one inch tall and 178 pounds (12 stone 10 pounds), with strong shoulders, long loose arms and exceptionally strong wrists and fingers. He was reputed to be able to send a cricket ball two storeys into the air with a snap of his fingers. One of the first cricketers to take physical fitness seriously, he was carefully toned by exercises that enabled him to play for over 25 years.[36]

He made his international debut in 1892 with matches against Canada and the Gentlemen of Ireland, but it was his bowling against the Australians in 1893 that established his reputation as a world-class player. He decimated their top order, including the Test players Charles Bannerman, George Giffen, Harry Trott and William Bruce in the Philadelphians' shock win. Giffen wrote afterwards that it was the American bowlers' use of 'baseball curves that upset our batsmen' – even though most also acknowledged that the Australians were worse for wear after an arduous English tour and a rough crossing of the Atlantic.

King followed this performance with outstanding tours of England with the Gentlemen of Philadelphia in 1897 and 1903 (nos 188–190), where he also secured his reputation as an all-rounder, for his batting was also of a high standard, mixing a big personality with a competitive spirit to win. He turned down all offers to join English county sides, including, it was rumoured, one that tried to entice him with an inducement of marriage to a wealthy widow fond enough of her county cricket side to set him up with a generous annual income.[37]

Of the many Bart King stories, true or exaggerated, one is often told that seems to best illustrate King's supreme self-confidence and mischievous sense of occasion. At a Belmont club match around 1902 against the visiting team from Trenton, New Jersey, the Trenton captain missed his train and arrived just as King bowled out the ninth batsman. He rushed onto the ground, saying to all

188 (opposite, left)
Signed photograph of Bart King posing at the batting crease

189 (opposite, right)
Bat signed by Bart King
King joined the Belmont CC in 1897 and played there for most of his career. The grounds became celebrated as the 'Lucky Belmont' after Philadelphia's decisive and surprising win over Australia there in 1893. King has signed this bat and added 'L.B.C.C', perhaps standing for Lucky Belmont Cricket Club.

190 (opposite, bottom)
Bowling Trophies of Bart King, 1897–1912
These balls mark some of King's greatest international bowling achievements. One ball celebrates his match-winning figures of 10–5–13–7 against Sussex on his first tour of England in 1897. The two trophy balls from the 1903 tour of England commemorate outstanding wins against Lancashire and Surrey. Against the Gentlemen of Ireland on 17–18 September 1909 he achieved the remarkable feat of taking all ten wickets in the first innings and a hat-trick (three wickets in three balls) in the second. The final trophy ball is from his last international match, against the touring Australians on 27–30 September 1912.

and sundry that if he had been there his team wouldn't have been in so much trouble. King made up his mind to pull the arrogant captain down a peg or two. King had recently seen the eccentric Philadelphia Athletics pitcher 'Rube' Waddell send all seven fielders off the ground, with a showman's confidence that he would strike out the man at bat. In much the same spirit, King decided to send all of his Belmont club mates back to the clubhouse, including the wicket keeper, leaving only King, the two New Jersey batsmen and two umpires on the field. The perplexed and uneasy Trenton captain protested, but the umpires ruled that King was within the laws as long as he did not have more than eleven men on the field. King now had to bowl the captain out or the ball was likely to go to the boundary for four runs. Relishing the drama of the moment, King decided to ask one fielder to return and, placing him in an unusual position, ran in and delivered a fast 'angler' that clean bowled the visiting captain, the ball landing exactly at the feet of the well-placed fielder.[38]

King's international career included three tours of England for the Gentlemen of Philadelphia, matches against the Australians, the Gentlemen of Ireland and top-quality touring amateur English sides at home, many of them at first-class level, as well as every USA–Canada fixture from 1892 to 1912. His playing appearances reduced considerably after 1912 when the Belmont club folded, but he still managed to win the domestic batting cup in 1914. Thereafter he became, as he remains today, a 'symbol of the bright days past' for Philadelphia cricket.[39] While he often carried the fortunes of his city's cricket on his shoulders, his reputation was not one of arrogance but of a ready wit and a warm heart (nos 191–194). His bottomless supply of cricket stories, no matter the truth of them, made him friends on both sides of the Atlantic.

191 (bottom right)
Hotel room keys from the 1897 Gentlemen of Philadelphia tour of England
King brought home souvenirs from his debut international tour, including, along with the more usual postcards and dinner programs, these two hotel keys.

192 (centre left)
Bowling Prize awarded to Bart King, 1908 tour of England

193 (bottom left)
Gold match case with single ruby inlay, c.1897–99
This lighter, with its tiger emblem and inlaid ruby, was a gift to King from Prince Ranjitsinhji. They had first met in 1897 when the Gentlemen of Philadelphia took on the strength of Sussex and won. The respect was mutual. King clean-bowled Ranjitsinhji first ball in the first innings, but in the second Ranji got going and King was at a loss as to how to get him out. Their friendship and friendly rivalry continued when Ranjitsinhji later brought an eleven on tour to North America in 1899.

194 (upper)
Cigarette and match cases belonging to Bart King

The decline of Philadephian cricket

Ironically, given the consistent focus on American-born players, the success of the Gentlemen of Philadelphia's international forays stemmed precisely from the fact that they played the game to English, indeed high Victorian standards. They played with a straight bat and, on tour at least, without the assistance of professionals. The English commented that they seemed as much a part of the 'honest freemasonry of the sport' as if they had been 'born and bred on an English village green'.[40] William Rotch Wister, the 'father of Philadelphian cricket', attributed this 'quality' to his old instructor, the well mannered and genial Sheffield cricketer William M. Bradshaw, who insisted on strict obedience to the captain and submission to the umpire. These attributes, instilled in subsequent generations, and a more homogenous and exclusive nature in Philadelphian cricket after the Civil War, combined to shift the character of the sport more in line with gentlemanly club cricket in southern England.[41] Yet Philadelphians, especially those of the 'great' families', truly embraced cricket, making it and all of its traditions an integral part of their lives for several generations. Their love of the game, and its many social aspects enjoyed by the whole family, can still be seen today in the grand pavilions and lush grounds of the Merion, Germantown and Philadelphia clubs. In many ways, the Philadelphians who visited England embodied the pure amateur spirit that English cricket itself then strove for, and this is what so impressed the English about the Gentlemen of Philadelphia. They played the game with zest and keen enthusiasm because they loved it, and the English found this spirit refreshing. As *Cricket* magazine concluded, 'They have made friends everywhere and not a single word has been said in their disfavour; there has been no necessity for it.'[42]

Even as the Gentlemen of Philadelphia were enjoying their highest success in 1903, finally reaping the rewards of decades of development, interest in the sport at home was waning. For years each visit by an international touring side had raised speculation about the health and future of the game in America, even in Philadelphia, its strongest centre. The weak showing against Ranjitsinhji's touring team in 1899 raised a 'turmoil of speculation' about the future of American cricket, with not enough promising young players, a lack of good slow bowlers and lack of full match experience. At a time when international matches lasted three days, half-day matches were increasingly common in American cricket by the 1890s.[43] A focus on the development of the domestic competition in Philadelphia brought a few years of increased competitive club matches, but the twin attractions of golf and tennis were already whittling away at cricket's support base. The *American Cricketer*, which began publication in 1877, expanded its coverage to include tennis and golf. By 1900, for example, two of the six golf clubs in the Philadelphia Golf Association were associated with cricket clubs, and a new golf trophy, the Patterson Cup, was introduced in memory of a popular cricketer.[44] Even Bart King had taken up golf by 1909.

There were still quality cricketers coming out of Philadelphia, and university and club sides toured England up to the outbreak of World War I, but without the popular support of the glory years. The Belmont Cricket Club folded and sold its grounds in 1913, and more and more tennis was played on the cricket grounds of the other major clubs. Members of the Philadelphia Cricket Club had starting playing tennis on the ground in 1884, and by 1902 the Club boasted 16 courts where all members could play – men, women and youths. The legacy of cricket was considered a great boon for tennis in Philadelphia, with the vast expanses of turf easily converted into courts.[45] In 1926, the last year of the inter-club Halifax Cup, only 42 matches in Philadelphia were reported in the *American Cricketer*, and none at all in 1928, the year before the publication ceased altogether. The cricket that was played was patchy and unreliable, sides showing up short-handed and forfeits common. A brief revival saw an amateur side, mostly made up of the old hands, form as the Philadelphia Pilgrims for a tour of England in 1921, and Haverford College continued to play, along with some dedicated minor clubs. University teams, allied to new interest from West Indian immigrants, changed the emphasis, and most tours by American sides in the 1920s and 1930s were to Bermuda.

In 1959, the same year that the Canada–USA annual matches were revived after a 51-year gap, MCC sent a team to tour North America, marking the centenary of the 1859 tourists. There was a visit by the 'Australian Old Collegians', who the next year played the first All-Philadelphia side formed in 20 years.[46] *The American Cricketer* was revived in 1965, and the playing of cricket at Merion Cricket Club in 1972. In 2006, two-thirds of the cricketers playing with the Philadelphia Cricket Club were US-born, and the British Officers' Cricket Club organised club matches to keep the cricketing heritage of Philadelphia alive.[47]

In 2008, Philadelphia boasted not only a champion baseball team, the World Series-winning Phillies, but also America's oldest country club, the Philadelphia Cricket Club. For a very long time, cricket and baseball have shared the summer in Philadelphia, vying for the leisure time of the populace. The first organised cricket club, the Union Club, followed after the Olympics of Philadelphia were formed in the early 1830s to play town ball. Clubs enthusiastically playing the 'New York' game sprang up in 1859 and 1860 and even the

Olympics shifted to the Knickerbocker rules in 1860.[48] All through the glory years of the Gentlemen of Philadelphia, professional baseball teams from Philadelphia also played their part in shaping the national game. Nowhere was the impact of the two sports more dramatic than at Haverford College, a Quaker university and heartland of university cricket where attempts by students to play baseball led to near 'athletic civil war' on campus between 1850 and 1920.[49]

Today cricket is a minor but growing sport and, although often seen as a relic of the city's history, it remains part of the Philadelphian summer. Haverford continues its strong cricketing tradition, raised to new levels by students from West Indies, India and Pakistan, and each year the Philadelphia International Cricket Festival draws over 150 players from around the region who compete in twelve teams for four days on the traditional cricketing grounds of the city, in the footsteps of so many great players.

The Hollywood Cricket Club

Later that same month [May 1933] the young Laurence Olivier sashayed into the Chateau Marmont Hotel to begin his first day as a film star in America. Waiting for him was a note: 'There will be nets tomorrow at 9am. I trust I shall see you there.' [50]

Cricket was first established in California by English and Australian immigrants, especially from the 1890s, when California agencies actively encouraged settlement. Although the competition was somewhat patchy, cricket attracted reasonable crowds and benefited from quality international players making the move to take advantage of California's opportunities, as well as from baseball players who often crossed between the two sports before professional baseball became fully established on the West Coast. San Francisco, where cricket had been played since the early 1850s, became the sport's early centre, and it was here that the California Cricket Association was formed in November 1891, presided over by Harold Webster from Philadelphia. The sport grew, slowly nursed along by players enthusiastic enough to adjust to hot conditions, hard pitches and brown fields – so different to how they played the game in England. In the early 20th century the focus shifted south to Los Angeles, where the Santa Monica Cricket Club dominated the local competition along with their rivals, the Los Angeles Cricket Club. But, as in northern California, cricket in Los Angeles suffered a decline in popularity after 1913 when the Santa Monica club lost its ground, the Los Angeles club pavilion burnt down and younger players stopped coming to the sport.[51]

A small cricket community in Los Angeles remained, centred around some good cricketers in Hollywood like Australian silent actor Sydney Deane and English actor Henry Pratt, better known as Boris Karloff. In the 1920s, Ernest Wright secured the first permanent cricket ground in Los Angeles, and then the English actor and accomplished cricketer Charles Aubrey Smith hit town 'like a bombshell'. He had played for Sussex and captained the first English cricket tour to South Africa in 1888–89, playing in what was later deemed to be South Africa's first ever Test match – and his only one (he took seven wickets). He made his stage debut in 1896, going on to a successful career in Hollywood as a character actor, appearing in films including *The Prisoner of Zenda* and Hitchcock's *Rebecca*. Forty-three years after his pioneering South African tour, at the age of 65 he spearheaded a resurgence of interest in cricket in California by helping to found the Hollywood Cricket Club in 1932 (nos 195–198). His strong character, organising ability and sway with local authorities gave the local cricket scene a much-needed boost. It helped that the Boer War movie *Cavalcade* was being filmed at the time, requiring 400 English extras. Wright's Venice Cricket Club, later the Los Angeles CC, was an early rival and soon other clubs sprang up in San Diego, Santa Barbara, Ventura and Montecito.[52]

Aubrey Smith gathered good quality cricketers around him, whether they liked it or not (as David Niven later recalled, 'when that Grand Old Man asked you to play, you played!'), and many illustrious film stars turned out for the club including Niven, Boris Karloff, Errol Flynn and Laurence Olivier. P. G. Wodehouse, writing scripts in Hollywood, also played. As president of the club, Aubrey Smith insisted on player decorum and punctuality. He was strictly traditional in his approach to the game, and observed all the social niceties. His house on Mulholland Drive was notable for being crowned by three stumps and a bat and ball serving as a weather vane.[53] The club colours of white, green and magenta that he chose were the same colours he had played under for the Actors Eleven in London, The Thespids. The club established itself in Griffith Park in May 1933 with an impressive pavilion and playing ground that had been seeded, under Smith's supervision, with five cases of imported English grass. Sadly neither still exists.[54]

197 (right)
C. Aubrey Smith, from Hollywood Cricket Club's scrapbook of its tour to Canada, 1936

195 (opposite)
Hollywood Cricket Club blazer worn by Tommy Freebairn-Smith, *c*.1930s
This blazer was worn by Thomas Freebairn-Smith, English-born like many other club members; he was a member of the Canadian tour to Vancouver in 1936. A radio announcer and producer, he was the founding executive secretary of the Academy of Television Arts and Sciences, the body responsible for the Emmy Awards.

196 (opposite)
Scrapbook, Hollywood Cricket Club tour to Canada, 1936
This scrapbook was presented to the captain, Aubrey Smith, by the members of the Hollywood CC tour to Canada, who all signed the frontispiece. They played four games in British Columbia and one in Seattle and attracted much press interest and attendance at their matches.

198

Hollywood Cricket Club team, from the scrapbook of the tour to Canada, 1936
Several well-known film actors took part in this tour, including Errol Flynn, Nigel Bruce (the label misspells him 'Nogel') and Claude King, as well as Aubrey Smith himself.

Smith's active promotion of the game not only led to a resurgence of interest and activity among other California cricket clubs, who started competing for the Williamson trophy in 1933, it also encouraged touring sides to visit, including Indians, the Canadian Legion and Gubby Allen's MCC team in 1936. Most memorably a top-flight Australian team, including the great Don Bradman, made a 'Good-Will' tour of Canada and the United States in 1932, playing exhibition matches in various large cities. Paramount made a featurette called *Cricket Flickers* highlighting the Australians and Aubrey Smith in Los Angeles. The Hollywood club toured up to Canada for a series of games around Vancouver, also in 1936, where their appeal on and off the field proved irresistible.

T. O'Hara   P.T.Dale EUGENE WALSH J.A.Hobday H. Booth JOE DRURY M. Berridge
    Umpire
S. Remnant A. Roughton Harry Warren F.Ward NICK DRACOPOLI FRANK LAWTON R.Burleigh DR.SEVERN

ERROL FLYNN. NOGEL BRUCE.F.J.Peers J.Fyfe-Smith C.AUBREY SMITH.STANLEY MANN.T.FREEBAIRN-SMITH
                                                                            CLAUDE KING

Hollywood Team in CAPS

United States Cricket Association tour, 1968

In a distant echo of the glory days of the Gentlemen of Philadelphia, a 17-man amateur side toured England in 1968 (nos 199–201). The first tour of a non-university team since the 1908 Gentlemen of Philadelphia, this was also the first tour under the auspices of the new national cricket association for the USA, formed in 1961. And it was, at long last, a fully representative side, with players chosen from 150 cricket clubs across the country. The players, whose occupations ranged from biochemist to stevedore, financed their own way to England. Three of the players were native-born Americans, and the rest were American residents from Commonwealth countries – two of them, Les Fernandes and Mike Stollmeyer, from prominent West Indian cricketing families. The continued strength of Californian cricket was apparent: the team was managed by Dr Tony Verity of the Westwood Cricket Club and captained by Dr Alf Cooper of the San Francisco CC, with five other players from that state. Five came from New York, one from New Jersey, two from Philadelphia, two from Washington DC and one from St Louis. As with the Gentlemen of Philadelphia, the USA side enjoyed generous hospitality; they were accommodated at John Gardiner's country house in Kent and honoured with an opening match at Arundel in Sussex against the Duke of Norfolk's Eleven. The team played 21 matches on the tour with underwhelming results. The aim, as with the 1884 Gentlemen of Philadelphia, was primarily educational. They were 'soundly and politely trounced' at Lord's, MCC winning by nine wickets, and one of the players admitted to being a bit nervous there, 'like an English team would be playing at Yankee Stadium for the first time'.[55]

Cricket in America today

The passing of the 'golden age' of American cricket and decline of the sport in Philadelphia was clearly not an irretrievable demise. The game continued at a local club level, encouraged by deep historical roots and the influx of immigrants from cricket-playing countries. Cricket in America today faces many of the same challenges as those tackled in Philadelphia in the 1850s and 1860s – how to simultaneously develop a competitive, representative senior team, in an amateur club environment, while also securing grass-roots and youth participation. At least some of the older stumbling blocks are now removed. The game is no longer exclusively identified as English; rather, its robust internationalism gives American cricket its greatest strength as immigrants from diverse

UNITED
STATES

UNITED STATES CRICKET TEAM
ENGLAND TOUR, 1968

countries join together and keep the game alive at a local and club level. Hundreds of cricket clubs play on weekends, usually in parks with matting wickets, disproving the perceived notion that the game can only be played on manicured lawns and expertly prepared wickets, a long-standing American reservation about the sport. There is even a new form of 'softball' cricket that is growing in popularity in New York and Florida.[56]

The United States national team, an associate member of the International Cricket Council since 1965, qualified for the ICC Champions Trophy for the first and only time in 2004 by winning the Six Nations Challenge, a competition the USA was only invited to participate in at the last minute when Kenya pulled out.[57] In an echo of the 1897 Gentlemen of Philadelphia's encounters against first-class opposition, the USA team travelled to England, the host of the 2004 Champions Trophy, to take on Test giants. In their first game against a full-strength New Zealand eleven, ten of the eleven Americans made their One Day International debut, and not surprisingly they lost heavily by 201 runs. They were likewise completely overwhelmed in the second match against Australia, a side many have described as among the best ever.[58] The USA national team have not since reached such levels in the international game.

More than a hundred years after American cricket administrators called for a shorter, more lively form of the game, international cricket now offers Twenty20, at its core a rapid game of aggressive batting that takes only about three hours to play and always has a winner. In fact, many of the atmospheric flourishes – music, cheerleaders, floodlit stadiums and flashy uniforms – are derided as 'Americana' in more traditional corners.[59] And it is Twenty20 that the USA Cricket Association, the governing body of the sport, hopes will tap into existing interest and bring new fans to the game in America. The most successful and financially lucrative Twenty20 competition, the Indian Premier League, has a plan to play some IPL games in America, either at the sole Florida stadium that meets ICC standards or at new venues, a prospect attracting some excitement.[60] Meanwhile New Zealand Cricket is partnering with USA Cricket to bring the first top-level cricket to America since the early 1900s – the New Zealand and Sri Lankan national T20 sides played against each other in Florida in May 2010. While New Zealand Cricket hopes to make this an annual visit, any international competition on American soil will surely require an American team that can achieve some on-field success if there is any chance of long-term popular support from the home audience. Therefore it remains to be seen if the proposed IPL venture, or any other such initiatives hoping to exploit the potential of a vast American market, will prove a success, or if they will rank alongside the many other previous attempts to popularise the game in the USA.[61]

199 (opposite)
USA team blazer and matching cap, 1968
This blazer with its distinctive pocket badge of an American eagle rampant over a horizontal cricket bat was donated to the C. C. Morris collection, Philadelphia by John Richard Gardiner, on whose country estate in Kent the USA team stayed and played during the 1968 tour.

200 (opposite, centre left)
Captains toss, 1968
The USA team captain, Alf Cooper, tosses the coin before a match on the tour.

201 (opposite, bottom)
USA Touring Team, 19 August 1968
All matches on this tour were played against minor county sides, but even these proved a high bar for the Americans. The match against Cambridgeshire at Fenner's, Cambridge, was one of only two won by the USA.

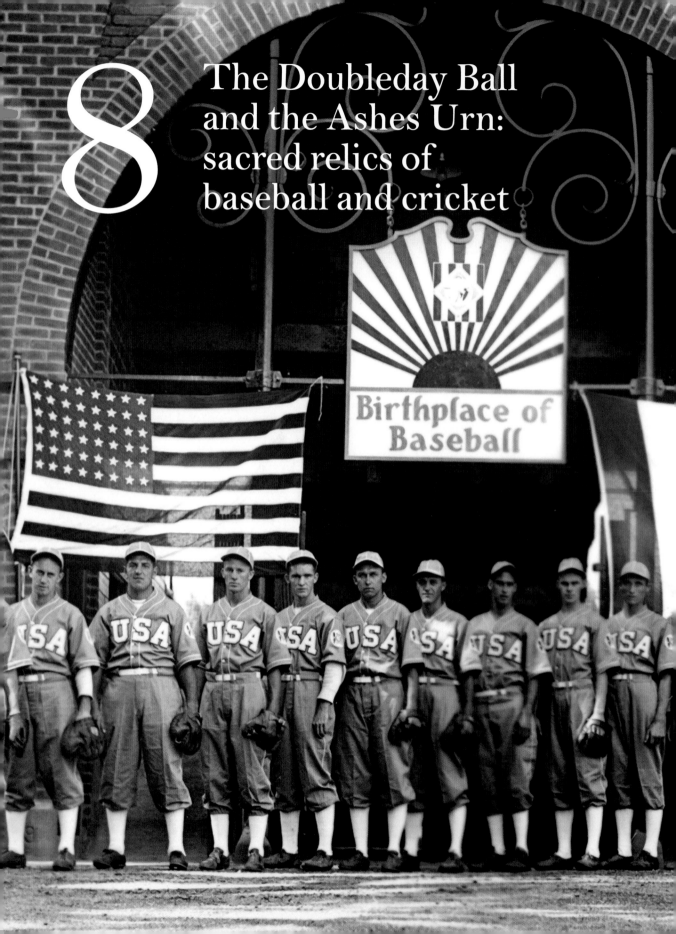

8

The Doubleday Ball and the Ashes Urn: sacred relics of baseball and cricket

Birthplace of Baseball

A curiosity of both baseball and cricket is that in both sports there exists a single object that is celebrated far above any other in the history of the game, to the point where it has become a kind of sacred relic. Baseball has the Doubleday ball. In cricket, there is the Ashes urn.

The Doubleday Ball

In 1860, writing in *Beadle's Dime Base-Ball Player*, sportswriter Henry Chadwick set out his thesis that baseball had in fact derived from rounders, the game of his English childhood. While ultimately disproved (see page 28), the idea that the American game grew out of rounders was actually reasonably well established in the 19th century. 'The game originated in Great Britain,' observed Charles Peverelly in 1866, 'and is familiarly known there as the game of Rounders.'[1]

In 1874 Albert Spalding, then the Boston Red Stockings' star 23-year-old pitcher, agreed when, during the baseball tour of England, spectators continually compared the two sports. 'The Englishmen who watched the American Clubs in England, and accused them of playing rounders were not so far out of the way,' he wrote. 'The game unquestionably thus originated.'[2] However by 1889, when Spalding, by now president of the Chicago White Stockings and head of a growing sporting goods franchise, brought his own baseball World Tourists to England, he had changed his mind and distanced baseball from rounders as much as possible. Writing in *The Cosmopolitan* after the tour, he recounted his experiences playing a game of rounders in England; this was, he concluded, very different from baseball. He was now convinced that baseball must have had an American origin.[3]

Chadwick again brought the issue to the surface in the 1903 edition of *Spalding's Official Base Ball Guide* when he reiterated his rounders theory and Spalding, embarking on something of a personal crusade now, spent much of 1904 refuting it. Spalding (no. 203) was a remarkable and driven man whose towering ambitions simply would not allow that the game that gave him a profession, then a sporting goods empire, baseball franchise and national and international recognition, could have come from a foreign children's game (he called

202 (opposite)
Amateur baseball players pose in front of the entrance to Doubleday Field, Cooperstown, New York, 1939.

203 (below)
Albert Goodwill Spalding, in an engraving based on a photograph of *c*.1896.

A.G. Spalding.

rounders 'that asinine pastime').[4] A man of his time, he shared with many other Americans at the dawn of the 20th century a yearning for grand national stories to match the burning patriotism of the day.[5] In the 1905 edition of his guide Spalding repeated his argument that baseball could only be of American origin, deriving from the American game of One Old Cat, and called for a 'commission to investigate the origin of baseball' in order to settle the question 'for all time'.[6]

And so, having agitated for a commission, Spalding duly set one up. This committee would have as its secretary James Sullivan, president of Spalding's publishing company, and among its members A. G. Mills, former National League president, whose name would later be attached to the commission report. Correspondence, testimony and other evidence were collected. Spalding gave one letter particular weight. This was from Abner Graves, an old miner living in Colorado but once a young boy growing up in the rural village of Cooperstown, New York, who reported that he himself had actually witnessed the invention of baseball as a boy.

Sixty-five years or so before, local teenager Abner Doubleday, home from the US Military Academy at West Point, took a stick and drew in the dust to teach a group of boys in Cooperstown his new game. Or so went the memory of Graves, who would have been about five years old at the time. The committee and Spalding seized on this rather perfect story. It showed that the National Game was invented by an American, and that this man was Major General Abner Doubleday, a Civil War hero who had taken part in nationally defining battles at Fort Sumter in 1861 and Gettysburg in 1863, and who had died over ten years before in 1893. Indeed Spalding discarded his previous position that baseball evolved from American Old Cat games, to embrace Doubleday's 'invention', never divulging his and Doubleday's mutual involvement in the Theosophical Society.[7] 'Base Ball had its origin in the United States.' The commission's final judgement comes as no surprise. It further concluded that 'the first scheme for playing [baseball], according to the best evidence available to date, was devised by Abner Doubleday at Cooperstown, N.Y., in 1839.'[8]

The scrapbooks put together by Sullivan on Spalding's commission were thought lost for many years until donated to the Hall of Fame in 2000. They show just how much Spalding himself manipulated the determination of baseball's origins. First he stacked the commission with like-minded members, while presenting them as respectable independent arbitrators. Then he prepared a heavily selective report for the commission to consider. Strategic omissions meant that the final report contained 66 pages in favour of the One Old Cat theory and only a page and a half supporting rounders.[9] The findings were meant to support Spalding's preference for an 'American Dad' for his favourite game.

Although almost immediately debunked, the Doubleday story soon settled into firm fact in the American imagination. Then an old ball was found in a dust-covered attic trunk in 1934. The small, misshapen, homemade ball was located in a farmhouse in Fly Creek, a village about three miles from Cooperstown. Wadded cloth could be seen inside the torn stitching of the dark leather cover (no. 204). With the centenary of the sport's 'invention' fast approaching, the link to Doubleday was irresistible, and the ball went from long-lost plaything, forgotten in an attic and perhaps never even used as a baseball, to *the* ball used by Abner Doubleday (no. 205) to 'invent' the game. Soon after its discovery, the ball was purchased for $5 by Stephen C. Clark, a Cooperstown resident and philanthropist, who put it on display with other baseball objects in a small one-room exhibition that attracted tremendous public interest and sowed the seed for a much grander edifice – a National Baseball Hall of Fame and Museum to celebrate baseball's first hundred years and commemorate the greatest players, which duly opened in 1939. The 'Doubleday Ball' would be its first treasure.

205
Major General Abner Doubleday, hero of the American Civil War, who was incorrectly deemed by the Mills Commission to have invented baseball in 1839

Swinging Away: How Cricket and Baseball Connect

The Ashes Urn

The Ashes urn started out as a small piece of good-natured fun. Some months after one of cricket's defining moments, when Australia beat England on English soil for the first time, a group of colonial ladies on an estate outside of Melbourne, Victoria had an entertaining idea. They were hosting some members of the English cricket team over the Christmas break during their Australian tour. When the English gentlemen won a social game against the estate staff, the ladies decided to present a memento to the English captain, Ivo Bligh. They found an empty jar that would do just the trick because, although tiny, its shape resembled an urn.

Why was an urn so appropriate? To understand this, we have to go back four months to 29 August 1882, the day Australia and England played the final day of a Test Match at the Kennington Oval in London. The Australians were nearing the end of what is now regarded the most successful 19th-century cricketing visit to England.[10] Australian cricket was still young at this time, as was the idea of playing as a national team on a continent then divided into separate, independent crown colonies. They had managed to come together to host the first English touring side in 1861, a mere 30 years or so after the sport itself became well established in Australia. In 1877, an Australian eleven triumphed over a professional English team in Melbourne, a contest now regarded as cricket's first ever Test match. Despite this and other wins, English cricketing authorities did not take Australian sides very seriously and there was little feeling that they could ever challenge a representative English side on home soil, in what was, after all, the cradle of the sport.

But over that unusually wet and cold summer of 1882, the Australians demonstrated exceptional skill on weather-affected pitches. Frederick 'the Demon' Spofforth showed himself to be perhaps the best pace bowler of the day (no. 206), the captain William Murdoch and Hugh Massie batted brilliantly, and Charles Bannerman proved a better wicket-keeper than anyone in England. All their talents were on display at the Oval where Australia met a strong England side in one of the most dramatic Test matches ever played.

On the second and final day of the match the English seemed certain of victory and started their second innings strongly; after all, they only needed to score 85 runs to win. Confidence grew when they reached 51 runs with only two batsmen out and the great W. G. Grace, considered the world's best batsman, still in at the wicket (no. 207). But Grace's dismissal triggered one of the most famous collapses in cricket history. Tension mounted, but surely the remaining five batsmen could get the mere 19 runs still required? But then, disastrously, one after another fell to the bowling of Spofforth and Harry Boyle. With the score at 75 for 9, tension among the spectators began to show – one died of heart failure, another bit through the handle of his umbrella. The last man was clean bowled and England were all out for 77, to lose by seven runs. Australia had achieved in spectacular manner its first victory in a Test match in England.

This unexpected defeat was considered a national calamity in England. A mock obituary notice, 'In Affectionate Remembrance of English Cricket', appeared in the *Sporting Times*, written by journalist Reginald Brooks (no. 208). English cricket, having 'died at The Oval', was 'deeply lamented by a large circle of sorrowing friends', and, he concluded, 'The body will be cremated and the ashes taken to Australia.' Amid the then current debate about the legitimacy of cremation, illegal in England at the time, the ashes analogy caught the imagination of the English cricketing public. So much so that, when the Hon. Ivo Bligh led an English team to Australia the following month, he vowed to 'recover those ashes'.

And this, the ladies at Rupertswood estate in Victoria decided, he would indeed do. After his victory over the staff in the social game, they are said to have burned one of the small bails from on top of the cricket stumps and placed its remains into the small urn-shaped jar – perhaps a ladies' cosmetic container – before presenting Bligh with the 'ashes' (no. 209). Over that Australian summer of 1882–83, three Test matches were played and Bligh's Englishmen avenged the earlier defeat at The Oval by winning the series by two Tests to one. A poem was pasted onto the urn and it is possible that the ashes of a bail used during the third Test were added to the urn and presented back to Ivo Bligh. Bligh could now indeed claim to be in possession of the Ashes – both symbolic and physical.

Most of the actors in this particular drama, none more so than the urn's owner Ivo Bligh, believed the Ashes would fade away, nothing more than an enjoyable play on words, while the serious business of cricket carried on as it should. And this was true for some time. The idea, however, was not easily abandoned and reappeared following England's Australian tour in 1903–04, when the

206
Portrait of Frederick 'the Demon' Spofforth by Henry Scott Tuke, 1906

English captain, Pelham Warner, wrote a memoir of the tour. Why exactly he chose the title *How We Recovered the Ashes* is unknown, as at this time 'Ashes' was not widely used in this way, but it started a slow trend. 'The Ashes' became a catch-all phrase for the Anglo-Australian competition, but it was a concept without concrete physical form. The urn remained in private hands and few had seen it or even knew of it. Not that anyone seemed to mind. Increasingly creative illustrations of the urn appeared, much in the tradition of the first 'Ashes' in a *Punch* cartoon in 1882 – an impressive and oversized soup-terrine-type cup – and winning was savoured, in the days of lavish banquets and long-winded speeches, without the need for a trophy. Indeed, in a game that often lauds the intangible, such as the so-called 'mental edge', playing for an ethereal prize raised little complaint.

For Ivo Bligh, this was doubtless a most personal relic as it was a memento of the budding love he had felt for one of the ladies he met at Rupertswood, Florence Rose Morphy, who in due course became his wife and life-long companion. Bligh, or Lord Darnley as he became after succeeding to his family's title, saw late in life that somehow the urn had come to represent one of the most keenly fought international sporting competitions. After his death in 1927, at his request his widow donated the urn, tiny and fragile, to MCC.

207
Portrait of W. G. Grace by Henry Scott Tuke, 1905

The Ashes urn itself slowly emerged from obscurity in the 1920s. It was put on public display at Lord's in 1929, seen by Australian cricketers for the first time on their tour in 1930. Only after the Second World War did the now well-known image of the Ashes urn begin to represent the universally understood concept of the Ashes. Over time a powerful, if erroneous, association grew between the urn itself and the Anglo-Australian cricketing competition.[11]

Generations of cricketers have battled on the pitch over the ashes of 'the body of English cricket'. What's more, when victorious captains took to holding a replica urn aloft, it had become by default the 'trophy' of the contest. As Australian dominance became entrenched from 1989 to 2005, and as trophies started appearing for other cricket compe-titions, many lost sight of, or never knew, the fact that this little urn was never meant to be a trophy.

For to hold the urn aloft, even in replica form, is to triumph in far more than just a game. After all, the urn symbolises all that it means to be English or Australian when the pitch is rolled, the bails are set on the wicket and the umpire calls 'Play!'

*   *   *

Sometimes, when significant meanings get attached to objects, these stories can run away in the popular imagination. After such a build-up, seeing the original can be something of a disappointment. 'It's an ugly little thing,' was the verdict of Steve Wulf in *Sports Illustrated* on the Doubleday ball, 'that looks more like a fossilized chaw of tobacco than a baseball... Hard to believe anybody saved the thing in the first place.' Similarly, Mike Selvey observed of the Ashes urn in 1995 that 'having seen what a pathetic totem they are the Australians might

208
'Obituary' notice by Reginald Brooks in the *Sporting Times*, 2 September 1882

In Affectionate Remembrance

OF

ENGLISH CRICKET,

WHICH DIED AT THE OVAL

ON

29th AUGUST, 1882,

Deeply lamented by a large circle of sorrowing friends and acquaintances.

R. I. P.

N.B.—The body will be cremated and the ashes taken to Australia.

deem them not worth the effort'.[12] Yet though these two very small and old everyday objects may appear ordinary, the pull of the myths has not diminished. That these powerful meanings are imposed, rather than intrinsic, does not distract from their significance; even the exposure of the myths is now thought key to understanding the history of each sport.

One reason behind the lasting appeal of both sporting myths is the transition they symbolise in each sport. For baseball, it is a move away from old-fashioned and folkish town ball to the 'first' game of baseball, and with it everything good about modernising America. Spalding's nationalistic overtones were unabashedly overt: 'I am determined to establish Base Ball as purely and entirely of American origin.'[13] When John Montgomery Ward dismissed the rounders theory by castigating 'persons who believed that everything good and beautiful in the world must be of English origin', he revealed just how much patriotic narratives had usurped the academic question of origins.[14]

209
The Ashes Urn, *c.*1882

The Ashes urn, likewise, marks the coming of age of Australian cricket. Cricket was no longer an English game, played to perfection by Englishmen to the admiration and envy of colonial pretenders. Pelham Warner revived the use of 'the Ashes' in 1903, soon after the Australian colonies federated into a single nation in 1901. The country now, not just the Australian cricketers, stood as a unified nation, and as time went on fewer and fewer Australians considered Mother England to be 'home'. Thus the rise of international cricket competition partnered the rise of an Australian national identity. It was in this long-term context, along with the dominance of Australian cricket in the late 1980s and 1990s, that pressure mounted for the Ashes urn to move from the abstract into the real. 'The Ashes is no longer a contest between a mother country and its colonial off-shoot, far from it,' wrote Matthew Engel in the 1995 edition of *Wisden*, 'it is a battle between two independent nations… [and] the trophy should be displayed in the country that holds them.' Former Australian Test cricketer Geoff Lawson agreed in 2002: 'Every other trophy is delivered to the winner, so this should be. [The Ashes urn] belongs in Australia.'

While the urn moved from the abstract to the real in popular imagining, the opposite was true of the Doubleday Ball. After initial reverence as *the* ball, much of the baseball-going public forgot about it sitting in the Hall of Fame, but the Doubleday myth continued. It should come as no surprise that heroic, expansive notions should overshadow muddled, plodding and prosaic truth. As John Thorn observes, 'to the question "How did baseball come to be," evolution seemed an unsatisfactory answer – messy, purposeless, and undramatic.'[15] The Doubleday myth, according to David Block, 'fooled several generations of Americans into accepting a deliberate historical falsehood' and stunted further research into the game's true origins.[16] It also propelled Doubleday himself into an internationally recognised relationship with baseball, the kind of popular if fact-poor idea that is very hard to break down.

Both myths have been debunked, loudly, many times and even by the two august bodies who hold these 'sacred relics'. The Hall of Fame stopped promoting Doubleday as the game's inventor and, as Senior Curator Tom Shieber said, 'We're comfortable with that.' As related on pages 28–30, the recent discovery of a social game of baseball in 1755 recorded in the diary of Englishman William Bray made headlines around the world. 'Major League Baseball told their sport was invented in Surrey, not America,' observed London's *Daily Telegraph*.[17] Yet, baseball remains America's game, no matter where it originated. And even without the weight of Doubleday behind it, the 'Doubleday ball' remains a special treasure at the National Baseball Hall of Fame and Museum, representing as it does this whole complex, intriguing story.

MCC never supported the idea that the urn was a trophy, but if it was a trophy the cricketers were after, MCC gave them one in 1998 – a super-sized Waterford crystal urn that now happily jets from England to Australia and back as winning fortunes decree (no. 210). Eventually MCC brought the urn back to Australia, not as a trophy, but celebrated, and more importantly explained, as the centrepiece in a significant travelling exhibition. As it made its way around the country over the Australian summer of 2006–07, the urn was soaked up by massive appreciative crowds enjoying their once-in-a-lifetime experience of seeing the real thing. A better understanding of the Ashes urn, what it is and more importantly isn't, hasn't diminished it in the public imagination. In the midst of exuberant, champagne-soaked celebrations at the end of every Ashes series, the winning captain triumphantly holds aloft, in carefully pinched fingers, an actual size replica of the urn (no. 211). Thousands flock to see the carefully showcased original at Lord's cricket ground and its image is still the ultimate symbol of Anglo-Australian cricketing rivalry.

211
England captain Michael Vaughan shows off the replica of the Ashes Urn at The Oval, 12 September 2005, after England had defeated Australia 2–1 in the series

Objects and illustrations appearing in the exhibition *Swinging Away*

119. Hull Giants v Leeds baseball programme from the short-lived 'outlaw' International Professional Baseball League, 4 June 1938

120. Hull baseball team photograph, n.d.

121. Hull Aces baseball jersey, 1980s

122. Hull Aces baseball batting helmet, 1980s

123. Baseball fielder's mitt, 1950s

124. Great Britain national team baseball jersey worn by Josh Chetwynd, 2000

125. Henry Barraud (1811–1874), *View of Lord's Pavilion*, c.1874, oil on canvas

126. MCC Member's Ticket, 1881, printed list of season matches in faux red leather pass

127. MCC Member's Ticket, 1899, printed list of season matches in faux red leather pass

128. MCC Member's Ticket belonging to Prime Minister Stanley Baldwin, 1926, printed list of season matches in faux red leather pass

129. MCC 'Life Member' token no. 7 belonging to J. Bradley Dyne, 1888–1922, ivory

130. MCC cap belonging to Brigadier General Edmond John Phipps-Hornby, 1886–1947, silk

132. Nicholas 'Felix' Wanostrocht (1804–1876), *The All-England Eleven*, 1847, pencil & watercolour on paper

133. English School (19th century), figures of George Parr and Julius Caesar, c.1860, Staffordshire pottery

134. Scrapbook by Felix of the All-England Eleven touring matches, 1850–51

135. English School (18th century), *Cricket Match Played by the Countess of Derby and Other Ladies*, 1779, watercolour on paper

136. White Heather Cricket Club blazer worn by Countess Brassey, President of the White Heather Club, 1910

137. Scorebook and scrapbook of the White Heather Cricket Club, 18 July 1888 to 30 May 1933

138. Uniform worn by Molly Beckenham of The Original English Lady Cricketers, 1890

139. *The Original English Lady Cricketers: The First Professional Elevens*, 1890, lithographic poster, David Allen and Sons

140. Commemorative miniature ball and bats, 1879, presented by fellow Knickerbocker Base Ball Club members to Samuel H. Kissam, silver

141. Trophy ball won on 29 September 1859, Excelsior BBC of Brooklyn defeating Gotham BBC of Hoboken, New Jersey

142. Belt worn by Jonas A. Polmatier, as catcher of the Eagle Base Ball Club of Florence, Massachusetts, 1868

143. Ribbons: Creighton of Norfolk, Virginia, late 1860s; Williston BBC of East Hampton, Massachusetts, c.1867; Pastime of Richmond, Virginia, late 1860s/early 1870s

144. Sheet Music for *Baseball Polka*, composed by James M. Goodman

145. The Knickerbockers of New York City and the Excelsiors of Brooklyn on the field, 2 August 1859, photograph by Charles H. Williamson

146. Harry Wright with his father Sam Wright (at left), photograph by Mathew Brady, early 1860s

147. New York Eleven (All New York). Photography studio John W. Hurn, 1865

149. Baseball from the Cincinnati Red Stockings' season of 1869

150. Sheet music cover for three compositions written in honour of the 1869 Cincinnati Red Stockings

151. Ticket to Union Grounds, 1 July 1869

152. Boston Red Stocking Pin, 1871

153. Levi Meyerle's National Association contract with Chicago for 1874 season, signed 7 August 1873

154. Illustration in *Harper's Weekly*, 24 July 1869, showing presentation of a Champion Bat to the 'Red Stocking' Base-Ball Club, Cincinnati, Ohio, on its Return Home

155. Cabinet card photograph of Young Ladies' Base Ball Club No. 1, c.1890

156. *Felix on the Bat* by Nicholas 'Felix' Wanostrocht, 1855

157. Baseball bat used by George Wright, 1879

158. Providence Grays championship pendant presented to George Wright, 1879

159. Cricket bat, signed by George Wright when he played for the Longwood Cricket Club, 1890

161. Babe Ruth with Australian cricketer Alan Fairfax in the nets at Thames House, London, 9 February 1935

162. New York Yankees baseball star Babe Ruth signs autographs for two bellboys on the roof of the Savoy Hotel during his visit to London, 8 February 1935

163. Cartoon by Burriss Jenkins titled 'H`a`yah Kid! The Babe is 40 years old', 1935, pencil on paper

164. Louisville Slugger baseball bat used by Babe Ruth to hit his last three home runs, 1935, ash wood

165. Young America Cricket Club, 1868, photograph with handwritten inscription in ornate wooden frame

166. Embroidered belt with decorative brass buckle, worn by Edward M. Davis Jr, c.1860s

167. George, Charlie, Dan and Robert Newhall, 1886, photograph

168. Young America cricket ground, Turnpike Bridge, Germantown, 4 July 1867, photograph with handwritten inscription

169. The Gentlemen of Philadelphia on their first tour of England, 1884, studio photograph

170. Lord Hawke's Eleven on their North American tour at Germantown Cricket Club in Philadelphia, 1891, photograph

171. J. B. King of the Gentlemen of Philadelphia bowling to Lord Hawke at Merion Cricket Ground, Haverford, 21 September 1894, from *Lord Hawke's XI: America and Canada 1894* scrapbook

172. General view of Merion Cricket Ground during Philadelphia's 1st innings, 22 September 1894, with Englishman William Whitwell bowling to Philadelphia's John Muir, from *Lord Hawke's XI: America and Canada 1894* scrapbook

173. 'The Coach Corner', Merion Cricket Ground, Haverford, September 1894, from *Lord Hawke's XI: America and Canada 1894* scrapbook

174. Scoreboard showing end of Philadelphia's 1st innings, Merion Cricket Ground, Haverford, 22 September 1894, from *Lord Hawke's XI: America and Canada 1894* scrapbook

175. Invitations and menus, from *Lord Hawke's XI: America and Canada 1894* scrapbook

176. Gentlemen of Philadelphia, 1897, photograph

177. W. G. Grace with G. S. Patterson during the 1897 tour of the Gentlemen of Philadelphia to England, 1897

178. Pelham Warner's Eleven at Belmont Cricket Club, September 1897, photograph

179. Prince Ranjitsinhji's Eleven at Merion Cricket Club, September 1899, photograph

180. Match poster advertising Ranjitsinhji's Eleven at Merion Cricket Club, 29–30 September and 2 October 1899, paper printed with red ink

182. Bat, signed by the Gentlemen of Philadelphia, 1903, wooden bat with twin wound handle inscribed and signed, maker: Angus, London

183. Gentlemen of Philadelphia blazer worn by Captain John Lester, c.1903, woollen blazer with gold trim and metallic thread pocket emblem

184. Cap, Gentlemen of Philadelphia, c.1903, woollen cap with metallic thread emblem

185. Gentlemen of Philadelphia in England, 1903, photograph

186. Bat used by C. C. Morris on tour of England, 1903, wooden bat with twine wound handle and twine repairs

187. J. Bart King bowling, n.d., sequence of three photographs

188. Bart King posing at the batting crease, n.d., signed photograph

189. Bat, signed by Bart King and inscribed 'L.B.C.C.', c.1897–1912, wooden bat with twine wound handle

190. Bowling trophies of Bart King, 1897–1912, wooden base with five mounted cricket balls

191. Hotel room keys from the 1897 Gentlemen of Philadelphia tour of England

192. Bowling Prize awarded to Bart King, 1908 tour of England, metal badge in two parts, connected by chain links

193. J.B. King's match case, a gift from Prince Ranjitsinhji, c.1897–99, gold with single ruby inlay

194. Cigarette and match cases belonging to Bart King, n.d., silver

195. Hollywood Cricket Club blazer worn by Tommy Freebairn-Smith, c.1930s, woollen blazer with pocket badge

196. Scrapbook, Hollywood Cricket Club tour to Canada, 1936

197. C. Aubrey Smith, from Hollywood Cricket Club scrapbook of tour to Canada, 1936

198. Hollywood Cricket Club team, from scrapbook of tour to Canada, 1936

199. USA team blazer and matching cap, 1968, woollen blazer with embroidered pocket emblem

200. Captains toss, 1968, photograph

201. US Touring Team 1968, photograph

Lenders

....

Notes

....

Chapter 1 (pages 12–23)

1. *New York Times*, 8 May 1879

2. *New York Times*, 2 October 1879

3. 'Baseball of the By-Gone Days' related by James Wood to Frank G. Menke in *The Evening Standard*, 16 August 1916; Peter Morris, *But Didn't We Have Fun? An Informal History of Baseball's Pioneer Era, 1843–1870* (Chicago: Ivan R. Dee, 2008), 70

4. E. T. Smith, *Playing Hard Ball* (London: Abacus, 2003), 11

5. See Melvin L. Adelman, *A Sporting Time: New York City and the Rise of Modern Athletics, 1820–70* (Urbana and Chicago: University of Illinois Press, 1986); Tom Melville, *The Tented Field: A History of Cricket in America* (Bowling Green, Ohio: Bowling Green State University Popular Press, 1998); George B. Kirsch, *Baseball and Cricket: the Creation of American Team Sports, 1838–72* (Urbana and Chicago: University of Illinois Press, 1989/2007)

6. Charles E. Clay in 1887 lists Sprague as both a 'familiar name' on the cricket team and 'the celebrated underhand pitcher' on the baseball team for the Staten Island Cricket and Baseball Club in the mid- to late 1870s. See Charles E. Clay, 'The Staten Island Cricket and Baseball Club', *Outing*, vol. XI, no 2 (November 1887), 103 and 105

7. www.cricinfo.com/afghanistan/content/story/449981.html (accessed 4 March 2010)

8. See 'World Series Cricket: Interesting Times', in Gideon Haigh, *Game for Anything: Writings on Cricket* (Melbourne: Black Inc, 2004), 163–167

9. Quoted in John Buchanan, *The Future of Cricket: The Rise of Twenty20* (Prahran, Victoria: Hardie Grant Books, 2009), 45

10. Peter J. Schwartz and Chris Smith, 'The World's Top Earning Cricketers', *Forbes*, 27 August 2009

11. Peter Roach, Manager, Cricket Operations and Membership, Australian Cricketers' Association, pers. comm., 5 March 2010

12. Alan M. Klein, *Growing the Game: The Globalization of Major League Baseball* (New Haven: Yale University Press, 2006)

13. *New York Times*, 28 February 2009

14. See for example, Baseball For All (www.baseballglory.com/Baseball_For_All), the American Women's Baseball Federation (www.awbf.org)

15. See web.usabaseball.com

Chapter 2 (pages 24–35)

1. Alfred T. Story, 'The Evolution of Cricket', *The Strand Magazine* (1895); Arthur B. Reeve, 'Beginnings of our Great Games: Birth of Baseball and Cricket', *Outing* (1910), 49–53

2. Charles Box, *English Game of Cricket; Comprising a Digest of its Origin, Character, History & Progress; Together With an Exposition of its Laws & Language* (London: 'The Field' Office, 1877), 19

3. Michael Rundell, *The Wisden Dictionary of Cricket* (London: A&C Black, 3rd edition, 2006)

4. David Terry, 'The Seventeenth Century Game of Cricket: A Reconstruction of the Game', *The Sports Historian*, vol. 20, no. 1 (May 2000), 37. Terry is referring to the work of Bonn University linguist Dr Heiner Gillmeister.

5. James Pycroft, *The Cricket Field: Or, The History and the Science of Cricket* (London: Longman, Brown, Green and Longmans, 1851), 11; Joseph Strutt, *The Sports and Pastimes of the People of England; Including the Rural and Domestic Recreations, May-games, Mummeries, Shows, Processions, Pageants and Pompous Spectacles from Earliest Period to the Present Time* (London: William Tegg, 1867; first published 1801), 106

6. Robert Henderson, *Ball, Bat and Bishop: The Origin of Ball Games* (Chicago: University of Illinois Press, 2001; originally published 1947)

7. Story, 'The Evolution of Cricket', 321; John Major, *More Than a Game: The Story of Cricket's Early Years* (London: Harper Collins, 2007), 17

8. Quoted in Major, *More than a Game*, 19

9. Major, *More than a Game*, 20–23

10. John Goulstone, 'Cricket', 1974, manuscript in MCC Library

11. *The Foreign Post* (London), 7 July 1697

12. Box, *English Game of Cricket*, 1

13. Terry asks 'Did the Flemish adapt stoolball and call it cricket?', in 'The Seventeenth Century Game of Cricket', 38.

14. Patrick Carroll, 'Filling in the Blanks' in *SABR UK Examiner* #4 (August 1994)

15. Patrick Carroll, 'The Chicken or the Egg?', in *SABR UK Examiner* #5 (January 1995)

16. David Block, *Baseball before We Knew It: A Search for the Roots of the Game* (Lincoln, NE: University of Nebraska, 2005), xxi

17. David Block, 'The Story of William Bray's Diary' in *Baseball: A Journal of the Early Game*, vol. 1, no. 2 (Fall 2007), 11; MLB Advanced Media documentary *Baseball Discovered* (dir. Sam Marchiano, 2008)

18. *Letters of May Lepel, Lady Hervey* (London: John Murray, 1821). Lady Hervey is discussed in Block, *Baseball before We Knew*, 189–90, and her letter was reprinted in *The Times* (London), 3 August 1874, during the first tour of American baseball players to England.

19. Block, 'The Story of William Bray's Diary', 10; David Block, pers. comm., 2 April 2010

20. Block, *Baseball before We Knew It*, 181–182; *The Times* (London), 18 August 1858

21. Block, *Baseball before We Knew It*, 119

22. John Myrc, *How Thow Schalt Thy Paresche Preche* (London, 1450), a translation of a 14th-century Latin text by William de Pagula that was shortly after publication annotated to detail banned sports in the churchyard including 'stoil ball'. See Block, *Baseball before We Knew It*, 165; Henderson, *Ball, Bat and Bishop*, 74–75; M. S. Russell-Goggs, 'Stoolball in Sussex' in *Sussex County Magazine* (July 1928), available at www.stoolball.org.uk/history/stoolball-in-sussex-by-russell-goggs (accessed 4 March 2010)

23. Russell-Goggs, 'Stoolball in Sussex'

24. Strutt, *The Sports and Pastimes of the People of England*, 108

25. Block, *Baseball before We Knew It*, 124–135

26. See Plates XIV, XV and XXIII in Robin Simon and Alastair Smart, *The Art of Cricket* (London: Secker & Warburg, 1983)

27. Block, *Baseball before We Knew It*, 125

Chapter 3 (pages 36–73)

1. *Gentlemen's Magazine*, September 1743, quoted in full in John Ford, *Cricket: A Social History 1700–1835* (Newton Abbot: David & Charles Publishers, 1972), 36–38

2. Block, *Baseball Before We Knew It*, 157–159; Morris, *But Didn't We Have Fun?*, 25

3. See Ford, *Cricket*, chapter 9

4. W. G. Grace, *Cricket* (Bristol and London, 1891), 237

5. http://exhibits.baseballhalloffame.org/dressed_to_the_nines/pants.htm (accessed 14 February 2010)

6. David Hopps, *Great Cricket Quotes: A Century of Cricket Quotations* (London: Robson Books, 2006)

7. This bat is very similar in shape and size to one conclusively dated to 1729 at Surrey County Cricket Club.

8. Nicholas Wanostrocht, *The Cricket-Bat and How to Use It* (London: Baily Brothers, 1861), 7

9. John Nyren quoted in Hugh Barty-King, *Quilt Winders and Pod Shavers: The History of Cricket Bat and Ball Manufacture* (London: Macdonald and Jane's Publishers Ltd, 1979), 40

10. Barty-King, *Quilt Winders and Pod Shavers*, 92

11. Arthur Haygarth in *Memoirs of the Old Cricketers* in John Nyren, *The Hambledon Men: being a new edition of John Nyren's 'Young Cricketer's Tutor' together with a collection of other matter drawn from various sources, all bearing upon the great batsmen and bowlers before round-arm came in*, ed. E. V. Lucas (London: Henry Frowde, 1907), 204–205; See also biographical notes by Martin Williamson, www.cricinfo.com/ci/content/player/19724.html (accessed 6 March 2010)

12. A. Craig, quoted in Barty-King, *Quilt Winders and Pod Shavers*, 115

13. www.cricinfo.com/ipl2010/content/story/454021.html (accessed 14 April 2010)

14. Eric Miklich, 'Evolution of Baseball Equipment', www.19cbaseball.com/equipment.html#the-bat (accessed 14 February 2010)

15. Major, *More Than a Game*, 95–96; 'Ponting's bat illegal, rules MCC', 16 February 2006, http://news.bbc.co.uk/sport2/hi/cricket/4720928.stm (accessed 6 March 2010)

16. Miklich, 'Evolution of Baseball Equipment'

17. Frederick Gale, *Echoes from Old Cricket Fields* (London: Simpkin and Marshall, 1871). The fire story is told by Arthur Haygarth in *Memoirs of the Old Cricketers* in Nyren, *The Hambledon Men*, 205; the ball theory is related in the periodical *The Ladies' Cabinet*, 1 June 1833

18. *The Ladies' Cabinet*, 1 June 1833

19. James Pycroft, *Cricketana, By the Author of 'The Cricket-Field'* (London: Longman, Green, Longman, Roberts & Green, 1865), 74

20. Barty-King, *Quilt Winders and Pod Shavers*, 30

21. Peter Morris, *A Game of Inches: The Stories Behind the Innovations That Shaped Baseball* (Chicago: Ivan R. Dee, 2006), 396, quoting the *Brooklyn Eagle* of 3 February 1884; Miklich, 'Evolution of Baseball Equipment', www.19cbaseball.com/equipment-3.html

22. Charles A. Peverelly, *The Book of American Pastimes: Containing a History of the Principal Base Ball, Cricket, Rowing and Yachting Clubs of the United States* (New York: published by the author, 1866), 415

23. Morris, *A Game of Inches*, quoting the *New York Clipper*, 4 December 1875

24. Morris, *A Game of Inches*, 45

25. Charles Dickens, *Martin Chuzzlewit* (London: Penguin Classics, 2004), 410

26. *The Washington Post*, 22 July 1938; *The Chicago Tribune*, 2 August 1938

27. *Chicago Daily Tribune*, 3 August 1938

28. Quoted in *Baseball Digest*, vol. 59, no 2 (February 2000), 65

29. Henry Chadwick, *The Sports and Pastimes of American Boys: A Guide and Text-book of Games of the Playground, the Parlor, and the Field. Adapted Especially for American Youth* (New York: G. Routledge and Sons, 1884), 37

30. Pycroft, *The Cricket Field*, 229

31. *Baseball Magazine*, March 1913

32. *New York Times*, 20 April 1926

33. http://mlb.mlb.com/
mlb/official_info/official_rules/
foreword.jsp (accessed 14 April 2010)

34. Quoted in Rundell, *The Wisden Dictionary of Cricket*, 195

35. Morris, *A Game of Inches*, 33–35

36. See http://icc-cricket.yahoo.net/
the-icc/match_officials/overview.php
(accessed 31 January 2010)

37. Rev. R. S. Holmes, *The History of Yorkshire County Cricket 1833–1903* (London: Archibald, Constable & Co Ltd, 1904), 23

38. Brian Winzor, statistician for *Howstat.com: The Cricket Statisticians*, pers. comm., 26 February 2010

39. Morris, *A Game of Inches*, 53–54

40. Andrew J. Schiff, *'The Father of Baseball': A Biography of Henry Chadwick* (Jefferson, NC: McFarland, 2008), 64

41. Andrew J. Schiff, 'Henry Chadwick: The "Father of Baseball" was a Sportswriter', *The National Pastime: A Review of Baseball History* (The Society of American Baseball Research), vol. 28 (2008), 26

42. Schiff, *'The Father of Baseball'*, 161

43. Henry Chadwick, *Chadwick's American Cricket Manual…* (New York: Robert M. De Witt Publisher, 1873), 4

44. *The American Chronicle*, 13 February 1868; Chadwick, *Chadwick's American Cricket Manual*, 3–4

45. Chadwick, *Chadwick's American Cricket Manual*, 26

46. Chadwick, *The Sports and Pastimes of American Boys*, 9

47. Peverelly, *The Book of American Pastimes*, 520

Chapter 4 (pages 74–111)

1. Frederick Lillywhite, *The English Cricketers' Trip to Canada and The United States*, (London: F. Lillywhite, 1860; reprinted 1980, ed. Robin Marlar), v–vi

2. American correspondent in *The Times* (London), 4 August 1874

3. *New York Gazette*, quoted in Martin Wilson, *Dawn's Early Light: Cricket in America before 1820* (Oxford: Christopher Saunders and Joshua Horgan, 2008), 10

4. *The New York Herald*, 1845, and *Brooklyn Daily Eagle*, 1846, quoted in Melville, *The Tented Field*, 18

5. 'Cricket in America', *Bell's Life in London and Sporting Chronicle*, 3 December 1843

6. As late as 1869, an English observer was able to write that 'rowing and other athletics, with the exception of skating and base-ball, are both neglected and despised in America'. Sir Charles Wentworth Dilke quoted in James Hunt, 'On the Acclimatisation of Europeans in the United States of America' in *Anthropological Review* (London), 1 April 1870

7. Kirsch, *Baseball and Cricket*, 21

8. Peverelly, *The Book of American Pastimes*, 529

9. Rowland Bowen, *North America in International Cricket* (self-published pamphlet, 1960), 2. See http://www.cricketarchive.com/
Archive/Scorecards/120/120631.htm
l for the full scorecard of this match (accessed 7 February 2009)

10. William Rotch Wister, *Some Reminiscences of Cricket in Philadelphia before 1861* (Philadelphia: Allen, Lane & Scott, 1904) and George B. Kirsch, 'American Cricket: Players and Clubs before the Civil War', *Journal of Sport History*, vol. 11, no. 1 (Spring 1984)

11. Kirsch, *Baseball and Cricket*, 37

12. John A. Lester (ed.), *A Century of Philadelphia Cricket* (Philadelphia: University of Pennsylvania Press, 1951), 17

13. Lillywhite, *The English Cricketers' Trip*, 45–46

14. *Rochester Union and Advertiser*, 17 September 1859; *Rochester Express*, 10 December 1859

15. Melville, *The Tented Field*, 51; Priscilla Astifan, pers. comm. 5 May 2008

16. *Rochester Union and Advertiser* 24 October 1859; *New York Times*, 24 October 1859, 1

17. Lillywhite, *The English Cricketers' Trip*, 50

18. Lillywhite, *The English Cricketers' Trip*, 7

19. *Bell's Life in London and Sporting Chronicle* (London), 1 January 1860

20. Lillywhite, *The English Cricketers' Trip*, 45 and 51; John Marder and Adrian Cole, 'Cricket in the USA' (on-line article on cricinfo.com adapted from an original in Barclays World of Cricket, 1980, www.cricinfo.com/
usa/content/story/261614.html
(accessed 18 April 2010); Melville, *The Tented Field*, 43

21. Melville, *The Tented Field*, 59; *New York Times*, 3 September 1868 and 21 October 1868

22. Melville, *The Tented Field*, 62

23. For details see Peter Wynne-Thomas, *The Complete History of Cricket Tours at Home and Abroad* (London: Hamlyn, 1989)

24. Henry Chadwick quoted in *Spalding's Official Base Ball Guide* (Chicago and New York: A. G. Spalding & Brothers, 1889), 92; A. G. Spalding's chapter, 'First Foreign Base Ball Tour', from his *America's National Game* (American Sports Publishing Company, 1911), quoted in *Sporting Life*, vol. 62, no. 14 (6 December 1913), 1

25. Eric Miklich, '1874 World Base Ball Tour', www.19cbaseball.com (downloaded 4 October 2009)

26. Harry Wright quoted in Christopher Devine, *Harry Wright: The Father of Professional Base Ball* (Jefferson, NC: McFarland, 2003), 104

27. *Bell's Life in London and Sporting Chronicle* (London), 14 February 1874, 4

28. *Bell's Life in London and Sporting Chronicle* (London), 21 March 1874; *New York Times*, 15 July 1874

29. *Sporting Gazette* (London), March 14, 1874; *Bell's Life in London and Sporting Chronicle* (London), 14 March

1874; and see Mark Lamster, *Spalding's World Tour: The Epic Adventure that Took Baseball Around the Globe – And Made It America's Game* (New York: Public Affairs, 2006), 27–30

30. Spalding, 'First Foreign Base Ball Tour', 1

31. *New York Times*, 13 July 1874

32. *New York Times*, 13 July 1874 and 12 September 1874

33. 'The Americans at Lord's', *Wisden Cricketers Almanack 1875*, 66

34. Cricket and baseball play as described in 'The Americans at Lord's', *Wisden 1875*, 66–67

35. *New York Times*, 12 September 1874. This paper concluded that the lack of enthusiasm for American victories was not because they faced second-string sides but because cricket did not have the 'hold on Englishmen that they would have us believe'.

36. *New York Times*, 12 September 1874; *Spalding's Official Base Ball Guide* (Chicago and New York: A. G. Spalding & Brothers, 1889), 93

37. *New York Times*, 12 September 1874

38. *Spalding's Official Base Ball Guide* (1889), 93; and see Melville, *The Tented Field*, 64

39. *The Times* (London), 31 July 1874; *The Field*, 11 July 1874

40. *Spalding's Official Base Ball Guide* (1889), 93

41. *Sporting Life: The World of Baseball*, 20 September 1913

42. This tour is covered in detail by Mark Lamster in *Spalding's World Tour*

43. Spalding, *America's National Game*, 251

44. Harry Palmer, 'Baseball in Australia', *Outing*, November 1888; *New York Clipper* quoted in 'Editor's Open Window', *Outing*, May 1888, 172

45. Spalding, *America's National Game*, 252

46. See Lamster, *Spalding's World Tour*, 66–70; Harry Clay Palmer, *Athletic Sports in America, England and Australia: The 1888–1889 World Tour of American Baseball Teams* (Jefferson, NC: McFarland, 2006), 160

47. *Spalding's Official Base Ball Guide* (1890), 121

48. Palmer, 'Baseball in Australia', 166

49. *Spalding's Official Base Ball Guide* (1890), 122

50. Lamster, *Spalding's World Tour*, 181

51. Spalding, *America's National Game*, 259

52. *The Times* (London), 11 February 1889

53. 'Between Ourselves', *The Licensed Victuallers' Mirror* (London), 12 March 1889

54. Spalding, *America's National Game*, 261

55. Lamster, *Spalding's World Tour*, 217

56. 'The American Baseball Players', *The Times* (London), 13 March 1889

57. Spalding, *America's National Game*, 263

58. Jimmy Ryan's tour diary, unpublished manuscript, National Baseball Hall of Fame and Museum

59. Spalding, *America's National Game*, 263

60. *Funny Folks* (London), 16 March 1889

61. *The Times* (London), 14 March 1889

62. *The Times* (London), 15 March 1889

63. *The Times* (London), 18 March 1889; *Western Mail* (Cardiff), 16 March 1889

64. Quoted in Lamster, *Spalding's World Tour*, 227

65. W. G. Grace, 'Cricket and Baseball', from *The English Illustrated Magazine*, reprinted in the *New York Times*, 15 June 1890

66. *The Times* (London), 19 March 1889; *The Sun* (New York), 19 March 1889; *The Dart: The Midland Figaro* (Birmingham), 22 March 1889

67. *The Sun* (New York), 20 March 1889

68. 'Sporting Intelligence', *The Newcastle Weekly* (Newcastle-upon-Tyne), 23 March 1889; 'The Great Trip', *The Sporting Life*, 17 April 1889

69. Andrew Welch, 'British Baseball: How a Curious Version of the Game Survives in Parts of England and Wales', *The National Pastime: A Review of Baseball History* (Society for American Baseball Research), vol. 28 (2008), 30

70. *The Sun* (New York), 24 March 1889

71. A. G. Spalding, 'What is the Origin of Base Ball?' in *Spalding's Official Base Ball Guide* (Chicago and New York: A.G. Spalding & Brothers, 1905), 7

72. *The Sun* (New York), 24 March 1889; *Daily News* (London), 25 March 1889

73. *The Sun* (New York), 25, 26 and 27 March 1889

74. *The Sun* (New York), 29 March 1889

75. Quoted in Lamster, *Spalding's World Tour*, 239

76. See Josh Chetwynd and Brian A. Belton, *British Baseball and the West Ham Club: History of a 1930s Professional Team in East London* (Jefferson, NC: McFarland, 2007), 14–15. Even the French press promoted baseball in 1914 as a way to keep footballers in shape in the summer off-season, as reported in *The Times* on 20 February 1914

77. William Morgan, '96 and counting: British baseball history', *First Base*, Autumn 1986

78. *The Times* (London), 22 August 1895

79. *Baily's Magazine of Sports and Pastimes*, 1 November 1895; 'Town and County Gossip', *Horse and Hound: A Journal of Sport and Agriculture*, 24 August 1895, 503; James Wilson, 'Baseball in England and its Rivals', *The Strand*, 1894, 185

80. *Sporting Life*, 18 October 1913

81. *Sporting Life*, 11 October 1913

82. *Baseball Magazine*, vol. XII, no. 4 (February 1914), 47–48; and *Sporting Life: The World of Baseball*, 20 September 1913. Comiskey also hosted the Australian national team of cricketers at White Sox Ball Park on 27–28 August 1913, and at Comiskey's Ball Yard on 29 August (see scorecards of the games at www.cricketarchive.com/cgi-bin/scorecard_oracle_reveals_results.cgi), playing three one-day matches against Chicago cricketers, a gesture intended to ensure a warm reception down under for his baseball tourists later that year.

83. *The Reach Official American League Base Ball Guide* (Philadelphia: A. J. Reach, 1925), 22

84. *The Reach Official American League Base Ball Guide* (Philadelphia: A. J. Reach, 1914) reports an estimated crowd of 37,000; *Sporting Life* reported 'between thirty and forty thousand' on 7 March 1914, although others have estimates.

85. *The Reach Official American League Baseball Guide* (1914)

86. Ben Toon, 'Five Million New Fans', *Baseball Magazine*, January 1914

87. *Spalding's Official Base Ball Guide* (Chicago: A. G. Spalding & Brothers, 1914), 51

88. Shaw, 'This Baseball Madness', *Evening Standard*, 4 November 1924

89. From a clipping in the *Wilson Cross Scrapbook* (untitled, 1924)

90. *The Times* (London), 28 October 1924

91. *Baseball Magazine*, vol. 12, no. 3 (January 1914), 15–16

92. *Sporting Life*, March 14, 1914

93. Andrew Weltch, 'British Baseball', 30–34

94. William Morgan, 'The Professional Leagues' in *Baseball Mercury*, no. 27 (May 1981), 1

95. For an overview of the establishment of baseball in England in the 1930s see Chetwynd and Belton *British Baseball and the West Ham Club*, 33–45

96. Keith Macklin, 'Baseball Returns to Home Base', *The Times* (London), 2 September 1980

97. William Kelly, 'Baseball in Japan: The National Pastime Beyond National Character', in *Baseball as America: Seeing Ourselves through our National Game* (National Geographic and the National Baseball Hall of Fame and Museum), 47

98. Herman Irving, 'Baseball Exile', in *Transatlantic Baseball Bulletin*, June/July 1987, 4

99. Josh Chetwynd, 'Great Britain: Baseball's Battle for Respect in the Land of Cricket, Rugby and Soccer' in George Gmelch (ed.), *Baseball Without Borders: The International Pastime* (Lincoln, NE: University of Nebraska Press, 2006), 263–287

100. www.guardian.co.uk/sport/blog/2008/oct/06/cricket.trescothick (accessed 9 February 2010)

101. Russell Dyas, 'The Man With The Weight Of Great Britain On His Shoulders', http://www.baseballgb.co.uk/?p=7505 (accessed 6 May 2010)

102. Matt Smith, 'British Baseball Beat: 2010 BBF League details published', http://www.baseballgb.co.uk/?p=7435 (accessed 6 May 2010)

Chapter 5 (pages 112–133)

1. Tony Lewis, *Double Century: 200 Years of the MCC* (London: Hodder and Stoughton, 1987), 29

2. Lewis, *Double Century*, 99

3. John Nyren, *The Young Cricketer's Tutor: comprising full directions for playing the elegant and manly game of cricket: with a complete version of its laws and regulations… to which is added The cricketers of my time, or, Recollections of the most famous old players / The whole collected and edited by Charles Cowden Clarke* (London: E. Wilson, 1833), 11

4. Wanostrocht, *The Cricket-Bat and How to Use It*, 11

5. W. F. Mandle, 'The Professional Cricketer in England in the Nineteenth Century', *Labour History: Journal of The Australian Society for the Study of Labour History*, no. 23 (November 1972), 1

6. Wanostrocht, *The Cricket-Bat and How to Use It*, 15

7. G. Derek West, *The Elevens of England* (London: Darf Publishers Limited, 1988), 142

8. Mandle, 'The Professional Cricketer', 14

9. Grace, *Cricket*, 97

10. Mandle, 'The Professional Cricketer', 1

11. English Cricket & Athletic Association advertisement, James Lillywhite's *Cricketers' Annual*, 1890, frontispiece

12. Morris, *But Didn't We Have Fun?*, 5

13. Morris, *But Didn't We Have Fun?*, 28; Block, *Baseball before We Knew It*, 74–75; John Thorn, 'Origins of the New York Game' in *Baseball: A Journal of the Early Game*, vol. 2, no. 2 (Fall 2009), 112

14. Devine, *Harry Wright*, 3

15. See chapter 5, 'The Failure of Cricket as an American Sport', in Adelman, *A Sporting Time*, especially page 103

16. Peter Wynne-Thomas, *The History of Nottinghamshire County Cricket Club* (London: Christopher Helm, 1992), 9

17. Melville, *The Tented Field*, 62; John Thorn, 'Jim Creighton', *The Baseball Biography Project* (Society of American Baseball Research), http://bioproj.sabr.org/bioproj.cfm?a=v&bid=770&pid=0; www.cricketarchive.com/Archive/Scorecards/121/121444.html (both accessed 18 February 2010)

18. Clay, 'The Staten Island Cricket and Baseball Club', 98

19. Devine, *Harry Wright*, 29

20. www.cricketarchive.com/Archive/Scorecards/134/134551.html (accessed 18 February 2010)

21. Paul Johnson, *A History of the American People* (London: Weidenfeld and Nicolson, 1997), 449

22. Eric Miklich, '1867–1870 Cincinnati Club; aka "Red Stockings" Tour', www.19cbaseball.com/tours-1867-1870-cincinnati-red-stockings-tour.html (accessed 18 February 2010). Depending on which games are counted, some sources give totals of up to 65 undefeated games for the Red Stockings in the 1869 season.

23. Devine, *Harry Wright*, 69–72

24. See Morris, *But Didn't We Have Fun?*, 184–201

25. *Sporting Life*, vol. 15, no. 23 (1890), 4

26. Gai Ingham Berlage, *Women in Baseball* (Westport, CT: Praeger Trade, 1994), 32

27. *The American Cricketer*, vol. XIV, no. 365 (13 May 1891), 1

28. *Chicago Times*, 17 April 1889

Chapter 6 (pages 134–141)

1. William Phelon in *Baseball Magazine*, vol. 12, no. 3 (January 1914), 15–16

2. *The American Chronicle*, 13 February 1868

3. *The Washington Post (1877–1922)*, 31 December 1911; *New York Times*, 13 July 1932;

4. Adelman holds that the Brooklyn Club were members of the Union Star who played baseball as a break from their usual cricket – see Adelman, 'The First Baseball Game, the First Newspaper References to Baseball, and the New York Club: A Note on the Early History of Baseball' in *Journal of Sport History*, vol. 7, no. 3 (Winter 1980), 133; Melville, *The Tented Field*, 18–19

5. Their first match was against the Satellite Club of Williamsburgh on 18 October 1860. The American Club was victorious. See *New York Times*, 17 October 1860, 1, and 20 October 1860, 8.

6. Melville, *The Tented Field*, 50; according to president Dakin, the club formed to make cricket 'popular among Americans, by making it a quicker game', *New York Times*, 20 October 1860

7. *The American Chronicle*, 13 February 1868

8. *The American Chronicle*, 13 February 1868; Kirsch, *Baseball and Cricket*, 105–06

9. www.dreamcricket.com/dreamcricket/news.hspl?nid=11194&ntid=4 (accessed 31 January 2010)

10. Henry Chadwick, 'A Revolution in the Cricket Field', *Outing* (June 1890), 228–29

11. Jerome Flannery, 'The Game of Cricket in America', *New York Times*, 22 September 1901

12. *The Country Gentleman: Sporting Gazette, Agricultural Journal, and 'The Man about Town'* (London), 23 March 1889

13. *Chicago Press and Tribune*, 12 October 1859

14. Jerome Flannery (ed.), *The American Cricket Annual* (Philadelphia, 1890), 8–9

15. *The Washington Post*, 18 April 1886

16. *New York Times*, 28 June 1903

17. *New York Times*, 25 December 1886

18. Thomas Wharton, 'Inter-City and International Cricket in America', *Outing* (June 1892), 179

19. Donald Bradman's introduction in Ric Sissons, *The Don Meets the Babe: The 1932 Australian Cricket Tour of North America* (Epsom: J. W. McKenzie, 1995)

20. Cliff Gewecke, 'Americans Don't Bother to Understand Cricket', *Christian Science Monitor*, 29 July 1968, 12

21. Ralph Nichols, 'Something Wicket This Way Comes', *Los Angeles Times*, 17 June 1988, 19

22. Gewecke, 'Americans Don't Bother', 12

23. *The Sporting Times* (London), 28 November 1896

24. *Los Angeles Times*, 5 July 1964

25. Flannery, 'The Game of Cricket in America', and *The Christian Science Monitor*, 6 May 1926

26. *Los Angeles Times*, 5 July 1964

27. *Los Angeles Times*, 17 June 1988

28. Simon Worrall, 'Cricket Anyone?' *Smithsonian Magazine*, October 2006 (www.smithsonianmag.com/people-places/cricket.html (accessed 19 April 2010)

29. Rick Marshall, 'The Gentlemen in White', in *Metroland: Capital Regions Alternative Newsweekly*, vol. 28, no. 36 (22 September 2005)

30. *Pittsburgh Tribune-Review*, 19 June 2008

31. Worrall, 'Cricket Anyone?'

32. Joseph O'Neill, *Netherland* (New York: Vintage Books, 2008), 120–21

Chapter 7 (pages 142–171)

1. *The Brisbane Courier*, 6 December 1878; the literature on gambling in baseball – a problem which culminated in the Black Sox scandal of 1919 – is extensive. See David Voigt, *American Baseball: From the Gentleman's Sport to the Commissioner System* (Pennsylvania State University Press, 1983); Harold Seymour, *Baseball: The Golden Age* (Oxford: Oxford University Press, 1971); Daniel E. Ginsburg, *The Fix Is In: A History of Baseball Gambling and Game Fixing Scandals* (Jefferson, NC: McFarland, 2004)

2. Quoted in Greg Kannerstein, 'A Tale of Two Sports: Haverford's Baseball-Cricket Wars', *HAVERFORD, The Alumni Magazine of Haverford College*, Fall 1995, 4

3. Wister, *Some Reminiscences*, 6

4. Wister, *Some Reminiscences*, 12

5. Wister, *Some Reminiscences*, 22

6. Melville, *The Tented Field*, 15–17

7. Germantown Cricket Club scorebook, quoted in Wister, *Some Reminiscences*, 47

8. Lester, *A Century of Philadelphia Cricket*, 8

9. Lester, *A Century of Philadelphia Cricket*, 24

10. Flannery (ed.), *The American Cricket Annual for 1891*, 2

11. Flannery, 'The Game of Cricket in America'

12. *New York Daily Times*, 11 August 1854; Wister, *Some Reminiscences*, 80

13. Flannery, 'The Game of Cricket in America'; Lester, *A Century of Philadelphia Cricket*, 57–66

14. B. A. Clarke, 'Cricket for 1897' in *Young England: An Illustrated Magazine for Boys Throughout the English-Speaking World* (London, n.d.), 133

15. These five clubs were Philadelphia, Germantown, Young America, Merion and Belmont.

16. See R. A. Fitzgerald, *Wickets in the West: Or, the Twelve in America* (London: Tinsley Brothers, 1873), 236–279

17. Fitzgerald, *Wickets in the West*, 243–244

18. *New York Times*, 15 September 1872

19. Wynne-Thomas, *The Complete History of Cricket Tours*, 28

20. Quoted in Ralph Barker, *Ten Great Bowlers* (London: Chatto & Windus, 1967), 134

21. See, for example, *Outing*, vol. XX, no. 3 (June 1892), 180

22. P. H. Clark, 'The Tour of England in 1897', in Lester, *A Century of Philadelphia Cricket*, 146; *Outing*, Vol. XLI, no. 1 (1902), 122

23. A.W., 'Lord Hawke and His Team Away from Home', clipping in *Lord Hawke's XI: America and Canada 1894* scrapbook (private collection)

24. Lester, *A Century of Philadelphia Cricket*, 182

25. For the scorecard, see http://cricketarchive.co.uk/Archive/Scorecards/6/6316.html (accessed 10 March 2010)

26. See Chapter 13, 'The English Tour of 1903' in Lester, *A Century of Philadelphia Cricket*

27. Wynne-Thomas, *The Complete History of Cricket Tours*, 235

28. *The American Cricketer,* vol. LI (November 1927; issued June, 1928)

29. *New York Times*, 21 August 1903

30. See Chapter 15, 'The Tour of England in 1908' in Lester, *A Century of Philadelphia Cricket*

31. Percy H. Clark, 'A Review of the Past Season' in *The American Cricketer*, vol. XXVII, no. 598 (1 December 1904), 2–4

32. John Barton King, 'The Angler and How I Bowled It' in Lester, *A Century of Philadelphia Cricket*, 165

33. Allen Synge, 'Baseball and Cricket: Cross-Currents', SABR UK Examiner (Society for American Baseball Research UK Chapter), no. 10 (2007)

34. 'Obituary of John Barton King', *Cricket Quarterly*, vol. 31, no. 1 (1966), 61; J. Thomas Jable, 'Social Class and the Sport of Cricket in Philadelphia, 1850–1880', *Journal of Sport History*, vol. 18, no. 2 (Summer 1991), ft. 24 & ft. 32

35. Barker, *Ten Great Bowlers*, 29

36. Lester, *A Century of Philadelphia Cricket*, 161–62

37. Barker, *Ten Great Bowlers*, 138

38. This story is told by Lester (*A Century of Philadelphia Cricket*) and Barker (*Ten Great Bowlers*) with some variations. Barker adds the supposed testimony of the Trenton captain who insisted he hit King for several boundaries, admitting only at the end of his tale to being the 'world's champion liar'.

39. Lester, *A Century of Philadelphia Cricket*, 255

40. *New York Times*, 2 September 1889

41. Wister, *Some Reminiscences*, 13; Jable, 'Social Class and the Sport of Cricket in Philadelphia, 1850–1880', 217

42. Quoted in Barker, *Ten Great Bowlers*, 137

43. Lester, *A Century of Philadelphia Cricket*, 176

44. *New York Times*, 25 March 1900

45. David R. Contosta, *Philadelphia Cricket Club: America's Oldest Country Club 1854–2004* (Philadelphia: Philadelphia Cricket Club, 2004), 20

46. Bowen, *North America in International Cricket*

47. See Worrall, 'Cricket Anyone?'

48. Morris, *But Didn't We Have Fun?*, 46

49. Greg Kannerstein, 'A Tale of Two Sports: Haverford's Baseball-Cricket Wars', 1

50. 'Caught Niven, bowled Flynn', *The Cricketer*, July 2001, reproduced at www.cricinfo.com/cricketer/content/story/210840.html (accessed 8 February 2010)

51. P. David Sentence, *Cricket in America 1710–2000* (Jefferson, NC: McFarland, 2006), 200–202

52. *Southern California Cricket Association Year Book* (Los Angeles, 1971)

53. David Niven, *The Moon's a Balloon* (London: Penguin, 1994; first published 1971), 182

54. David Rayvern Allen, *Sir Aubrey: A Biography of C. Aubrey Smith, England Cricketer, West End Actor, Hollywood Film Star* (London: Elm Tree Books, 1982), 142

55. *New York Times*, 28 July 1968; Sentence, *Cricket in America*, 257

56. From the USA Cricket Association, http://usaca.org/the-organization

57. Deb K. Das, 'To the "Lamps of Samarquand"?', *Cricinfo*, 4 January 2004, www.cricinfo.com/usa/content/story/137987.html (accessed 19 February 2010)

58. www.cricketarchive.com/Archive/Scorecards/80/80591.html; www.cricketarchive.com/Archive/Scorecards/80/80655.html

59. Rhys Blakely, 'Indian Premier League unveils plans to hit America for six', *The Times* (London), 18 January 2010, available at www.timesonline.co.uk/tol/sport/cricket/article6991616.ece (accessed 19 February 2010)

60. Blakely, 'Indian Premier League unveils plans'; Andrew Miller, 'Champions League in USA Sights?', *Cricinfo*, 10 February 2010,

www.cricinfo.com/usa/content/story/447810.html?CMP=OTC-RSS (accessed 19 February 2010)

61. Kristin Dizon, 'Take Me Out to the Cricket Game', *Seattle Post*, 13 September 2001

Chapter 8 (pages 172–183)

1. Peverelly, *The Book of American Pastimes*, 338

2. *Spalding's Official Base Ball Guide for 1878*, 5

3. Block, *Baseball before We Knew It*, 10

4. Spalding, 'What is the Origin of Base Ball?', 9

5. Tom Shieber and Ted Spencer, 'Spalding's Commission' in *Baseball as America*, 41

6. Spalding, 'What is the Origin of Base Ball?', 3, 13

7. Philip Block exposed the direct connection between Spalding's eagerness to accept the Doubleday story and both men's involvement in the Eastern spiritualism movement. See Philip Block, 'Abner and Albert, the Missing Link' in Block, *Baseball before We Knew It*, 32–46

8. Quoted in Shieber and Spencer, 'Spalding's Commission', 43

9. Shieber and Spencer, 'Spalding's Commission', 43

10. Wynne-Thomas, *The Complete History of Cricket Tours*, 212

11. David Studham and Glenys Williams, 'The Evolution of an Image' in *MCC Travelex Ashes Exhibition* (London: Marylebone Cricket Club, 2006), 42–43

12. Steve Wulf, 'A Home of Their Own', *Sports Illustrated*, 12 June 1989, available at http://sportsillustrated.cnn.com/vault/article/magazine/MAG1115584; Mike Selvey, Review of 1995 *Wisden Almanack*, first published in *The Guardian*, available online at www.cricinfo.com/ci/content/story/67569.html

13. Quoted in Shieber and Spencer, 'Spalding's Commission', 42

14. Quoted in William J. Ryczek, *Baseball's First Inning: A History of the National Pastime Through the Civil War* (Jefferson, NC: McFarland, 2009), 22

15. John Thorn, *Treasures of the Baseball Hall of Fame: The Official Companion to the Collection at Cooperstown* (New York: Villard Books, 1998), 3

16. Block, *Baseball before We Knew It*, xix

17. *Daily Telegraph* (London), 11 September 2008

Index

Picture credits

British Library: page 1; nos 15–17
Associated Press: page 2; no. 161
Patrick Eagar: page 4; nos 3, 4, 211
Courtesy of National Baseball Hall of Fame Library, Cooperstown, NY and John Grieshop/MLB: page 9
Getty Images: nos 1, 11
Matt Bright: nos 2, 7, 8
Courtesy of Marylebone Cricket Club: nos 5, 6, 18, 19–20, 21, 22, 26, 30–35, 39, 40, 46–50, 51, 59, 60, 65, 67–69, 79, 82, 83, 99, 106, 107, 126–130, 131, 136–139, 181, 182, 206–208
Graham Morris/cricketpix.com: nos 9, 57
Courtesy of National Baseball Hall of Fame Library, Cooperstown, NY and Bryan Yablonsky: no. 10
Courtesy of Milo Stewart Jr./National Baseball Hall of Fame and Museum, Cooperstown, NY: nos 12, 25, 28, 36–38, 41–45, 52, 54, 61, 62, 64, 72–75, 86–88, 92–93, 94–96, 100, 102–105, 108, 111, 140–144, 148–153, 156–159, 163, 164, 204
© Marylebone Cricket Club, London, UK/The Bridgeman Art Library: nos 13, 23, 24, 58, 66, 80, 81, 132–135
Courtesy of the Surrey History Centre: no. 14
Courtesy of the C. C. Morris Cricket Library and Collection: nos 27, 56, 63, 70, 71, 147, 165–170, 176–180, 183–201
Courtesy of National Baseball Hall of Fame Library, Cooperstown, NY: nos 29, 55, 76, 89–92, 94, 97, 98, 101, 110, 145, 148, 155, 202, 203
Courtesy of the San Francisco Giants and Andy Kuno: no. 53
Collection of Tom Shieber: nos 77, 78, 84, 85, 154
Courtesy SABR UK (Wilson Cross scrapbook): no. 109
Fox Photos/Getty Images: nos 112, 113, 115–117
George W. Hales/Fox Photos/Getty Images: no. 114
Private Collection of Dennis Newton, photograph courtesy of Marylebone Cricket Club: nos. 118–123
Private Collection of Josh Chetwynd, photograph courtesy of Marylebone Cricket Club: no. 124
Museum of London: no. 125
New York Public Library: no. 146
Courtesy of the State Library of South Australia (Bradman Digital Library). Scrapbook Vol. 14 – Don Bradman & Babe Ruth watching baseball in New York, 1932: no. 160
Allsport Hulton Archive/Getty Images: no. 162
Priory Collection, courtesy of Nick Potter: nos 171–175
Courtesy of Library of Congress: no. 205
Courtesy of Terry Murphy: no. 209
Courtesy of Patrick Eagar: no. 210

An incomplete credit is given on the cover for the photograph that appears on the front cover (right). The full credit is: **Courtesy of National Baseball Hall of Fame and Museum, Cooperstown, NY/New York Daily News, L.P.**

Swinging Away silhouettes (cover and page 1) designed by Owen Snee

'Cricket and Baseball' by W. G. Grace (page 98) was first published in *The English Illustrated Magazine* and reprinted in the *New York Times*, 15 June 1890

Acknowledgements

Some of the strongest memories of my youth are of the old Cleveland Stadium in the 1980s where I cheered on the Cleveland Indians. And watched them lose, as often as not. Unlike many baseball fans, I have recollections just as vivid of the Sydney Cricket Ground where I barracked for Australia in the early 1990s. And watched them win, as often as not. For 20 years, as I built my museum career in Australia and visited family in America, I took every opportunity I could to get to cricket grounds and baseball parks and spent endless hours following both sports on radio and television, never imagining that such private obsessions might one day pay professional dividends.

My personal sporting passions combined with my museum 'day job' for the first time at the Museum of Sydney when MCC brought *The Ashes Exhibition* to Australia in 2006. What a thrill. The oddity of an American-Australian museum curator pontificating about one of the most significant moments in cricket history was lost on no one. My love of cricket, I would explain again and again, was not only heartfelt but actually came from growing up loving baseball.

There are many, many people to thank. I am extraordinarily grateful to Adam Chadwick for the opportunity to take an enticing idea – a comparison of cricket and baseball – and forge it into a ridiculously ambitious exhibition and accompanying publication. It has been an immense privilege and I thank Adam for his vision, stewardship, trust and willingness to juggle time zones and overcome the tyranny of distance between London and Sydney. Others at MCC provided hands-on help and specialist advice including Charlotte Goodhew and her volunteers, Neil Robinson and Glenys Williams. Owen Snee's inspired exhibition design and Oliver Craske's unflagging work on the catalogue, with James Alexander's elegant graphic design, brought a huge mass of material into concrete form. Sir Mervyn Dunnington-Jefferson provided invaluable support and helpful introductions.

This would have been a truly one-sided endeavour without the enthusiastic participation of the National Baseball Hall of Fame and Museum. I'll never forget the moment senior curator Tom Shieber bounded in to meet me on my first trip to Cooperstown, so excited about cricket that I was momentarily stunned. I couldn't have hoped for a more animated, intelligent or professional curatorial collaborator. Many other staff assisted in one way or another, but special thanks are due to Erik Strohl, Jenny Ambrose, Milo Stewart Jr., Helen Stiles and Sara DeGaetano. The catalogue text benefited from Tom's team of fact checkers at the Hall of Fame as well as the discerning Davids – David Block in America, David Rayvern Allen in England and David Studham in Australia.

The Society for American Baseball Research (SABR) is an impressive body of researchers and baseball enthusiasts and I've benefited from the Origins and 19th Century research committees and received many stimulating ideas from Larry McCray, John Thorn, Richard Hershberger, Pricilla Astifan, David Block, Deb Shattuck, Dorothy Mills and Eric Miklich. The UK branch of SABR has been similarly helpful and special thanks are due to Mike Ross, Martin Hoerchner and Patrick Carroll; John and Kay Price from Stoolball England provided friendly advice, and Patricia St John Barry, Julian Pooley and Sam Marchiano enabled the inclusion of the Bray image.

Baseball in Britain, in both its indigenous and American formats, attracts dedicated followers and I've received support from all corners: William Morgan, who organised, researched and chronicled American baseball in England for decades, was kind enough to share his memories and knowledge; Dennis Newton, who shared the same, as well as his collection, as did former player, commentator and author Josh Chetwynd; Bob Fromer, Mark Mullins and John Walmsley from British Baseball Federation and BaseballSoftballUK; Joe Gray from Project Cobb; and Andrew Weltch, who generously offered more Welsh/British Baseball material than could fit in the exhibition, as well as his thorough knowledge of this fascinating game.

It has been a delight to explore the fascinating history of cricket in America through the collection of the C. C. Morris Cricket Library, and I am grateful to Paul Hensley, Alfred and Betty Reeves and Joe Lynn for their hospitality and support. In Australia, I must thank David Studham, Librarian of the Melbourne Cricket Club, and his staff, whose superb facilities and valued friendship have provided a research oasis, and David Wells, curator at the Bradman Museum of Cricket.

Finally, thanks to my dad, who took me to my first baseball game, and to my husband, who took me to my first cricket match.
Beth Hise
Sydney, May 2010

Recommended reading

David Block, *Baseball before We Knew It: A Search for the Roots of the Game* (Lincoln, NE: University of Nebraska, 2005)
Rowland Bowen, *Cricket: A History of its Growth and Development Throughout the World* (London: Eyre & Spottiswoode, 1970)
Josh Chetwynd and Brian A. Belton, *British Baseball and the West Ham Club: History of a 1930s Professional Team in East London* (Jefferson, NC: McFarland, 2007)
R. A. Fitzgerald, *Wickets in the West: Or, the Twelve in America* (London: Tinsley Brothers, 1873)
John Ford, *Cricket: A Social History 1700–1835* (Newton Abbot: David & Charles Publishers, 1972),
W. G. Grace, *Cricket* (Bristol and London, 1891)
George B. Kirsch, *Baseball and Cricket: the Creation of American Team Sports, 1838–72* (Urbana and Chicago: University of Illinois Press, 2007; first published 1989)
Mark Lamster, *Spalding's World Tour: The Epic Adventure that Took Baseball Around the Globe – And Made It America's Game* (New York: Public Affairs, 2006)
John A. Lester (ed.), *A Century of Philadelphia Cricket* (Philadelphia: University of Pennsylvania Press, 1951)
Peter Levine, *A. G. Spalding and the Rise of Baseball: The Promise of American Sport* (New York: Oxford University Press, 1985)
Frederick Lillywhite, *The English Cricketers' Trip to Canada and The United States*, (London: F. Lillywhite, 1860; reprinted 1980, ed. Robin Marlar)
John Major, *More Than a Game: The Story of Cricket's Early Years* (London: Harper Collins, 2007)
Tom Melville, *The Tented Field: A History of Cricket in America* (Bowling Green, Ohio: Bowling Green State University Popular Press, 1998)
Peter Morris, *But Didn't We Have Fun? An Informal History of Baseball's Pioneer Era, 1843–1870* (Chicago: Ivan R. Dee, 2008)
John Nyren, *The Young Cricketer's Tutor: comprising full directions for playing the elegant and manly game of cricket: with a complete version of its laws and regulations… to which is added The cricketers of my time, or, Recollections of the most famous old players / The whole collected and edited by Charles Cowden Clarke* (London: E. Wilson, 1833),
Harry Clay Palmer, *Athletic Sports in America, England and Australia: The 1888–1889 World Tour of American Baseball Teams* (Jefferson, NC: McFarland, 2006)
Charles A. Peverelly, *The Book of American Pastimes: Containing a History of the Principal Base Ball, Cricket, Rowing and Yachting Clubs of the United States* (New York: published by the author, 1866)
Simon Rae, *W. G. Grace: A Life* (London: Faber and Faber, 1998)
Robin Simon and Alastair Smart, *The Art of Cricket* (London: Secker & Warburg, 1983)
Nicholas ['Felix'] Wanostrocht, *The Cricket-Bat and How to Use It: A Treatise on the Game of Cricket. With practical and scientific instructions in batting, bowling, and fielding. The laws of cricket, match-playing, single-wicket, &c. By an old cricketer* (London: Baily Brothers, 1861)
Peter Wynne-Thomas, *The Complete History of Cricket Tours at Home and Abroad* (London: Hamlyn, 1989)